# THE MESSAGE

# THE WISDOM BOOKS

The Message is a contemporary rendering
of the Bible from the original languages,
crafted to present its tone, rhythm, events,
and ideas in everyday speech.

Other editions of *The Message:*
   *The New Testament with Psalms and Proverbs*
   *The New Testament*
   *Psalms*
   *Proverbs*
   *Job*

# *The* MESSAGE

## THE WISDOM BOOKS

### EUGENE H. PETERSON

NAVPRESS

BRINGING TRUTH TO LIFE

NavPress Publishing Group

P.O. Box 35001, Colorado Springs, Colorado 80935

*Old Testament Exegetical Consultant:*
    Dr. Robert L. Alden
    Denver Seminary

*Stylistic Consultant:*
    Luci Shaw
    senior editor, Shaw Publishers; writer-in-residence, Regent College

Library of Congress Catalog Card Number:
    96-67606
ISBN 08910-99603

Printed in the United States of America

1 2 3 4 5 6 7 8 9 10 11 12 13 14 15 / 00 99 98 97 96

---

Published in association with the literary agency of Alive Communications, Inc., 1465 Kelly Johnson Blvd., Suite 320, Colorado Springs, CO 80920.

---

# CONTENTS

# INTRODUCTION TO
# THE WISDOM BOOKS

There is a distinctive strain of writing in the Bible that more or less specializes in dealing with human experience—as is. *This* is what is involved in being human, and don't you forget it. "Wisdom" is the common designation given to this aspect of biblical witness and writing.

The word in this context refers more to a kind of attitude, a distinctive stance, than to any particular ideas or doctrines or counsel. As such, Wisdom is wide-ranging, collecting under its umbrella diverse and unlikely fellow travelers. What keeps the feet of these faith-travelers on common ground is Wisdom's unrelenting insistence that nothing in human experience can be omitted or slighted if we decide to take God seriously and respond to him believingly.

God and God's ways provide the comprehensive plot and sovereign action in the Holy Scriptures, but human beings—every last man and woman of us, including every last detail involved in our daily living—are invited and honored participants in all of it. There are no spectator seats provided for the drama of salvation. There is no "bench" for incompetent players.

It is fairly common among people who get interested in religion or God to get proportionately *dis*interested in their jobs and families, their communities and their colleagues—the more of God, the less of the human. But that is not the way God intends it. Wisdom counters this tendency by giving witness to the precious nature of human experience in all its forms, whether or not it feels or appears "spiritual."

Job, Psalms, Proverbs, Ecclesiastes, and the Song of Songs serve as our primary witnesses to biblical Wisdom. It is not as if wisdom is confined to these books, for its influence is pervasive throughout Scripture. But in these books human experience as the arena in which God is present and working is placed front and center.

The comprehensiveness of these five witnesses becomes evident when we set Psalms at the center, and then crisscross that center with the other four arranged as two sets of polarities: first Job and Proverbs, and then Ecclesiastes and the Song of Songs.

Psalms is a magnetic center, pulling every scrap and dimension of human experience into the presence of God. The Psalms are indiscriminate in their subject matter—complaint and thanks, doubt and anger, outcries of pain and outbursts of joy, quiet reflection and boisterous worship. If it's *human*, it qualifies. Any human experience, feeling, or thought *can* be prayed. Eventually it all *must* be prayed if it is to retain—or recover—its essential humanity. The totality of God's concern with the totality of our humanity is then elaborated by means of the two polarities.

The Job-Proverbs polarity sets the crisis experience of extreme suffering opposite the routine experience of getting along as best we can in the ordinary affairs of work and family, money and sex, the use of language and the expression of emotions. The life of faith has to do with extraordinary experience; the life of faith has to do with ordinary experience. Neither cancels out the other; neither takes precedence over the other. As Job rages in pain and protest, we find that the worst that can happen to us has been staked out as God's territory. As the pithy Proverbs sharpen our observations and insights regarding what is going on all around us, we realize that all this unobtrusive, undramatic dailiness is also God's country.

The Song-Ecclesiastes polarity sets the ecstatic experience of love in tension with the boredom of the same old round. The life of faith has to do with the glories of discovering far more in life than we ever dreamed of; the life of faith has to do with doggedly putting one flat foot in front of the other, wondering what the point of it all is. Neither cancels out the other; neither takes precedence over the other. As we sing and pray the lyrics of the Song of Songs, we become convinced that God blesses the best that human experience is capable of; as we ponder the sardonic verses of Ecclesiastes, we recognize the limits inherent in all human experience, appreciate it for what it is, but learn not to confuse it with God.

In such ways, these Wisdom writers keep us honest with and attentive to the entire range of human experience that God the Spirit uses to fashion a life of holy salvation in each of us.

# JOB

# JOB

Job suffered. His name is synonymous with suffering. He asked, "Why?" He asked, "Why me?" And he put his questions to God. He asked his questions persistently, passionately, and eloquently. He refused to take silence for an answer. He refused to take clichés for an answer. He refused to let God off the hook.

Job did not take his sufferings quietly or piously. He disdained going for a second opinion to outside physicians or philosophers. Job took his stance before *God*, and there he protested his suffering, protested mightily.

It is not only because Job suffered that he is important to us. It is because he suffered in the same ways that *we* suffer—in the vital areas of family, personal health, and material things. Job is also important to us because he searchingly questioned and boldly protested his suffering. Indeed, he went "to the top" with his questions.

It is not suffering as such that troubles us. It is undeserved suffering.

Almost all of us in our years of growing up have the experience of disobeying our parents and getting punished for it. When that discipline was connected with wrongdoing, it had a certain sense of justice to it: *When we do wrong, we get punished.*

One of the surprises as we get older, however, is that we come to see that there is no real correlation between the amount of wrong we commit and the amount of pain we experience. An even larger surprise is that very often there is something quite the opposite: We do right and get knocked down. We do the best we are capable of doing, and just as we are reaching out to receive our reward we are hit from the blind side and sent reeling.

*This* is the suffering that first bewilders and then outrages us. This is the kind of suffering that bewildered and outraged Job, for Job was doing everything right when suddenly everything went wrong. And it is this kind of suffering to which Job gives voice when he protests to God.

Job gives voice to his sufferings so well, so accurately and honestly, that anyone who has ever suffered—which includes every last one of us—can recognize his or her personal pain in the voice of Job. Job says boldly what some of us are too timid to say. He makes poetry out of what in many of us is only a tangle of confused whimpers. He shouts out to God what a lot of us mutter behind our sleeves. He refuses to accept the role of a defeated victim.

It is also important to note what Job does *not* do, lest we expect something from him that he does not intend. Job does not curse God as his wife suggests he should do, getting rid of the problem by getting rid of God. But neither does Job *explain* suffering. He does not instruct us in how to live so that we can avoid suffering. Suffering is a mystery, and Job comes to respect the mystery.

In the course of facing, questioning, and respecting suffering, Job finds himself in an even larger mystery—the mystery of God. Perhaps the greatest mystery in suffering is how it can bring a person into the presence of God in a state of worship, full of wonder, love, and praise. Suffering does not inevitably do that, but it does it far more often than we would expect. It certainly did that for Job. Even in his answer to his wife he speaks the language of an uncharted irony, a dark and difficult kind of truth: "We take the good days from God—why not also the bad days?"

But there is more to the book of Job than Job. There are Job's friends. The moment we find ourselves in trouble of any kind—sick in the hospital, bereaved by a friend's death, dismissed from a job or relationship, depressed or bewildered—people start showing up telling us exactly what is wrong with us and what we must do to get better. Sufferers attract fixers the way road-kills attract vultures. At first we are impressed that they bother with us and amazed at their facility with answers. They know so much! How did they get to be such experts in living?

More often than not, these people use the Word of God frequently and loosely. They are full of spiritual diagnosis and prescription. It all sounds so hopeful. But then we begin to wonder, "Why is it that for all their apparent compassion we feel worse instead of better after they've said their piece?"

The book of Job is not only a witness to the dignity of suffering and God's presence in our suffering but is also our primary biblical protest against religion that has been reduced to explanations or "answers." Many of the answers that Job's so-called friends give him are technically true. But it is the "technical" part that ruins them. They are answers without personal relationship, intellect without intimacy. The answers are slapped onto Job's ravaged

11

life like labels on a specimen bottle. Job rages against this secularized wisdom that has lost touch with the living realities of God.

In every generation there are men and women who pretend to be able to instruct us in a way of life that guarantees that we will be "healthy, wealthy, and wise." According to the propaganda of these people, anyone who lives intelligently and morally is exempt from suffering. From their point of view, it is lucky for us that they are now at hand to provide the intelligent and moral answers we need.

On behalf of all of us who have been misled by the platitudes of the nice people who show up to tell us everything is going to be just all right if we simply think such-and-such and do such-and-such, Job issues an anguished rejoinder. He rejects the kind of advice and teaching that has God all figured out, that provides glib explanations for every circumstance. Job's honest defiance continues to be the best defense against the clichés of positive thinkers and the prattle of religious small talk.

The honest, innocent Job is placed in a setting of immense suffering and then surrounded by the conventional religious wisdom of the day in the form of speeches by Eliphaz, Bildad, Zophar, and Elihu. The contrast is unforgettable. The counselors methodically and pedantically recite their bookish precepts to Job. At first Job rages in pain and roars out his protests, but then he becomes silent in awestruck faith before God, who speaks from out of a storm—a "whirlwind" of Deity. Real faith cannot be reduced to spiritual bromides and merchandised in success stories. It is refined in the fires and the storms of pain.

The book of Job does not reject answers as such. There *is* content to biblical religion. It is the *secularization* of answers that is rejected— answers severed from their Source, the living God, the Word that both batters us and heals us. We cannot have truth *about* God divorced from the mind and heart *of* God.

In our compassion, we don't like to see people suffer. And so our instincts are aimed at preventing and alleviating suffering. No doubt that is a good impulse. But if we really want to reach out to others who are suffering, we should be careful not to be like Job's friends, not to do our "helping" with the presumption that we can fix things, get rid of them, or make them "better." We may look at our suffering friends and imagine how they could have better marriages, better behaved children, better mental and emotional health. But when we rush in to fix suffering, we need to keep in mind several things.

First, no matter how insightful we may be, we don't *really* understand the full nature of our friends' problems. Second, our friends may not *want* our advice. Third, the ironic fact of the matter is that more often than not, people do not suffer *less* when they are committed to following God, but *more*. When these people go through suffering, their lives are often transformed, deepened, marked with beauty and holiness, in remarkable ways that could never have been anticipated before the suffering.

So, instead of continuing to focus on preventing suffering—which we simply won't be very successful at anyway—perhaps we should begin *entering* the suffering, participating insofar as we are able—entering the mystery and looking around for God. In other words, we need to quit feeling sorry for people who suffer and instead look up to them, learn from them, and—if they will let us—join them in protest and prayer. Pity can be nearsighted and condescending; shared suffering can be dignifying and life-changing. As we look at Job's suffering and praying and worshiping, we see that he has already blazed a trail of courage and integrity for us to follow.

But sometimes it's hard to know just how to follow Job's lead when we feel so alone in our suffering, unsure of what God wants us to do. What we must realize during those times of darkness is that the God who appeared to Job in the whirlwind is calling out to all of us. Although God may not appear to us in a vision, he makes himself known to us in all the many ways that he describes to Job—from the macro to the micro, from the wonders of the galaxies to the little things we take for granted. He is the Creator of the unfathomable universe all around us—and he is also the Creator of the universe inside of us. And so we gain hope—not from the darkness of our suffering, not from pat answers in books, but from the God who sees our suffering and shares our pain.

Reading Job prayerfully and meditatively leads us to face the questions that arise when our lives don't turn out the way we expect them to. First we hear all the stock answers. Then we ask the questions again, with variations—and hear the answers again, with variations. Over and over and over. Every time we let Job give voice to our own questions, our suffering gains in dignity and we are brought a step closer to the threshold of the voice and mystery of God. Every time we persist with Job in rejecting the quick-fix counsel of people who see us and hear us but do not understand us, we deepen our availability and openness to the revelation that comes only out of the tempest. The mystery of God eclipses the darkness and the struggle. We realize that suffering calls *our* lives into question, not God's. The tables are turned: God-Alive is present to us. God is speaking to us. And so Job's experience is confirmed and repeated once again in our suffering and our vulnerable humanity.

13

# JOB

# 1

## A MAN DEVOTED TO GOD

Job was a man who lived in Uz. He was honest inside and out, a man of his word, who was totally devoted to God and hated evil with a passion. He had seven sons and three daughters. He was also very wealthy—seven thousand head of sheep, three thousand camels, five hundred teams of oxen, five hundred donkeys, and a huge staff of servants—the most influential man in all the East!

His sons used to take turns hosting parties in their homes, always inviting their three sisters to join them in their merrymaking. When the parties were over, Job would get up early in the morning and sacrifice a burnt offering for each of his children, thinking, "Maybe one of them sinned by defying God inwardly." Job made a habit of this sacrificial atonement, just in case they'd sinned.

## THE FIRST TEST: FAMILY AND FORTUNE

One day when the angels came to report to GOD, Satan, who was the Designated Accuser, came along with them. GOD singled out Satan and said, "What have you been up to?"

Satan answered GOD, "Going here and there, checking things out on earth."

GOD said to Satan, "Have you noticed my friend Job? There's no one quite like him—honest and true to his word, totally devoted to God and hating evil."

Satan retorted, "So do you think Job does all that out of the sheer goodness of his heart? Why, no one ever had it so good! You pamper him like a pet, make sure nothing bad ever happens to him or his family or his possessions, bless everything he does—he can't lose!

"But what do you think would happen if you reached down and took away everything that is his? He'd curse you right to your face, that's what."

GOD replied, "We'll see. Go ahead—do what you want with all that is his. Just don't hurt *him*." Then Satan left the presence of GOD.

Sometime later, while Job's children were having one of their parties at the home of the oldest son, a messenger came to Job and said,

"The oxen were plowing and the donkeys grazing in the field next to us when Sabeans attacked. They stole the animals and killed the field hands. I'm the only one to get out alive and tell you what happened."

While he was still talking, another messenger arrived and said, "Bolts of lightning struck the sheep and the shepherds and fried them—burned them to a crisp. I'm the only one to get out alive and tell you what happened."

While he was still talking, another messenger arrived and said, "Chaldeans coming from three directions raided the camels and massacred the camel drivers. I'm the only one to get out alive and tell you what happened."

While he was still talking, another messenger arrived and said, "Your children were having a party at the home of the oldest brother when a tornado swept in off the desert and struck the house. It collapsed on the young people and they died. I'm the only one to get out alive and tell you what happened."

Job got to his feet, ripped his robe, shaved his head, then fell to the ground and worshiped:

"Naked I came from my mother's womb,
    naked I'll return to the womb of the earth.
GOD gives, GOD takes.
    God's name be ever blessed."

Not once through all this did Job sin; not once did he blame God.

# 2

THE SECOND TEST: HEALTH

One day when the angels came to report to GOD, Satan also showed up. GOD singled out Satan, saying, "And what have you been up to?"

Satan answered GOD, "Oh, going here and there, checking things out."

Then GOD said to Satan, "Have you noticed my friend Job? There's no one quite like him, is there—honest and true to his word, totally devoted to God and hating evil? He still has a firm grip on his integrity! You tried to trick me into destroying him, but it didn't work."

Satan answered, "A human would do anything to save his life. But what do you think would happen if you reached down and took away his health? He'd curse you to your face, that's what."

GOD said, "All right. Go ahead—you can do what you like with him. But mind you, don't kill him."

Satan left GOD and struck Job with terrible sores. Job was ulcers and scabs from head to foot. They itched and oozed so badly that he took a piece of broken pottery to scrape himself, then went and sat on a trash heap, among the ashes.

His wife said, "Still holding on to your precious integrity, are you? Curse God and be done with it!"

He told her, "You're talking like an empty-headed fool. We take the good days from God—why not also the bad days?"

Not once through all this did Job sin. He said nothing against God.

### JOB'S THREE FRIENDS

Three of Job's friends heard of all the trouble that had fallen on him. Each traveled from his own country—Eliphaz from Teman, Bildad from Shuah, Zophar from Naamath—and went together to Job to keep him company and comfort him. When they first caught sight of him, they couldn't believe what they saw—they hardly recognized him! They cried out in lament, ripped their robes, and dumped dirt on their heads as a sign of their grief. Then they sat with him on the ground. Seven days and nights they sat there without saying a word. They could see how rotten he felt, how deeply he was suffering.

# 3          JOB CRIES OUT

### WHAT'S THE POINT OF LIFE?

Then Job broke the silence. He spoke up and cursed his fate:

"Obliterate the day I was born.
    Blank out the night I was conceived!
Let it be a black hole in space.
    May God above forget it ever happened.
    Erase it from the books!
May the day of my birth be buried in deep darkness,
    shrouded by the fog,
    swallowed by the night.

And the night of my conception—the devil take it!
    Rip the date off the calendar,
    delete it from the almanac.
Oh, turn that night into pure nothingness—
    no sounds of pleasure from that night, ever!
May those who are good at cursing curse that day.
    Unleash the sea beast, Leviathan, on it.
May its morning stars turn to black cinders,
    waiting for a daylight that never comes,
    never once seeing the first light of dawn.
And why? Because it released me from my mother's womb
    into a life with so much trouble.

"Why didn't I die at birth,
    my first breath out of the womb my last?
Why were there arms to rock me,
    and breasts for me to drink from?
I could be resting in peace right now,
    asleep forever, feeling no pain,
In the company of kings and statesmen
    in their royal ruins,
Or with princes resplendent
    in their gold and silver tombs.
Why wasn't I stillborn and buried
    with all the babies who never saw light,
Where the wicked no longer trouble anyone
    and bone-weary people get a long-deserved rest?
Prisoners sleep undisturbed,
    never again to wake up to the bark of the guards.
The small and the great are equals in that place,
    and slaves are free from their masters.

"Why does God bother giving light to the miserable,
    why bother keeping bitter people alive,
Those who want in the worst way to die, and can't,
    who can't imagine anything better than death,
Who count the day of their death and burial
    the happiest day of their life?
What's the point of life when it doesn't make sense,
    when God blocks all the roads to meaning?

"Instead of bread I get groans for my supper,
    then leave the table and vomit my anguish.
The worst of my fears has come true,
    what I've dreaded most has happened.
My repose is shattered, my peace destroyed.
    No rest for me, ever—death has invaded life."

# 4     ELIPHAZ SPEAKS OUT

### NOW *YOU'RE* THE ONE IN TROUBLE

Then Eliphaz from Teman spoke up:

"Would you mind if I said something to you?
    Under the circumstances it's hard to keep quiet.
You yourself have done this plenty of times, spoken words
    that clarify, encouraged those who were about to quit.
Your words have put stumbling people on their feet,
    put fresh hope in people about to collapse.
But now *you're* the one in trouble—you're hurting!
    You've been hit hard and you're reeling from the blow.
But shouldn't your devout life give you confidence now?
    Shouldn't your exemplary life give you hope?

"Think! Has a truly innocent person ever ended up on
        the scrap heap?
    Do genuinely upright people ever lose out in the end?
It's my observation that those who plow evil
    and sow trouble reap evil and trouble.
One breath from God and they fall apart,
    one blast of his anger and there's nothing left of them.
The mighty lion, king of the beasts, roars mightily,
    but when he's toothless he's useless—
No teeth, no prey—and the cubs
    wander off to fend for themselves.

"A word came to me in secret—
    a mere whisper of a word, but I heard it clearly.
It came in a scary dream one night,
    after I had fallen into a deep, deep sleep.

Dread stared me in the face, and Terror.
   I was scared to death—I shook from head to foot.
A spirit glided right in front of me—
   the hair on my head stood on end.
I couldn't tell what it was that appeared there—
   a blur . . . and then I heard a muffled voice:

"'How can mere mortals be more righteous than God?
   How can humans be purer than their Creator?
Why, God doesn't even trust his own servants,
   doesn't even cheer his angels,
So how much less these bodies composed of mud,
   fragile as moths?
These bodies of ours are here today and gone tomorrow,
   and no one even notices—gone without a trace.
When the tent stakes are ripped up, the tent collapses—
   we die and are never the wiser for having lived.'

# 5

## DON'T BLAME FATE WHEN THINGS GO WRONG

"Call for help, Job, if you think anyone will answer!
   To which of the holy angels will you turn?
The hot temper of a fool eventually kills him,
   the jealous anger of a simpleton does her in.
I've seen it myself—seen fools putting down roots,
   and then, suddenly, their houses are cursed.
Their children out in the cold, abused and exploited,
   with no one to stick up for them.
Hungry people off the street plunder their harvests,
   cleaning them out completely, taking thorns and all,
   insatiable for everything they have.
Don't blame fate when things go wrong—
   trouble doesn't come from nowhere.
It's human! Mortals are born and bred for trouble,
   as certainly as sparks fly upward.

### WHAT A BLESSING WHEN GOD CORRECTS YOU!

"If I were in your shoes, I'd go straight to God,
    I'd throw myself on the mercy of God.
After all, he's famous for great and unexpected acts;
    there's no end to his surprises.
He gives rain, for instance, across the wide earth,
    sends water to irrigate the fields.
He raises up the down-and-out,
    gives firm footing to those sinking in grief.
He aborts the schemes of conniving crooks,
    so that none of their plots come to term.
He catches the know-it-alls in their conspiracies—
    all that intricate intrigue swept out with the trash!
Suddenly they're disoriented, plunged into darkness;
    they can't see to put one foot in front of the other.
But the downtrodden are saved by God,
    saved from the murderous plots, saved from the iron fist.
And so the poor continue to hope,
    while injustice is bound and gagged.

"So, what a blessing when God steps in and corrects you!
    Mind you, don't despise the discipline of Almighty God!
True, he wounds, but he also dresses the wound;
    the same hand that hurts you, heals you.
From one disaster after another he delivers you;
    no matter what the calamity, the evil can't touch you—

"In famine, he'll keep you from starving,
    in war, from being gutted by the sword.
You'll be protected from vicious gossip
    and live fearless through any catastrophe.
You'll shrug off disaster and famine,
    and stroll fearlessly among wild animals.
You'll be on good terms with rocks and mountains;
    wild animals will become your good friends.
You'll know that your place on earth is safe,
    you'll look over your goods and find nothing amiss.
You'll see your children grow up,
    your family lovely and lissome as orchard grass.

21

You'll arrive at your grave ripe with many good years,
    like sheaves of golden grain at harvest.

"Yes, this is the way things are—my word of honor!
    Take it to heart and you won't go wrong."

# 6         JOB REPLIES TO ELIPHAZ

## GOD HAS DUMPED THE WORKS ON ME

Job answered:

"If my misery could be weighed,
    if you could pile the whole bitter load on the scales,
It would be heavier than all the sand of the sea!
    Is it any wonder that I'm screaming like a caged cat?
The arrows of God Almighty are in me,
    poison arrows—and I'm poisoned all through!
    God has dumped the whole works on me.
Donkeys bray and cows moo when they run out of pasture—
    so don't expect me to keep quiet in this.
Do you see what God has dished out for me?
    It's enough to turn anyone's stomach!
Everything in me is repulsed by it—
    it makes me sick.

## PRESSED PAST THE LIMITS

"All I want is an answer to one prayer,
    a last request to be honored:
Let God step on me—squash me like a bug,
    and be done with me for good.
I'd at least have the satisfaction
    of not having blasphemed the Holy God,
    before being pressed past the limits.
Where's the strength to keep my hopes up?
    What future do I have to keep me going?
Do you think I have nerves of steel?
    Do you think I'm made of iron?
Do you think I can pull myself up by my bootstraps?
    Why, I don't even have any boots!

## My So-Called Friends

"When desperate people give up on God Almighty,
    their friends, at least, should stick with them.
But my brothers are fickle as a gulch in the desert—
    one day they're gushing with water
From melting ice and snow
    cascading out of the mountains,
But by midsummer they're dry,
    gullies baked dry in the sun.
Travelers who spot them and go out of their way for a drink,
    end up in a waterless gulch and die of thirst.
Merchant caravans from Tema see them and expect water,
    tourists from Sheba hope for a cool drink.
They arrive so confident—but what a disappointment!
    They get there, and their faces fall!
And you, my so-called friends, are no better—
        there's nothing to you!
    One look at a hard scene and you shrink in fear.
It's not as though I asked you for anything—
    I didn't ask you for one red cent—
Nor did I beg you to go out on a limb for me.
    So why all this dodging and shuffling?

"Confront me with the truth and I'll shut up,
    show me where I've gone off the track.
Honest words never hurt anyone,
    but what's the point of all this pious bluster?
You pretend to tell me what's wrong with my life,
    but treat my words of anguish as so much hot air.
Are people mere things to you?
    Are friends just items of profit and loss?

"Look me in the eyes!
    Do you think I'd lie to your face?
Think it over—no double-talk!
    Think carefully—my integrity is on the line!
Can you detect anything false in what I say?
    Don't you trust me to discern good from evil?

# 7

## THERE'S NOTHING TO MY LIFE

"Human life is a struggle, isn't it?
>It's a life sentence to hard labor.
Like field hands longing for quitting time
>and working stiffs with nothing to hope for but payday,
I'm given a life that meanders and goes nowhere—
>months of aimlessness, nights of misery!
I go to bed and think, 'How long till I can get up?'
>I toss and turn as the night drags on—and I'm fed up!
I'm covered with maggots and scabs.
>My skin gets scaly and hard, then oozes with pus.
My days come and go swifter than the click of knitting needles,
>and then the yarn runs out—an unfinished life!

"God, don't forget that I'm only a puff of air!
>These eyes have had their last look at goodness.
And your eyes have seen the last of me;
>even while you're looking, there'll be nothing left to look at.
When a cloud evaporates, it's gone for good;
>those who go to the grave never come back.
They don't return to visit their families;
>never again will friends drop in for coffee.

"And so I'm not keeping one bit of this quiet,
>I'm laying it all out on the table;
>my complaining to high heaven is bitter, but honest.
Are you going to put a muzzle on me,
>the way you quiet the sea and still the storm?
If I say, 'I'm going to bed, then I'll feel better.
>A little nap will lift my spirits,'
You come and so scare me with nightmares
>and frighten me with ghosts
That I'd rather strangle in the bedclothes
>than face this kind of life any longer.
I hate this life! Who needs any more of this?
>Let me alone! There's nothing to my life—it's nothing
>>but smoke.

"What are mortals anyway, that you bother with them,
    that you even give them the time of day?
That you check up on them every morning,
    looking in on them to see how they're doing?
Let up on me, will you?
    Can't you even let me spit in peace?
Even suppose I'd sinned—how would that hurt you?
    You're responsible for every human being.
Don't you have better things to do than pick on me?
    Why make a federal case out of me?
Why don't you just forgive my sins
    and start me off with a clean slate?
The way things are going, I'll soon be dead.
    You'll look high and low, but I won't be around."

# 8           BILDAD'S RESPONSE

## DOES GOD MESS UP?

Bildad from Shuah was next to speak:

"How can you keep on talking like this?
    You're talking nonsense, and noisy nonsense at that.
Does God mess up?
    Does God Almighty ever get things backwards?
It's plain that your children sinned against him—
    otherwise, why would God have punished them?
Here's what you must do—and don't put it off any longer:
    Get down on your knees before God Almighty.
If you're as innocent and upright as you say,
    it's not too late—he'll come running;
    he'll set everything right again, reestablish your fortunes.
Even though you're not much right now,
    you'll end up better than ever.

## TO HANG YOUR LIFE FROM ONE THIN THREAD

"Put the question to our ancestors,
    study what they learned from their ancestors.

For we're newcomers at this, with a lot to learn,
    and not too long to learn it.
So why not let the ancients teach you, tell you what's what,
    instruct you in what they knew from experience?
Can mighty pine trees grow tall without soil?
    Can luscious tomatoes flourish without water?
Blossoming flowers look great before they're cut or picked,
    but without soil or water they wither more quickly than grass.
That's what happens to all who forget God—
    all their hopes come to nothing.
They hang their life from one thin thread,
    they hitch their fate to a spider web.
One jiggle and the thread breaks,
    one jab and the web collapses.
Or they're like weeds springing up in the sunshine,
    invading the garden,
Spreading everywhere, overtaking the flowers,
    getting a foothold even in the rocks.
But when the gardener rips them out by the roots,
    the garden doesn't miss them one bit.
The sooner the godless are gone, the better;
    then good plants can grow in their place.

"There's no way that God will reject a good person,
    and there is no way he'll help a bad one.
God will let you laugh again;
    you'll raise the roof with shouts of joy,
With your enemies thoroughly discredited,
    their house of cards collapsed."

# 9 JOB CONTINUES

## How Can Mere Mortals Get Right With God?

Job continued by saying:

"So what's new? I know all this.
    The question is, 'How can mere mortals get right with God?'
If we wanted to bring our case before him,
    what chance would we have? Not one in a thousand!

God's wisdom is so deep, God's power so immense,
    who could take him on and come out in one piece?
He moves mountains before they know what's happened,
    flips them on their heads on a whim.
He gives the earth a good shaking up,
    rocks it down to its very foundations.
He tells the sun, 'Don't shine,' and it doesn't;
    he pulls the blinds on the stars.
All by himself he stretches out the heavens
    and strides on the waves of the sea.
He designed the Big Dipper and Orion,
    the Pleiades and Alpha Centauri.
We'll never comprehend all the great things he does;
    his miracle-surprises can't be counted.
Somehow, though he moves right in front of me, I don't see him;
    quietly but surely he's active, and I miss it.
If he steals you blind, who can stop him?
    Who's going to say, 'Hey, what are you doing?'
God doesn't hold back on his anger;
    even dragon-bred monsters cringe before him.

"So how could I ever argue with him,
    construct a defense that would influence God?
Even though I'm innocent I could never prove it;
    I can only throw myself on the Judge's mercy.
If I called on God and he himself answered me,
    then, and only then, would I believe that he'd heard me.
As it is, he knocks me about from pillar to post,
    beating me up, black and blue, for no good reason.
He won't even let me catch my breath,
    piles bitterness upon bitterness.
If it's a question of who's stronger, he wins, hands down!
    If it's a question of justice, who'll serve him the subpoena?
Even though innocent, anything I say incriminates me;
    blameless as I am, my defense just makes me sound worse.

IF GOD'S NOT RESPONSIBLE, WHO IS?

"Believe me, I'm blameless.
    I don't understand what's going on.

I hate my life!
Since either way it ends up the same, I can only conclude
    that God destroys the good right along with the bad.
When calamity hits and brings sudden death,
    he folds his arms, aloof from the despair of the innocent.
He lets the wicked take over running the world,
    he installs judges who can't tell right from wrong.
    If he's not responsible, who is?

"My time is short—what's left of my life races off
    too fast for me to even glimpse the good.
My life is going fast, like a ship under full sail,
    like an eagle plummeting to its prey.
Even if I say, 'I'll put all this behind me,
    I'll look on the bright side and force a smile,'
All these troubles would still be like grit in my gut
    since it's clear you're not going to let up.
The verdict has already been handed down—'Guilty!'—
    so what's the use of protests or appeals?
Even if I scrub myself all over
    and wash myself with the strongest soap I can find,
It wouldn't last—you'd push me into a pigpen, or worse,
    so nobody could stand me for the stink.

"God and I are not equals; I can't bring a case against him.
    We'll never enter a courtroom as peers.
How I wish we had an arbitrator
    to step in and let me get on with life—
To break God's death grip on me,
    to free me from this terror so I could breathe again.
Then I'd speak up and state my case boldly.
    As things stand, there is no way I can do it.

# 10

To Find Some Skeleton in My Closet

"I can't stand my life—I hate it!
    I'm putting it all out on the table,
    all the bitterness of my life—I'm holding back nothing."

Job prayed:

"Here's what I want to say:
Don't, God, bring in a verdict of guilty
    without letting me know the charges you're bringing.
How does this fit into what you once called 'good'—
    giving me a hard time, spurning me,
    a life you shaped by your very own hands,
    and then blessing the plots of the wicked?
You don't look at things the way we mortals do.
    You're not taken in by appearances, are you?
Unlike us, you're not working against a deadline.
    You have all eternity to work things out.
So what's this all about, anyway—this compulsion
    to dig up some dirt, to find some skeleton in my closet?
You know good and well I'm not guilty.
    You also know no one can help me.

"You made me like a handcrafted piece of pottery—
    and now are you going to smash me to pieces?
Don't you remember how beautifully you worked my clay?
    Will you reduce me now to a mud pie?
Oh, that marvel of conception as you stirred together
    semen and ovum—
What a miracle of skin and bone,
    muscle and brain!
You gave me life itself, and incredible love.
    You watched and guarded every breath I took.

"But you never told me about this part.
    I should have known that there was more to it—
That if I so much as missed a step, you'd notice and pounce,
    wouldn't let me get by with a thing.
If I'm truly guilty, I'm doomed.
    But if I'm innocent, it's no better—I'm still doomed.
My belly is full of bitterness.
    I'm up to my ears in a swamp of affliction.
I try to make the best of it, try to brave it out,
    but you're too much for me,

relentless, like a lion on the prowl.
You line up fresh witnesses against me.
    You compound your anger
    and pile on the grief and pain!

"So why did you have me born?
    I wish no one had ever laid eyes on me!
I wish I'd never lived—a stillborn,
    buried without ever having breathed.
Isn't it time to call it quits on my life?
    Can't you let up, and let me smile just once
Before I die and am buried,
    before I'm nailed into my coffin, sealed in the ground,
And banished for good to the land of the dead,
    blind in the final dark?"


# 11    ZOPHAR'S COUNSEL

## How Wisdom Looks From the Inside

Now it was the turn of Zophar from Naamath:

"What a flood of words! Shouldn't we put a stop to it?
    Should this kind of loose talk be permitted?
Job, do you think you can carry on like this and we'll say nothing?
    That we'll let you rail and mock and not step in?
You claim, 'My doctrine is sound
    and my conduct impeccable.'
How I wish God would give you a piece of his mind,
    tell you what's what!
I wish he'd show you how wisdom looks from the inside,
    for true wisdom is mostly 'inside.'
But you can be sure of this,
    you haven't gotten half of what you deserve.

"Do you think you can explain the mystery of God?
    Do you think you can diagram God Almighty?
God is far higher than you can imagine,
    far deeper than you can comprehend,

30

Stretching farther than earth's horizons,
>    far wider than the endless ocean.
If he happens along, throws you in jail
>    then hauls you into court, can you do anything about it?
He sees through vain pretensions,
>    spots evil a long way off—
>    no one pulls the wool over *his* eyes!
Hollow men, hollow women, will wise up
>    about the same time mules learn to talk.

### REACH OUT TO GOD

"Still, if you set your heart on God
>    and reach out to him,
If you scrub your hands of sin
>    and refuse to entertain evil in your home,
You'll be able to face the world unashamed
>    and keep a firm grip on life, guiltless and fearless.
You'll forget your troubles;
>    they'll be like old, faded photographs.
Your world will be washed in sunshine,
>    every shadow dispersed by dayspring.
Full of hope, you'll relax, confident again;
>    you'll look around, sit back, and take it easy.
Expansive, without a care in the world,
>    you'll be hunted out by many for your blessing.
But the wicked will see none of this.
>    They're headed down a dead-end road
>    with nothing to look forward to—nothing."

# 12      JOB ANSWERS ZOPHAR

### PUT YOUR EAR TO THE EARTH

Job answered:

"I'm sure you speak for all the experts,
>    and when you die there'll be no one left to tell us how to live.
But don't forget that I also have a brain—
>    I don't intend to play second fiddle to you.

31

It doesn't take an expert to know these things.

"I'm ridiculed by my friends:
    'So that's the man who had conversations with God!'
Ridiculed without mercy:
    'Look at the man who never did wrong!'
It's easy for the well-to-do to point their fingers in blame,
    for the well-fixed to pour scorn on the strugglers.
Crooks reside safely in high-security houses,
    insolent blasphemers live in luxury;
    they've bought and paid for a god who'll protect them.

"But ask the animals what they think—let them teach you;
    let the birds tell you what's going on.
Put your ear to the earth—learn the basics.
    Listen—the fish in the ocean will tell you their stories.
Isn't it clear that they all know and agree
    that GOD is sovereign, that he holds all things in his hand—
Every living soul, yes,
    every breathing creature?
Isn't this all just common sense,
    as common as the sense of taste?
Do you think the elderly have a corner on wisdom,
    that you have to grow old before you understand life?

FROM GOD WE LEARN HOW TO LIVE
"True wisdom and real power belong to God;
    from him we learn how to live,
    and also what to live for.
If he tears something down, it's down for good;
    if he locks people up, they're locked up for good.
If he holds back the rain, there's a drought;
    if he lets it loose, there's a flood.
Strength and success belong to God;
    both deceived and deceiver must answer to him.
He strips experts of their vaunted credentials,
    exposes judges as witless fools.
He divests kings of their royal garments,
    then ties a rag around their waists.
He strips priests of their robes,

32

and fires high officials from their jobs.
He forces trusted sages to keep silence,
      deprives elders of their good sense and wisdom.
He dumps contempt on famous people,
      disarms the strong and mighty.
He shines a spotlight into caves of darkness,
      hauls deepest darkness into the noonday sun.
He makes nations rise and then fall,
      builds up some and abandons others.
He robs world leaders of their reason,
      and sends them off into no man's land.
They grope in the dark without a clue,
      lurching and staggering like drunks.

# 13

I'm Taking My Case to God

"Yes, I've seen all this with my own eyes,
      heard and understood it with my very own ears.
Everything you know, I know,
      so I'm not taking a back seat to any of you.
I'm taking my case straight to God Almighty;
      I've had it with you—I'm going directly to God.
You graffiti my life with lies.
      You're a bunch of pompous quacks!
I wish you'd shut your mouths—
      silence is your only claim to wisdom.

"Listen now while I make my case,
      consider my side of things for a change.
Or are you going to keep on lying 'to do God a service'?
      to make up stories 'to get him off the hook'?
Why do you always take his side?
      Do you think he needs a lawyer to defend himself?
How would you fare if you were in the dock?
      Your lies might convince a jury—but would they
            convince *God*?
He'd reprimand you on the spot
      if he detected a bias in your witness.

33

Doesn't his splendor put you in awe?
>     Aren't you afraid to speak cheap lies before him?
Your wise sayings are knickknack wisdom,
>     good for nothing but gathering dust.

"So hold your tongue while I have my say,
>     then I'll take whatever I have coming to me.
Why do I go out on a limb like this
>     and take my life in my hands?
Because even if he killed me, I'd keep on hoping.
>     I'd defend my innocence to the very end.
Just wait, this is going to work out for the best—my salvation!
>     If I were guilt-stricken do you think I'd be doing this—
>     laying myself on the line before God?
You'd better pay attention to what I'm telling you,
>     listen carefully with both ears.
Now that I've laid out my defense,
>     I'm sure that I'll be acquitted.
Can anyone prove charges against me?
>     I've said my piece. I rest my case.

## WHY DOES GOD STAY HIDDEN AND SILENT?

"Please, God, I have two requests;
>     grant them so I'll know I count with you:
First, lay off the afflictions;
>     the terror is too much for me.
Second, address me directly so I can answer you,
>     or let me speak and then you answer me.
How many sins have been charged against me?
>     Show me the list—how bad is it?
Why do you stay hidden and silent?
>     Why treat me like I'm your enemy?
Why kick me around like an old tin can?
>     Why beat a dead horse?
You compile a long list of mean things about me,
>     even hold me accountable for the sins of my youth.
You hobble me so I can't move about.
>     You watch every move I make,
>     and brand me as a dangerous character.

"Like something rotten, human life fast decomposes,
    like a moth-eaten shirt or a mildewed blouse.

# 14

## If We Die, Will We Live Again?

"We're all adrift in the same boat:
    too few days, too many troubles.
We spring up like wildflowers in the desert and then wilt,
    transient as the shadow of a cloud.
Do you occupy your time with such fragile wisps?
    Why even bother hauling me into court?
There's nothing much to us to start with;
    how do you expect us to amount to anything?
Mortals have a limited life span.
    You've already decided how long we'll live—
    you set the boundary and no one can cross it.
So why not give us a break? Ease up!
    Even ditchdiggers get occasional days off.
For a tree there is always hope.
    Chop it down and it still has a chance—
    its roots can put out fresh sprouts.
Even if its roots are old and gnarled,
    its stump long dormant,
At the first whiff of water it comes to life,
    buds and grows like a sapling.
But men and women? They die and stay dead.
    They breathe their last, and that's it.
Like lakes and rivers that have dried up,
    parched reminders of what once was,
So mortals lie down and never get up,
    never wake up again—never.
Why don't you just bury me alive,
    get me out of the way until your anger cools?
But don't leave me there!
    Set a date when you'll see me again.
If we humans die, will we live again? That's my question.
    All through these difficult days I keep hoping,

waiting for the final change—for resurrection!
Homesick with longing for the creature you made,
 you'll call—and I'll answer!
You'll watch over every step I take,
 but you won't keep track of my missteps.
My sins will be stuffed in a sack
 and thrown into the sea—sunk in deep ocean.

"Meanwhile, mountains wear down
 and boulders break up,
Stones wear smooth
 and soil erodes,
 as you relentlessly grind down our hope.
You're too much for us.
 As always, you get the last word.
We don't like it and our faces show it,
 but you send us off anyway.
If our children do well for themselves, we never know it;
 if they do badly, we're spared the hurt.
Body and soul, that's it for us—
 a lifetime of pain, a lifetime of sorrow."

# 15     ELIPHAZ ATTACKS AGAIN

## You Trivialize Religion

Eliphaz of Teman spoke a second time:

"If you were truly wise, would you sound so much like a windbag,
 belching hot air?
Would you talk nonsense in the middle of a serious argument,
 babbling baloney?
Look at you! You trivialize religion,
 turn spiritual conversation into empty gossip.
It's your sin that taught you to talk this way.
 You chose an education in fraud.
Your own words have exposed your guilt.
 It's nothing I've said—you've incriminated yourself!
Do you think you're the first person to have to deal with
  these things?

Have you been around as long as the hills?
Were you listening in when God planned all this?
    Do you think you're the only one who knows anything?
What do you know that we don't know?
    What insights do you have that we've missed?
Gray beards and white hair back us up—
    old folks who've been around a lot longer than you.
Are God's promises not enough for you,
    spoken so gently and tenderly?
Why do you let your emotions take over,
    lashing out and spitting fire,
Pitting your whole being against God
    by letting words like this come out of your mouth?
Do you think it's possible for any mere mortal to be sinless
      in God's sight,
    for anyone born of a human mother to get it all together?
Why, God can't even trust his holy angels.
    He sees the flaws in the very heavens themselves,
So how much less we humans, smelly and foul,
    who lap up evil like water?

## ALWAYS AT ODDS WITH GOD

"I've a thing or two to tell you, so listen up!
    I'm letting you in on my views;
It's what wise men and women have always taught,
    holding nothing back from what *they* were taught
By their parents, back in the days
    when they had this land all to themselves:
Those who live by their own rules, not God's, can expect
      nothing but trouble,
    and the longer they live, the worse it gets.
Every little sound terrifies them.
    Just when they think they have it made, disaster strikes.
They despair of things ever getting better—
    they're on the list of people for whom things always turn out
      for the worst.
They wander here and there,
    never knowing where the next meal is coming from—
    every day is doomsday!

They live in constant terror,
    always with their backs up against the wall
Because they insist on shaking their fists at God,
    defying God Almighty to his face,
Always and ever at odds with God,
    always on the defensive.

"Even if they're the picture of health,
    trim and fit and youthful,
They'll end up living in a ghost town
    sleeping in a hovel not fit for a dog,
    a ramshackle shack.
They'll never get ahead,
    never amount to a hill of beans.
And then death—don't think they'll escape that!
    They'll end up shriveled weeds,
    brought down by a puff of God's breath.
There's a lesson here: Whoever invests in lies,
    gets lies for interest,
Paid in full before the due date.
    Some investment!
They'll be like fruit frost-killed before it ripens,
    like buds sheared off before they bloom.
The godless are fruitless—a barren crew;
    a life built on bribes goes up in smoke.
They have sex with sin and give birth to evil.
    Their lives are wombs for breeding deceit."

# 16      JOB DEFENDS HIMSELF

IF YOU WERE IN MY SHOES

Then Job defended himself:

"I've had all I can take of your talk.
    What a bunch of miserable comforters!
Is there no end to your windbag speeches?
    What's your problem that you go on and on like this?

If you were in my shoes,
    I could talk just like you.
I could put together a terrific harangue
    and really let you have it.
But I'd never do that. I'd console and comfort,
    make things better, not worse!

"When I speak up, I feel no better;
    if I say nothing, that doesn't help either.
I feel worn down.
    God, you have wasted me totally—me and my family!
You've shriveled me like a dried prune,
    showing the world that you're against me.
My gaunt face stares back at me from the mirror,
    a mute witness to your treatment of me.
Your anger tears at me,
    your teeth rip me to shreds,
    your eyes burn holes in me—God, my enemy!
People take one look at me and gasp.
    Contemptuous, they slap me around
    and gang up against me.
And God just stands there and lets them do it,
    lets wicked people do what they want with me.
I was contentedly minding my business when God beat me up.
    He grabbed me by the neck and threw me around.
He set me up as his target,
    then rounded up archers to shoot at me.
Merciless, they shot me full of arrows;
    bitter bile poured from my gut to the ground.
He burst in on me, onslaught after onslaught,
    charging me like a mad bull.

"I sewed myself a shroud and wore it like a shirt;
    I lay face down in the dirt.
Now my face is blotched red from weeping;
    look at the dark shadows under my eyes,
Even though I've never hurt a soul
    and my prayers are sincere!

THE ONE WHO REPRESENTS MORTALS BEFORE GOD

"Oh Earth, don't cover up the wrong done to me!
    Don't muffle my cry!
There must be Someone in heaven who knows the truth about me,
    in highest heaven, some Attorney who can clear my name—
My Champion, my Friend,
    while I'm weeping my eyes out before God.
I appeal to the One who represents mortals before God
    as a neighbor stands up for a neighbor.

"Only a few years are left
    before I set out on the road of no return.

# 17

"My spirit is broken,
    my days used up,
    my grave dug and waiting.
See how these mockers close in on me?
    How long do I have to put up with their insolence?

"O God, pledge your support for me.
    Give it to me in writing, with your signature.
    You're the only one who can do it!
These people are so useless!
    You know firsthand how stupid they can be.
    You wouldn't let them have the last word, would you?
Those who betray their own friends
    leave a legacy of abuse to their children.

"God, you've made me the talk of the town—
    people spit in my face;
I can hardly see from crying so much;
    I'm nothing but skin and bones.
Decent people can't believe what they're seeing;
    the good-hearted wake up and insist I've given up on God.

"But principled people hold tight, keep a firm grip on life,
    sure that their clean, pure hands will get stronger and stronger!

"Maybe you'd all like to start over,
   to try it again, the bunch of you.
So far I haven't come across one scrap
   of wisdom in anything you've said.
My life's about over. All my plans are smashed,
   all my hopes are snuffed out—
My hope that night would turn into day,
   my hope that dawn was about to break.
If all I have to look forward to is a home in the graveyard,
   if my only hope for comfort is a well-built coffin,
If a family reunion means going six feet under,
   and the only family that shows up is worms,
Do you call that hope?
   Who on earth could find any hope in that?
No. If hope and I are to be buried together,
   I suppose you'll all come to the double funeral!"

# 18     BILDAD'S SECOND ATTACK

PLUNGED FROM LIGHT INTO DARKNESS

Bildad from Shuhah chimed in:

"How monotonous these word games are getting!
   Get serious! We need to get down to business.
Why do you treat your friends like slow-witted animals?
   You look down on us as if we don't know anything.
Why are you working yourself up like this?
   Do you want the world redesigned to suit you?
   Should reality be suspended to accommodate you?

"Here's the rule: The light of the wicked is put out.
   Their flame dies down and is extinguished.
Their house goes dark—
   every lamp in the place goes out.
Their strong strides weaken, falter;
   they stumble into their own traps.
They get all tangled up

in their own red tape,
Their feet are grabbed and caught,
    their necks in a noose.
They trip on ropes they've hidden,
    and fall into pits they've dug themselves.
Terrors come at them from all sides.
    They run helter-skelter.
The hungry grave is ready
    to gobble them up for supper,
To lay them out for a gourmet meal,
    a treat for ravenous Death.
They are snatched from their home sweet home
    and marched straight to the death house.
Their lives go up in smoke;
    acid rain soaks their ruins.
Their roots rot
    and their branches wither.
They'll never again be remembered—
    nameless in unmarked graves.
They are plunged from light into darkness,
    banished from the world.
And they leave empty-handed—not one single child—
    nothing to show for their life on this earth.
Westerners are aghast at their fate,
    easterners are horrified:
'Oh no! So this is what happens to perverse people.
    This is how the God-ignorant end up!'"

## 19       JOB ANSWERS BILDAD

### I CALL FOR HELP AND NO ONE BOTHERS

Job answered:

"How long are you going to keep battering away at me,
    pounding me with these harangues?
Time after time after time you jump all over me.
    Do you have no conscience, abusing me like this?
Even if I have, somehow or other, gotten off the track,

42

what business is that of yours?
Why do you insist on putting me down,
    using my troubles as a stick to beat me?
Tell it to God—he's the one behind all this,
    he's the one who dragged me into this mess.

"Look at me—I shout 'Murder!' and I'm ignored;
    I call for help and no one bothers to stop.
God threw a barricade across my path—I'm stymied;
    he turned out all the lights—I'm stuck in the dark.
He destroyed my reputation,
    robbed me of all self-respect.
He tore me apart piece by piece—I'm ruined!
    Then he yanked out hope by the roots.
He's angry with me—oh, how he's angry!
    He treats me like his worst enemy.
He has launched a major campaign against me,
    using every weapon he can think of,
    coming at me from all sides at once.

I KNOW THAT GOD LIVES

"God alienated my family from me;
    everyone who knows me avoids me.
My relatives and friends have all left;
    houseguests forget I ever existed.
The servant girls treat me like a bum off the street,
    look at me like they've never seen me before.
I call my attendant and he ignores me,
    ignores me even though I plead with him.
My wife can't stand to be around me anymore.
    I'm repulsive to my family.
Even street urchins despise me;
    when I come out, they taunt and jeer.
Everyone I've ever been close to abhors me;
    my dearest loved ones reject me.
I'm nothing but a bag of bones;
    my life hangs by a thread.

"Oh, friends, dear friends, take pity on me.

God has come down hard on me!
Do you have to be hard on me too?
> Don't you ever tire of abusing me?

"If only my words were written in a book—
> better yet, chiseled in stone!
Still, I know that God lives—the One who gives me back my life—
> and eventually he'll take his stand on earth.
And I'll see him—even though I get skinned alive!—
> see God myself, with my very own eyes.
> Oh, how I long for that day!

"If you're thinking, 'How can we get through to him,
> get him to see that his trouble is all his own fault?'
Forget it. Start worrying about *yourselves*.
> Worry about your own sins and God's coming judgment,
> for judgment is most certainly on the way."

## 20  ZOPHAR ATTACKS JOB— THE SECOND ROUND

SAVORING EVIL AS A DELICACY

Zophar from Naamath again took his turn:

"I can't believe what I'm hearing!
> You've put my teeth on edge, my stomach in a knot.
How dare you insult my intelligence like this!
> Well, here's a piece of my mind!

"Don't you even know the basics,
> how things have been since the earliest days,
> when Adam and Eve were first placed on earth?
The good times of the wicked are short-lived;
> godless joy is only momentary.
The evil might become world famous,
> strutting at the head of the celebrity parade,
But still end up in a pile of dung.
> Acquaintances look at them with disgust and say, 'What's that?'
They fly off like a dream that can't be remembered,

like a shadowy illusion that vanishes in the light.
Though once notorious public figures, now they're nobodies,
    unnoticed, whether they come or go.
Their children will go begging on skid row,
    and they'll have to give back their ill-gotten gain.
Right in the prime of life,
    and youthful and vigorous, they'll die.

"They savor evil as a delicacy,
    roll it around on their tongues,
Prolong the flavor, a dalliance in decadence—
    real gourmets of evil!
But then they get stomach cramps,
    a bad case of food poisoning.
They gag on all that rich food;
    God makes them vomit it up.
They gorge on evil, make a diet of that poison—
    a deadly diet—and it kills them.
No quiet picnics for them beside gentle streams
    with fresh-baked bread and cheese, and tall, cool drinks.
They spit out their food half-chewed,
    unable to relax and enjoy anything they've worked for.
And why? Because they exploited the poor,
    took what never belonged to them.

"Such God-denying people are never content with what they have
        or who they are;
    their greed drives them relentlessly.
They plunder everything
    but they can't hold on to any of it.
Just when they think they have it all, disaster strikes;
    they're served up a plate full of misery.
When they've filled their bellies with that,
    God gives them a taste of his anger,
    and they get to chew on that for a while.
As they run for their lives from one disaster,
    they run smack into another.
They're knocked around from pillar to post,
    beaten to within an inch of their lives.

They're trapped in a house of horrors,
    and see their loot disappear down a black hole.
Their lives are a total loss—
    not a penny to their name, not so much as a bean.
God will strip them of their sin-soaked clothes
    and hang their dirty laundry out for all to see.
Life is a complete wipe-out for them,
    nothing surviving God's wrath.
There! That's God's blueprint for the wicked—
    what they have to look forward to."

# 21         JOB'S RESPONSE

### WHY DO THE WICKED HAVE IT SO GOOD?

Job replied:

"Now listen to me carefully, please listen,
    at least do me the favor of listening.
Put up with me while I have my say—
    then you can mock me later to your heart's content.

"It's not *you* I'm complaining to—it's *God*.
    Is it any wonder I'm getting fed up with his silence?
Take a good look at me. Aren't you appalled by what's happened?
    No! Don't say anything. I can do without your comments.
When I look back, I go into shock,
    my body is racked with spasms.
Why do the wicked have it so good,
    live to a ripe old age and get rich?
They get to see their children succeed,
    get to watch and enjoy their grandchildren.
Their homes are peaceful and free from fear;
    they never experience God's disciplining rod.
Their bulls breed with great vigor
    and their cows calve without fail.
They send their children out to play
    and watch them frolic like spring lambs.
They make music with fiddles and flutes,

have good times singing and dancing.
They have a long life on easy street,
    and die painlessly in their sleep.
They say to God, 'Get lost!
    We've no interest in you or your ways.
Why should we have dealings with God Almighty?
    What's there in it for us?'
But they're wrong, dead wrong—they're not gods.
    It's beyond me how they can carry on like this!

"Still, how often does it happen that the wicked fail,
    or disaster strikes,
    or they get their just deserts?
How often are they blown away by bad luck?
    Not very often.
You might say, 'God is saving up the punishment for their children.'
    I say, 'Give it to them right now so they'll know what
        they've done!'
They deserve to experience the effects of their evil,
    feel the full force of God's wrath firsthand.
What do they care what happens to their families
    after they're safely tucked away in the grave?

Fancy Funerals With All the Trimmings

"But who are we to tell God how to run his affairs?
    He's dealing with matters that are way over our heads.
Some people die in the prime of life,
    with everything going for them—
    fat and sassy.
Others die bitter and bereft,
    never getting a taste of happiness.
They're laid out side by side in the cemetery,
    where the worms can't tell one from the other.

"I'm not deceived. I know what you're up to,
    the plans you're cooking up to bring me down.
Naively you claim that the castles of tyrants fall to pieces,
    that the achievements of the wicked collapse.
Have you ever asked world travelers how they see it?

Have you not listened to their stories
Of evil men and women who got off scot-free,
    who never had to pay for their wickedness?
Did anyone ever confront them with their crimes?
    Did they ever have to face the music?
Not likely—they're given fancy funerals
    with all the trimmings,
Gently lowered into expensive graves,
    with everyone telling lies about how wonderful they were.

"So how do you expect me to get any comfort from your nonsense?
    Your so-called comfort is a tissue of lies."

## ELIPHAZ ATTACKS JOB— THE THIRD ROUND

# 22

### COME TO TERMS WITH GOD

Once again Eliphaz the Temanite took up his theme:

"Are any of us strong enough to give God a hand,
    or smart enough to give him advice?
So what if you were righteous—would God Almighty even notice?
    Even if you gave a perfect performance, do you think
        he'd applaud?
Do you think it's because he cares about your purity
    that he's disciplining you, putting you on the spot?
Hardly! It's because you're a first-class moral failure,
    because there's no end to your sins.
When people came to you for help,
    you took the shirts off their backs, exploited their helplessness.
You wouldn't so much as give a drink to the thirsty,
    or food, not even a scrap, to the hungry.
And there you sat, strong and honored by everyone,
    surrounded by immense wealth!
You turned poor widows away from your door;
    heartless, you crushed orphans.
Now *you're* the one trapped in terror, paralyzed by fear.
    Suddenly the tables have turned!
How do you like living in the dark, sightless,

up to your neck in flood waters?

"You agree, don't you, that God is in charge?
    He runs the universe—just look at the stars!
Yet you dare raise questions: 'What does God know?
    From that distance and darkness, how can he judge?
He roams the heavens wrapped in clouds,
    so how can he see us?'

"Are you going to persist in that tired old line
    that wicked men and women have always used?
Where did it get them? They died young,
    flash floods sweeping them off to their doom.
They told God, 'Get lost!
    What good is God Almighty to us?'
And yet it was God who gave them everything they had.
    It's beyond me how they can carry on like this!

"Good people see bad people crash, and call for a celebration.
    Relieved, they crow,
'At last! Our enemies—wiped out.
    Everything they had and stood for is up in smoke!'

"Give in to God, come to terms with him
    and everything will turn out just fine.
Let him tell you what to do;
    take his words to heart.
Come back to God Almighty
    and he'll rebuild your life.
Clean house of everything evil.
    Relax your grip on your money
    and abandon your gold-plated luxury.
God Almighty will be your treasure,
    more wealth than you can imagine.

"You'll take delight in God, the Mighty One,
    and look to him joyfully, boldly.
You'll pray to him and he'll listen;
    he'll help you do what you've promised.

49

You'll decide what you want and it will happen;
    your life will be bathed in light.
To those who feel low you'll say, 'Chin up! Be brave!'
    and God will save them.
Yes, even the guilty will escape,
    escape through God's grace in your life."

# 23     JOB'S DEFENSE

## I'M COMPLETELY IN THE DARK

Job replied:

"I'm not letting up—I'm standing my ground.
    My complaint is legitimate.
God has no right to treat me like this—
    it isn't fair!
If I knew where on earth to find him,
    I'd go straight to him.
I'd lay my case before him face-to-face,
    give him all my arguments firsthand.
I'd find out exactly what he's thinking,
    discover what's going on in his head.
Do you think he'd dismiss me or bully me?
    No, he'd take me seriously.
He'd see a straight-living man standing before him;
    my Judge would acquit me for good of all charges.

"I travel East looking for him—I find no one;
    then West, but not a trace;
I go North, but he's hidden his tracks;
    then South, but not even a glimpse.

"But he knows where I am and what I've done.
    He can cross-examine me all he wants, and I'll pass the test
        with honors.
I've followed him closely, my feet in his footprints,
    not once swerving from his way.

I've obeyed every word he's spoken,
     and not just obeyed his advice—I've *treasured* it.

"But he is singular and sovereign. Who can argue with him?
     He does what he wants, when he wants to.
He'll complete in detail what he's decided about me,
     and whatever else he determines to do.
Is it any wonder that I dread meeting him?
     Whenever I think about it, I get scared all over again.
God makes my heart sink!
     God Almighty gives me the shudders!
I'm completely in the dark,
     I can't see my hand in front of my face.

# 24

AN ILLUSION OF SECURITY

"But if Judgment Day isn't hidden from the Almighty,
     why are we kept in the dark?
There are people out there getting by with murder—
     stealing and lying and cheating.
They rip off the poor
     and exploit the unfortunate,
Push the helpless into the ditch,
     bully the weak so that they fear for their lives.
The poor, like stray dogs and cats,
     scavenge for food in back alleys.
They sort through the garbage of the rich,
     eke out survival on handouts.
Homeless, they shiver through cold nights on the street;
     they've no place to lay their heads.
Exposed to the weather, wet and frozen,
     they huddle in makeshift shelters.
Nursing mothers have their babies snatched from them;
     the infants of the poor are kidnapped and sold.
They go about patched and threadbare;
     even the hard workers go hungry.
No matter how back-breaking their labor,
     they can never make ends meet.

51

People are dying right and left, groaning in torment.
    The wretched cry out for help
    and God does nothing, acts like nothing's wrong!

"Then there are those who avoid light at all costs,
    who scorn the light-filled path.
When the sun goes down, the murderer gets up—
    kills the poor and robs the defenseless.
Sexual predators can't wait for nightfall,
    thinking, 'No one can see us now.'
Burglars do their work at night,
    but keep well out of sight through the day.
    They want nothing to do with light.
Deep darkness is morning for that bunch;
    they make the terrors of darkness their companions in crime.

"They are scraps of wood floating on the water—
    useless, cursed junk, good for nothing.
As surely as snow melts under the hot, summer sun,
    sinners disappear in the grave.
The womb has forgotten them, worms have relished them—
    nothing that is evil lasts.
Unscrupulous,
    they prey on those less fortunate.
However much they strut and flex their muscles,
    there's nothing to them. They're hollow.
They may have an illusion of security,
    but God has his eye on them.
They may get their brief successes,
    but then it's over, nothing to show for it.
Like yesterday's newspaper,
    they're used to wrap up the garbage.
You're free to try to prove me a liar,
    but you won't be able to do it."

# 25     BILDAD'S THIRD ATTACK

EVEN THE STARS AREN'T PERFECT IN GOD'S EYES
Bildad the Shuhite again attacked Job:

"God is sovereign, God is fearsome—
    everything in the cosmos fits and works in his plan.
Can anyone count his angel armies?
    Is there any place where his light doesn't shine?
How can a mere mortal presume to stand up to God?
    How can an ordinary person pretend to be guiltless?
Why, even the moon has its flaws,
    even the stars aren't perfect in God's eyes,
So how much less, plain men and women—
    slugs and maggots by comparison!"

# 26 JOB'S DEFENSE

### GOD SETS A BOUNDARY BETWEEN LIGHT AND DARKNESS

Job answered:

"Well, you've certainly been a great help to a helpless man!
    You came to the rescue just in the nick of time!
What wonderful advice you've given to a mixed-up man!
    What amazing insights you've provided!
Where in the world did you learn all this?
    How did you become so inspired!

"All the buried dead are in torment,
    and all who've been drowned in the deep, deep sea.
Hell is ripped open before God,
    graveyards dug up and exposed.
He spreads the skies over unformed space,
    hangs the earth out in empty space.
He pours water into cumulus cloud-bags
    and the bags don't burst.
He makes the moon wax and wane,
    putting it through its phases.
He draws the horizon out over the ocean,
    sets a boundary between light and darkness.
Thunder crashes and rumbles in the skies.
    Listen! It's God raising his voice!
By his power he stills sea storms,
    by his wisdom he tames sea monsters.

With one breath he clears the sky,
    with one finger he crushes the sea serpent.
And this is only the beginning,
    a mere whisper of his rule.
    Whatever would we do if he *really* raised his voice!"

# 27

No Place to Hide

Having waited for Zophar, Job now resumed his defense:

"God-Alive! He's denied me justice!
    God Almighty! He's ruined my life!
But for as long as I draw breath,
    and for as long as God breathes life into me,
I refuse to say one word that isn't true.
    I refuse to confess to any charge that's false.
There is no way I'll ever agree to your accusations.
    I'll not deny my integrity even if it costs me my life.
I'm holding fast to my integrity and not loosening my grip—
    and, believe me, I'll never regret it.

"Let my enemy be exposed as wicked!
    Let my adversary be proven guilty!
What hope do people without God have when life is cut short?
    when God puts an end to life?
Do you think God will listen to their cry for help
    when disaster hits?
What interest have they ever shown in the Almighty?
    Have they ever been known to pray before?

"I've given you a clear account of God in action,
    suppressed nothing regarding God Almighty.
The evidence is right before you. You can all see it for yourselves,
    so why do you keep talking nonsense?

"I'll quote your own words back to you:

"'This is how God treats the wicked,

this is what evil people can expect from God Almighty:
Their children—all of them—will die violent deaths;
    they'll never have enough bread to put on the table.
They'll be wiped out by the plague,
    and none of the widows will shed a tear when they're gone.
Even if they make a lot of money
    and are resplendent in the latest fashions,
It's the good who will end up wearing the clothes
    and the decent who will divide up the money.
They build elaborate houses
    that won't survive a single winter.
They go to bed wealthy
    and wake up poor.
Terrors pour in on them like flash floods—
    a tornado snatches them away in the middle of the night,
A cyclone sweeps them up—gone!
    Not a trace of them left, not even a footprint.
Catastrophes relentlessly pursue them;
    they run this way and that, but there's no place to hide—
Pummeled by the weather,
    blown to kingdom come by the storm.'

# 28

## Where Does Wisdom Come From?

"We all know how silver seams the rocks,
    we've seen the stuff from which gold is refined,
We're aware of how iron is dug out of the ground
    and copper is smelted from rock.
Miners penetrate the earth's darkness,
    searching the roots of the mountains for ore,
    digging away in the suffocating darkness.
Far from civilization, far from the traffic,
    they cut a shaft,
    and are lowered into it by ropes.
Earth's surface is a field for grain,
    but its depths are a forge
Firing sapphires from stones

and chiseling gold from rocks.
Vultures are blind to its riches,
    hawks never lay eyes on it.
Wild animals are oblivious to it,
    lions don't know it's there.
Miners hammer away at the rock,
    they uproot the mountains.
They tunnel through the rock
    and find all kinds of beautiful gems.
They discover the origins of rivers,
    and bring earth's secrets to light.

"But where, oh where, will they find Wisdom?
    Where does Insight hide?
Mortals don't have a clue,
    haven't the slightest idea where to look.
Earth's depths say, 'It's not here';
    ocean deeps echo, 'Never heard of it.'
It can't be bought with the finest gold;
    no amount of silver can get it.
Even famous Ophir gold can't buy it,
    not even diamonds and sapphires.
Neither gold nor emeralds are comparable;
    extravagant jewelry can't touch it.
Pearl necklaces and ruby bracelets—why bother?
    None of this is even a down payment on Wisdom!
Pile gold and African diamonds as high as you will,
    they can't hold a candle to Wisdom.

"So where does Wisdom come from?
    And where does Insight live?
It can't be found by looking, no matter
    how deep you dig, no matter how high you fly.
If you search through the graveyard and question the dead,
    they say, 'We've only heard rumors of it.'

"God alone knows the way to Wisdom,
    he knows the exact place to find it.
He knows where everything is on earth,

he sees everything under heaven.
After he commanded the winds to blow
    and measured out the waters,
Arranged for the rain
    and set off explosions of thunder and lightning,
He focused on Wisdom,
    made sure it was all set and tested and ready.
Then he addressed the human race: 'Here it is!
    Fear-of-the-Lord—that's Wisdom,
    and Insight means shunning evil.'"

# 29

## WHEN GOD WAS STILL BY MY SIDE

Job now resumed his response:

"Oh, how I long for the good old days,
    when God took such very good care of me.
He always held a lamp before me
    and I walked through the dark by its light.
Oh, how I miss those golden years
    when God's friendship graced my home,
When the Mighty One was still by my side
    and my children were all around me,
When everything was going my way,
    and nothing seemed too difficult.

"When I walked downtown
    and sat with my friends in the public square,
Young and old greeted me with respect;
    I was honored by everyone in town.
When I spoke, everyone listened;
    they hung on my every word.
People who knew me, spoke well of me;
    my reputation went ahead of me.
I was known for helping people in trouble
    and standing up for those who were down on their luck.
The dying blessed me,

and the bereaved were cheered by my visits.
All my dealings with people were good.
    I was known for being fair to everyone I met.
I was eyes to the blind
    and feet to the lame,
Father to the needy,
    and champion of abused aliens.
I grabbed street thieves by the scruff of the neck
    and made them give back what they'd stolen.
I thought, 'I'll die peacefully in my own bed,
    grateful for a long and full life,
A life deep-rooted and well-watered,
    a life limber and dew-fresh,
My soul suffused with glory
    and my body robust until the day I die.'

"Men and women listened when I spoke,
    hung expectantly on my every word.
After I spoke, they'd be quiet,
    taking it all in.
They welcomed my counsel like spring rain,
    drinking it all in.
When I smiled at them, they could hardly believe it;
    their faces lit up, their troubles took wing!
I was their leader, establishing the mood
    and setting the pace by which they lived.
    Where I led, they followed.

# 30

THE PAIN NEVER LETS UP

"But no longer. Now I'm the butt of their jokes—
    young ruffians! whippersnappers!
Why, I considered their fathers
    mere inexperienced pups.
But they are worse than dogs—good for nothing,
    stray, mangy animals,
Half-starved, scavenging the back alleys,
    howling at the moon;

Homeless guttersnipes
    chewing on old bones and licking old tin cans;
Outcasts from the community,
    cursed as dangerous delinquents.
Nobody would put up with them;
    they were driven from the neighborhood.
You could hear them out there at the edge of town,
    yelping and barking, huddled in junkyards,
A gang of beggars and no-names,
    thrown out on their ears.

"But now I'm the one they're after,
    mistreating me, taunting and mocking.
They abhor me, they abuse me.
    How dare those scoundrels—they spit in my face!
Now that God has undone me and left me in a heap,
    they hold nothing back. Anything goes.
They come at me from my blind side,
    trip me up, then jump on me while I'm down.
They throw every kind of obstacle in my path,
    determined to ruin me—
    and no one lifts a finger to help me!
They violate my broken body,
    trample through the rubble of my ruined life.
Terrors assault me—
    my dignity in shreds,
    salvation up in smoke.

"And now my life drains out,
    as suffering seizes and grips me hard.
Night gnaws at my bones;
    the pain never lets up.
I am tied hand and foot, my neck in a noose.
    I twist and turn.
Thrown facedown in the muck,
    I'm a muddy mess, inside and out.

WHAT DID I DO TO DESERVE THIS?

"I shout for help, God, and get nothing, no answer!
    I stand to face you in protest, and you give me a blank stare!

You've turned into my tormenter—
    you slap me around, knock me about.
You raised me up so I was riding high
    and then dropped me, and I crashed.
I know you're determined to kill me,
    to put me six feet under.

"What did I do to deserve this?
    Did I ever hit anyone who was calling for help?
Haven't I wept for those who live a hard life,
    been heartsick over the lot of the poor?
But where did it get me?
    I expected good but evil showed up.
    I looked for light but darkness fell.
My stomach's in a constant churning, never settles down.
    Each day confronts me with more suffering.
I walk under a black cloud. The sun is gone.
    I stand in the congregation and protest.
I howl with the jackals,
    I hoot with the owls.
I'm black and blue all over,
    burning up with fever.
My fiddle plays nothing but the blues;
    my mouth harp wails laments.

# 31

WHAT CAN I EXPECT FROM GOD?

"I made a solemn pact with myself
    never to undress a girl with my eyes.
So what can I expect from God?
    What do I deserve from God Almighty above?
Isn't calamity reserved for the wicked?
    Isn't disaster supposed to strike those who do wrong?
Isn't God looking, observing how I live?
    Doesn't he mark every step I take?

"Have I walked hand in hand with falsehood,
    or hung out in the company of deceit?

Weigh me on a set of honest scales
    so God has proof of my integrity.
If I've strayed off the straight and narrow,
    wanted things I had no right to,
    messed around with sin,
Go ahead, then—
    give my portion to someone who deserves it.

"If I've let myself be seduced by a woman
    and conspired to go to bed with her,
Fine, my wife has every right to go ahead
    and sleep with anyone she wants to.
For disgusting behavior like that,
    I'd deserve the worst punishment you could hand out.
Adultery is a fire that burns the house down;
    I wouldn't expect anything I count dear to survive it.

"Have I ever been unfair to my employees
    when they brought a complaint to me?
What, then, will I do when God confronts me?
    When God examines my books, what can I say?
Didn't the same God who made me, make them?
    Aren't we all made of the same stuff, equals before God?

"Have I ignored the needs of the poor,
    turned my back on the indigent,
Taken care of my own needs and fed my own face
    while they languished?
Wasn't my home always open to them?
    Weren't they always welcome at my table?

"Have I ever left a poor family shivering in the cold
    when they had no warm clothes?
Didn't the poor bless me when they saw me coming,
    knowing I'd brought coats from my closet?

"If I've ever used my strength and influence
    to take advantage of the unfortunate,
Go ahead, break both my arms,

61

cut off all my fingers!
The fear of God has kept me from these things—
  how else could I ever face him?

## IF ONLY SOMEONE WOULD GIVE ME A HEARING!

"Did I set my heart on making big money
  or worship at the bank?
Did I boast about my wealth,
  show off because I was well-off?
Was I ever so awed by the sun's brilliance
  and moved by the moon's beauty
That I let myself become seduced by them
  and worshiped them on the sly?
If so, I would deserve the worst of punishments,
  for I would be betraying God himself.

"Did I ever crow over my enemy's ruin?
  Or gloat over my rival's bad luck?
No, I never said a word of detraction,
  never cursed them, even under my breath.

"Didn't those who worked for me say,
  'He fed us well. There were always second helpings'?
And no stranger ever had to spend a night in the street;
  my doors were always open to travelers.
Did I hide my sin the way Adam did,
  or conceal my guilt behind closed doors
Because I was afraid what people would say,
  fearing the gossip of the neighbors so much
That I turned myself into a recluse?
  You know good and well that I didn't.

"Oh, if only someone would give me a hearing!
  I've signed my name to my defense—let the
    Almighty One answer!
  I want to see my indictment in writing.
Anyone's welcome to read my defense;
  I'll write it on a poster and carry it around town.

I'm prepared to account for every move I've ever made—
    to anyone and everyone, prince or pauper.

"If the very ground that I farm accuses me,
    if even the furrows fill with tears from my abuse,
If I've ever raped the earth for my own profit
    or dispossessed its rightful owners,
Then curse it with thistles instead of wheat,
    curse it with weeds instead of barley."

The words of Job to his three friends were finished.

# 32     ELIHU SPEAKS

GOD'S SPIRIT MAKES WISDOM POSSIBLE

Job's three friends now fell silent. They were talked out, stymied because Job wouldn't budge an inch—wouldn't admit to an ounce of guilt. Then Elihu lost his temper. (Elihu was the son of Barakel the Buzite from the clan of Ram.) He blazed out in anger against Job for pitting his righteousness against God's. He was also angry with the three friends because they had neither come up with an answer nor proved Job wrong. Elihu had waited with Job while they spoke because they were all older than he. But when he saw that the three other men had exhausted their arguments, he exploded with pent-up anger.

This is what Elihu, son of Barakel the Buzite, said:

"I'm a young man,
    and you are all old and experienced.
That's why I kept quiet
    and held back from joining the discussion.
I kept thinking, 'Experience will tell.
    The longer you live, the wiser you become.'
But I see I was wrong—it's God's Spirit in a person,
    the breath of the Almighty One, that makes wise human
        insight possible.
The experts have no corner on wisdom;
    getting old doesn't guarantee good sense.

So I've decided to speak up. Listen well!
 I'm going to tell you exactly what I think.

"I hung on your words while you spoke,
 listened carefully to your arguments.
While you searched for the right words,
 I was all ears.
And now what have you proved? Nothing.
 Nothing you say has even touched Job.
And don't excuse yourselves by saying, 'We've done our best.
 Now it's up to God to talk sense into him.'
Job has yet to contend with me.
 And rest assured, I won't be using *your* arguments!

"Do you three have nothing else to say?
 Of *course* you don't! You're total frauds!
Why should I wait any longer,
 now that you're stopped dead in your tracks?
I'm ready to speak my piece. That's right!
 It's my turn—and it's about time!
I've got a lot to say,
 and I'm bursting to say it.
The pressure has built up, like lava beneath the earth.
 I'm a volcano ready to blow.
I *have* to speak—I have no choice.
 I have to say what's on my heart,
And I'm going to say it straight—
 the truth, the whole truth, and nothing but the truth.
I was never any good at bootlicking;
 my Maker would make short work of me if I started in now!

# 33

"So please, Job, hear me out,
 honor me by listening to me.
What I'm about to say
 has been carefully thought out.
I have no ulterior motives in this;

I'm speaking honestly from my heart.
The Spirit of God made me what I am,
    the breath of God Almighty gave me life!

## GOD ALWAYS ANSWERS, ONE WAY OR ANOTHER

"And if you think you can prove me wrong, do it.
    Lay out your arguments. Stand up for yourself!
Look, I'm human—no better than you;
    we're both made of the same kind of mud.
So let's work this through together;
    don't let my aggressiveness overwhelm you.

"Here's what you said.
    I heard you say it with my own ears.
You said, 'I'm pure—I've done nothing wrong.
    Believe me, I'm clean—my conscience is clear.
But God keeps picking on me;
    he treats me like I'm his enemy.
He's thrown me in jail;
    he keeps me under constant surveillance.'

"But let me tell you, Job, you're wrong, dead wrong!
    God is far greater than any human.
So how dare you haul him into court,
    and then complain that he won't answer your charges?
God always answers, one way or another,
    even when people don't recognize his presence.

"In a dream, for instance, a vision at night,
    when men and women are deep in sleep,
    fast asleep in their beds—
God opens their ears
    and impresses them with warnings
To turn them back from something bad they're planning,
    from some reckless choice,
And keep them from an early grave,
    from the river of no return.

"Or, God might get their attention through pain,
    by throwing them on a bed of suffering,
So they can't stand the sight of food,
    have no appetite for their favorite treats.
They lose weight, wasting away to nothing,
    reduced to a bag of bones.
They hang on the cliff-edge of death,
    knowing the next breath may be their last.

"But even then an angel could come,
    a champion—there are thousands of them!—
    to take up your cause,
A messenger who would mercifully intervene,
    canceling the death sentence with the words:
    'I've come up with the ransom!'
Before you know it, you're healed,
    the very picture of health!

"Or, you may fall on your knees and pray—to God's delight!
    You'll see God's smile and celebrate,
    finding yourself set right with God.
You'll sing God's praises to everyone you meet,
    testifying, 'I messed up my life—
    and let me tell you, it wasn't worth it.
But God stepped in and saved me from certain death.
    I'm alive again! Once more I see the light!'

"This is the way God works.
    Over and over again
He pulls our souls back from certain destruction
    so we'll see the light—and *live* in the light!

"Keep listening, Job.
    Don't interrupt—I'm not finished yet.
But if you think of anything I should know, tell me.
    There's nothing I'd like better than to see your name cleared.
Meanwhile, keep listening. Don't distract me with interruptions.
    I'm going to teach you the basics of wisdom."

# 34     ELIHU'S SECOND SPEECH

## IT'S IMPOSSIBLE FOR GOD TO DO EVIL

Elihu continued:

"So, my fine friends—listen to me,
    and see what you think of this.
Isn't it just common sense—
    as common as the sense of taste—
To put our heads together
    and figure out what's going on here?

"We've all heard Job say, 'I'm in the right,
    but God won't give me a fair trial.
When I defend myself, I'm called a liar to my face.
    I've done nothing wrong, and I get punished anyway.'
Have you ever heard anything to beat this?
    Does nothing faze this man Job?
Do you think he's spent too much time in bad company,
    hanging out with the wrong crowd,
So that now he's parroting their line:
    'It doesn't pay to try to please God'?

"You're veterans in dealing with these matters;
    certainly we're of one mind on this.
It's impossible for God to do anything evil;
    no way can the Mighty One do wrong.
He makes us pay for exactly what we've done—no more, no less.
    Our chickens always come home to roost.
It's impossible for God to do anything wicked,
    for the Mighty One to subvert justice.
He's the one who runs the earth!
    He cradles the whole world in his hand!
If he decided to hold his breath,
    every man, woman, and child would die for lack of air.

### GOD IS WORKING BEHIND THE SCENES

"So, Job, use your head;
    this is all pretty obvious.
Can someone who hates order, keep order?
    Do you dare condemn the righteous, mighty God?
Doesn't God always tell it like it is,
    exposing corrupt rulers as scoundrels and criminals?
Does he play favorites with the rich and famous and
        slight the poor?
    Isn't he equally responsible to everybody?
Don't people who deserve it die without notice?
    Don't wicked rulers tumble to their doom?
When the so-called great ones are wiped out,
    we know God is working behind the scenes.

"He has his eyes on every man and woman.
    He doesn't miss a trick.
There is no night dark enough, no shadow deep enough,
    to hide those who do evil.
God doesn't need to gather any more evidence;
    their sin is an open-and-shut case.
He deposes the so-called high and mighty without
        asking questions,
    and replaces them at once with others.
Nobody gets by with anything; overnight,
    judgment is signed, sealed, and delivered.
He punishes the wicked for their wickedness
    out in the open where everyone can see it,
Because they quit following him,
    no longer even thought about him or his ways.
Their apostasy was announced by the cry of the poor;
    the cry of the afflicted got God's attention.

### BECAUSE YOU REFUSE TO LIVE ON GOD'S TERMS

"If God is silent, what's that to you?
    If he turns his face away, what can you do about it?
But whether silent or hidden, he's there, ruling,

so that those who hate God won't take over
and ruin people's lives.

"So why don't you simply confess to God?
Say, 'I sinned, but I'll sin no more.
Teach me to see what I still don't see.
Whatever evil I've done, I'll do it no more.'
Just because you refuse to live on God's terms,
do you think he should start living on yours?
You choose. I can't do it for you.
Tell me what you decide.

"All right-thinking people say—
and the wise who have listened to me concur—
'Job is an ignoramus.
He talks utter nonsense.'
Job, you need to be pushed to the wall and called to account
for wickedly talking back to God the way you have.
You've compounded your original sin
by rebelling against God's discipline,
Defiantly shaking your fist at God,
piling up indictments against the Almighty One."

# 35       ELIHU'S THIRD SPEECH

### When God Makes Creation a Classroom

Elihu lit into Job again:

"Does this kind of thing make any sense?
First you say, 'I'm perfectly innocent before God.'
And then you say, 'It doesn't make a bit of difference
whether I've sinned or not.'

"Well, I'm going to show you
that you don't know what you're talking about,
neither you nor your friends.
Look up at the sky. Take a long hard look.
See those clouds towering above you?

If you sin, what difference could that make to God?
    No matter how much you sin, will it matter to him?
Even if you're good, what would God get out of that?
    Do you think he's dependent on your accomplishments?
The only ones who care whether you're good or bad
    are your family and friends and neighbors.
    God's not dependent on your behavior.

"When times get bad, people cry out for help.
    They cry for relief from being kicked around,
But never give God a thought when things go well,
    when God puts spontaneous songs in their hearts,
When God sets out the entire creation as a science classroom,
    using birds and beasts to teach wisdom.
People are arrogantly indifferent to God—
    until, of course, they're in trouble,
    and then God is indifferent to them.
There's nothing behind such prayers except panic;
    the Almighty pays them no mind.
So why would he notice you
    just because you say you're tired of waiting to be heard,
Or waiting for him to get good and angry
    and do something about the world's problems?

"Job, you talk sheer nonsense—
    nonstop nonsense!"

# 36

THOSE WHO LEARN FROM THEIR SUFFERING

Here Elihu took a deep breath, but kept going:

"Stay with me a little longer. I'll convince you.
    There's still more to be said on God's side.
I learned all this firsthand from the Source;
    everything I know about justice I owe to my Maker himself.
Trust me, I'm giving you undiluted truth;
    believe me, I know these things inside and out.

70

"It's true that God is all-powerful,
    but he doesn't bully innocent people.
For the wicked, though, it's a different story—
    he doesn't give them the time of day,
    but champions the rights of their victims.
He never takes his eyes off the righteous;
    he honors them lavishly, promotes them endlessly.
When things go badly,
    when affliction and suffering descend,
God tells them where they've gone wrong,
    shows them how their pride has caused their trouble.
He forces them to heed his warning,
    tells them they must repent of their bad life.
If they obey and serve him,
    they'll have a good, long life on easy street.
But if they disobey, they'll be cut down in their prime
    and never know the first thing about life.
Angry people without God pile grievance upon grievance,
    always blaming others for their troubles.
Living it up in sexual excesses,
    virility wasted, they die young.
But those who learn from their suffering,
    God delivers from their suffering.

OBSESSED WITH PUTTING THE BLAME ON GOD

"Oh, Job, don't you see how God's wooing you
    from the jaws of danger?
How he's drawing you into wide-open places—
    inviting you to feast at a table laden with blessings?
And here you are laden with the guilt of the wicked,
    obsessed with putting the blame on *God*!
Don't let your great riches mislead you;
    don't think you can bribe your way out of this.
Did you plan to buy your way out of this?
    Not on your life!
And don't think that night,
    when people sleep off their troubles,
    will bring you any relief.

Above all, don't make things worse with more evil—
    that's what's behind your suffering as it is!

"Do you have any idea how powerful God is?
    Have you ever heard of a teacher like him?
Has anyone ever had to tell him what to do,
    or correct him, saying, 'You did that all wrong!'?
Remember, then, to praise his workmanship,
    which is so often celebrated in song.
Everybody sees it;
    nobody is too far away to see it.

No One Can Escape From God

"Take a long, hard look. See how great he is—infinite,
    greater than anything you could ever imagine or figure out!

"He pulls water up out of the sea,
    distills it, and fills up his rain-cloud cisterns.
Then the skies open up
    and pour out soaking showers on everyone.
Does anyone have the slightest idea how this happens?
    How he arranges the clouds, how he speaks in thunder?
Just look at that lightning, his sky-filling light show
    illumining the dark depths of the sea!
These are the symbols of his sovereignty,
    his generosity, his loving care.
He hurls arrows of light,
    taking sure and accurate aim.
The High God roars in the thunder,
    angry against evil.

# 37

"Whenever this happens, my heart stops—
    I'm stunned, I can't catch my breath.
Listen to it! Listen to his thunder,
    the rolling, rumbling thunder of his voice.
He lets loose his lightnings from horizon to horizon,

lighting up the earth from pole to pole.
In their wake, the thunder echoes his voice,
    powerful and majestic.
He lets out all the stops, he holds nothing back.
    No one can mistake that voice—
His word thundering so wondrously,
    his mighty acts staggering our understanding.
He orders the snow, 'Blanket the earth!'
    and the rain, 'Soak the whole countryside!'
No one can escape the weather—it's *there*.
    And no one can escape from God.
Wild animals take shelter,
    crawling into their dens,
When blizzards roar out of the north
    and freezing rain crusts the land.
It's God's breath that forms the ice,
    it's God's breath that turns lakes and rivers solid.
And yes, it's God who fills clouds with rainwater
    and hurls lightning from them every which way.
He puts them through their paces—first this way, then that—
    commands them to do what he says all over the world.
Whether for discipline or grace or extravagant love,
    he makes sure they make their mark.

## A TERRIBLE BEAUTY STREAMS FROM GOD

"Job, are you listening? Have you noticed all this?
    Stop in your tracks! Take in God's miracle-wonders!
Do you have any idea how God does it all,
    how he makes bright lightning from dark storms,
How he piles up the cumulus clouds—
    all these miracle-wonders of a perfect Mind?
Why, you don't even know how to keep cool
    on a sweltering hot day,
So how could you even dream
    of making a dent in that hot-tin-roof sky?

"If you're so smart, give us a lesson in how to address God.
    We're in the dark and can't figure it out.

73

Do you think I'm dumb enough to challenge God?
    Wouldn't that just be asking for trouble?
No one in his right mind stares straight at the sun
    on a clear and cloudless day.
As gold comes from the northern mountains,
    so a terrible beauty streams from God.

"Mighty God! Far beyond our reach!
    Unsurpassable in power and justice!
    It's unthinkable that he'd treat anyone unfairly.
So bow to him in deep reverence, one and all!
    If you're wise, you'll most certainly worship him."

# 38    GOD CONFRONTS JOB

## HAVE YOU GOTTEN TO THE BOTTOM OF THINGS?

And now, finally, GOD answered Job from the eye of a violent storm.
He said:

"Why do you confuse the issue?
    Why do you talk without knowing what you're talking about?
Pull yourself together, Job!
    Up on your feet! Stand tall!
I have some questions for you,
    and I want some straight answers.
Where were you when I created the earth?
    Tell me, since you know so much!
Who decided on its size? Certainly you'll know that!
    Who came up with the blueprints and measurements?
How was its foundation poured,
    and who set the cornerstone,
While the morning stars sang in chorus
    and all the angels shouted praise?
And who took charge of the ocean
    when it gushed forth like a baby from the womb?
That was me! I wrapped it in soft clouds,
    and tucked it in safely at night.

Then I made a playpen for it,
      a strong playpen so it couldn't run loose,
And said, 'Stay here, this is your place.
      Your wild tantrums are confined to this place.'

"And have you ever ordered Morning, 'Get up!'
      told Dawn, 'Get to work!'
So you could seize Earth like a blanket
      and shake out the wicked like cockroaches?
As the sun brings everything to light,
      brings out all the colors and shapes,
The cover of darkness is snatched from the wicked—
      they're caught in the very act!

"Have you ever gotten to the true bottom of things,
      explored the labyrinthine caves of deep ocean?
Do you know the first thing about death?
      Do you have one clue regarding death's dark mysteries?
And do you have any idea how large this earth is?
      Speak up if you have even the beginning of an answer.

"Do you know where Light comes from
      and where Darkness lives
So you can take them by the hand
      and lead them home when they get lost?
Why, of *course* you know that.
      You've known them all your life,
      grown up in the same neighborhood with them!

"Have you ever traveled to where snow is made,
      seen the vault where hail is stockpiled,
The arsenals of hail and snow that I keep in readiness
      for times of trouble and battle and war?
Can you find your way to where lightning is launched,
      or to the place from which the wind blows?
Who do you suppose carves canyons
      for the downpours of rain, and charts
      the route of thunderstorms
That bring water to unvisited fields,
      deserts no one ever lays eyes on,

75

Drenching the useless wastelands
    so they're carpeted with wildflowers and grass?
And who do you think is the father of rain and dew,
    the mother of ice and frost?
You don't for a minute imagine
    these marvels of weather just happen, do you?

"Can you catch the eye of the beautiful Pleiades sisters,
    or distract Orion from his hunt?
Can you get Venus to look your way,
    or get the Great Bear and her cubs to come out and play?
Do you know the first thing about the sky's constellations
    and how they affect things on Earth?

"Can you get the attention of the clouds,
    and commission a shower of rain?
Can you take charge of the lightning bolts
    and have them report to you for orders?

WHAT DO YOU HAVE TO SAY FOR YOURSELF?

"Who do you think gave weather-wisdom to the ibis,
    and storm-savvy to the rooster?
Does anyone know enough to number all the clouds
    or tip over the rain barrels of heaven
When the earth is cracked and dry,
    the ground baked hard as a brick?

"Can you teach the lioness to stalk her prey
    and satisfy the appetite of her cubs
As they crouch in their den,
    waiting hungrily in their cave?
And who sets out food for the ravens
    when their young cry to God,
        fluttering about because they have no food?

# 39

"Do you know the month when mountain goats give birth?
    Have you ever watched a doe bear her fawn?

Do you know how many months she is pregnant?
    Do you know the season of her delivery,
    when she crouches down and drops her offspring?
Her young ones flourish and are soon on their own;
    they leave and don't come back.

"Who do you think set the wild donkey free,
    opened the corral gates and let him go?
I gave him the whole wilderness to roam in,
    the rolling plains and wide-open places.
He laughs at his city cousins, who are harnessed and harried.
    He's oblivious to the cries of teamsters.
He grazes freely through the hills,
    nibbling anything that's green.

"Will the wild buffalo condescend to serve you,
    volunteer to spend the night in your barn?
Can you imagine hitching your plow to a buffalo
    and getting him to till your fields?
He's hugely strong, yes, but could you trust him,
    would you dare turn the job over to him?
You wouldn't for a minute depend on him, would you,
    to do what you said when you said it?

"The ostrich flaps her wings futilely—
    all those beautiful feathers, but useless!
She lays her eggs on the hard ground,
    leaves them there in the dirt, exposed to the weather,
Not caring that they might get stepped on and cracked
    or trampled by some wild animal.
She's negligent with her young, as if they weren't even hers.
    She cares nothing about anything.
She wasn't created very smart, that's for sure,
    wasn't given her share of good sense.
But when she runs, oh, how she runs,
    laughing, leaving horse and rider in the dust.

"Are you the one who gave the horse his prowess
    and adorned him with a shimmering mane?

77

Did you create him to prance proudly
    and strike terror with his royal snorts?
He paws the ground fiercely, eager and spirited,
    then charges into the fray.
He laughs at danger, fearless,
    doesn't shy away from the sword.
The banging and clanging
    of quiver and lance don't faze him.
He quivers with excitement, and at the trumpet blast
    races off at a gallop.
At the sound of the trumpet he neighs mightily,
    smelling the excitement of battle from a long way off,
    catching the rolling thunder of the war cries.

"Was it through your knowhow that the hawk learned to fly,
    soaring effortlessly on thermal updrafts?
Did you command the eagle's flight,
    and teach her to build her nest in the heights,
Perfectly at home on the high cliff-face,
    invulnerable on pinnacle and crag?
From her perch she searches for prey,
    spies it at a great distance.
Her young gorge themselves on carrion;
    wherever there's a road kill, you'll see her circling."

# 40

God then confronted Job directly:

"Now what do you have to say for yourself?
    Are you going to haul me, the Mighty One, into court and press
      charges?"

## JOB ANSWERS GOD

### I'm Ready to Shut Up and Listen

Job answered:

"I'm speechless, in awe—words fail me.
    I should never have opened my mouth!

I've talked too much, way too much.
    I'm ready to shut up and listen."

## GOD'S SECOND SET OF QUESTIONS

### I WANT STRAIGHT ANSWERS

GOD addressed Job next from the eye of the storm, and this is what he said:

"I have some more questions for you,
    and I want straight answers.

"Do you presume to tell me what I'm doing wrong?
    Are you calling me a sinner so you can be a saint?
Do you have an arm like my arm?
    Can you shout in thunder the way I can?
Go ahead, show your stuff.
    Let's see what you're made of, what you can do.
Unleash your outrage.
    Target the arrogant and lay them flat.
Target the arrogant and bring them to their knees.
    Stop the wicked in their tracks—make mincemeat of them!
Dig a mass grave and dump them in it—
    faceless corpses in an unmarked grave.
I'll gladly step aside and hand things over to you—
    you can surely save yourself with no help from me!

"Look at the land beast, Behemoth. I created him as well as you.
    Grazing on grass, docile as a cow—
Just look at the strength of his back,
    the powerful muscles of his belly.
His tail sways like a cedar in the wind;
    his huge legs are like beech trees.
His skeleton is made of steel,
    every bone in his body hard as steel.
Most magnificent of all my creatures,
    but I still lead him around like a lamb!
The grass-covered hills serve him meals,
    while field mice frolic in his shadow.

79

He takes afternoon naps under shade trees,
    cools himself in the reedy swamps,
Lazily cool in the leafy shadows
    as the breeze moves through the willows.
And when the river rages he doesn't budge,
    stolid and unperturbed even when the Jordan goes wild.
But you'd never want him for a pet—
    you'd never be able to housebreak him!

# 41

## I RUN THIS UNIVERSE

"Or can you pull in the sea beast, Leviathan, with a fly rod
    and stuff him in your creel?
Can you lasso him with a rope,
    or snag him with an anchor?
Will he beg you over and over for mercy,
    or flatter you with flowery speech?
Will he apply for a job with you
    to run errands and serve you the rest of your life?
Will you play with him as if he were a pet goldfish?
    Will you make him the mascot of the neighborhood children?
Will you put him on display in the market
    and have shoppers haggle over the price?
Could you shoot him full of arrows like a pin cushion,
    or drive harpoons into his huge head?
If you so much as lay a hand on him,
    you won't live to tell the story.
What hope would you have with such a creature?
    Why, one look at him would do you in!
If you can't hold your own against his glowering visage,
    how, then, do you expect to stand up to *me*?
Who could confront me and get by with it?
    I'm in *charge* of all this—I *run* this universe!

"But I've more to say about Leviathan, the sea beast,
    his enormous bulk, his beautiful shape.
Who would even dream of piercing that tough skin

or putting those jaws into bit and bridle?
And who would dare knock at the door of his mouth
    filled with row upon row of fierce teeth?
His pride is invincible;
    nothing can make a dent in that pride.
Nothing can get through that proud skin—
    impervious to weapons and weather,
The thickest and toughest of hides,
    impenetrable!

"He snorts and the world lights up with fire,
    he blinks and the dawn breaks.
Comets pour out of his mouth,
    fireworks arc and branch.
Smoke erupts from his nostrils
    like steam from a boiling pot.
He blows and fires blaze;
    flames of fire stream from his mouth.
All muscle he is—sheer and seamless muscle.
    To meet him is to dance with death.
Sinewy and lithe,
    there's not a soft spot in his entire body—
As tough inside as out,
    rock-hard, invulnerable.
Even angels run for cover when he surfaces,
    cowering before his tail-thrashing turbulence.
Javelins bounce harmlessly off his hide,
    harpoons ricochet wildly.
Iron bars are so much straw to him,
    bronze weapons beneath notice.
Arrows don't even make him blink;
    bullets make no more impression than raindrops.
A battle axe is nothing but a splinter of kindling;
    he treats a brandished harpoon as a joke.
His belly is armor-plated, inexorable—
    unstoppable as a barge.
He roils deep ocean the way you'd boil water,
    he whips the sea like you'd whip an egg into batter.
With a luminous trail stretching out behind him,

you might think Ocean had grown a gray beard!
There's nothing on this earth quite like him,
  not an ounce of fear in *that* creature!
He surveys all the high and mighty—
  king of the ocean, king of the deep!"

# 42      JOB WORSHIPS GOD

I BABBLED ON ABOUT THINGS FAR BEYOND ME

Job answered GOD:

"I'm convinced: You can do anything and everything.
  Nothing and no one can upset your plans.
You asked, 'Who is this muddying the water,
  ignorantly confusing the issue, second-guessing my purposes?'
I admit it. I was the one. I babbled on about things far beyond me,
  made small talk about wonders way over my head.
You told me, 'Listen, and let me do the talking.
  Let me ask the questions. *You* give the answers.'
I admit I once lived by rumors of you;
  now I have it all firsthand—from my own eyes and ears!
I'm sorry—forgive me. I'll never do that again, I promise!
  I'll never again live on crusts of hearsay, crumbs of rumor."

## GOD RESTORES JOB

I WILL ACCEPT HIS PRAYER

After GOD had finished addressing Job, he turned to Eliphaz the Temanite and said, "I've had it with you and your two friends. I'm fed up! You haven't been honest either with me or about me—not the way my friend Job has. So here's what you must do. Take seven bulls and seven rams, and go to my friend Job. Sacrifice a burnt offering on your own behalf. My friend Job will pray for you, and I will accept his prayer. He will ask me not to treat you as you deserve for talking nonsense about me, and for not being honest with me, as he has."

They did it. Eliphaz the Temanite, Bildad the Shuhite, and Zophar the Naamathite did what GOD commanded. And GOD accepted Job's prayer.

After Job had interceded for his friends, God restored his fortune—and then doubled it! All his brothers and sisters and friends came to his house and celebrated. They told him how sorry they were, and consoled him for all the trouble God had brought him. Each of them brought generous house-warming gifts.

God blessed Job's later life even more than his earlier life. He ended up with fourteen thousand sheep, six thousand camels, one thousand teams of oxen, and one thousand donkeys. He also had seven sons and three daughters. He named the first daughter Dove, the second, Cinnamon, and the third, Darkeyes. There was not a woman in that country as beautiful as Job's daughters. Their father treated them as equals with their brothers, providing the same inheritance.

Job lived on another hundred and forty years, living to see his children and grandchildren—four generations of them! Then he died—an old man, a full life.

# PSALMS

INTRODUCTION
# PSALMS

Most Christians for most of the Christian centuries have learned to pray by praying the Psalms. The Hebrews, with several centuries of a head start on us in matters of prayer and worship, provided us with this prayer book that gives us a language adequate for responding to the God who speaks to us.

The stimulus to paraphrase the Psalms into a contemporary idiom comes from my lifetime of work as a pastor. As a pastor I was charged with, among other things, teaching people to pray, helping them to give voice to the entire experience of being human, and to do it both honestly and thoroughly. I found that it was not as easy as I expected. Getting started is easy enough. The impulse to pray is deep within us, at the very center of our created being, and so practically anything will do to get us started—"Help" and "Thanks!" are our basic prayers. But honesty and thoroughness don't come quite as spontaneously.

Faced with the prospect of conversation with a holy God who speaks worlds into being, it is not surprising that we have trouble. We feel awkward and out of place: "I'm not good enough for this. I'll wait until I clean up my act and prove that I am a decent person." Or we excuse ourselves on the grounds that our vocabulary is inadequate: "Give me a few months—or years!—to practice prayers that are polished enough for such a sacred meeting. Then I won't feel so stuttery and ill at ease."

My usual response when presented with these difficulties is to put the Psalms in a person's hand and say, "Go home and pray these. You've got wrong ideas about prayer; the praying you find in these Psalms will dispel the wrong ideas and introduce you to the real thing." A common response of those who do what I ask is surprise—they don't expect this kind of thing in the Bible. And then I express surprise at their surprise: "Did you think these would be the prayers of *nice* people? Did you think the psalmists' language would be polished and polite?"

Untutored, we tend to think that prayer is what good people do when they are doing their best. It is not. Inexperienced, we suppose that there must be an "insider" language that must be acquired before God takes us seriously in our prayer. There is not. Prayer is elemental, not advanced, language. It is the means by which our language becomes honest, true, and personal in response to God. It is the means by which we get everything in our lives out in the open before God.

But even with the Psalms in their hands and my pastoral encouragement, people often tell me that they still don't get it. In English translation, the Psalms often sound smooth and polished, sonorous with Elizabethan rhythms and diction. As literature, they are beyond compare. But as *prayer*, as the utterances of men and women passionate for God in moments of anger and praise and lament, these translations miss something. *Grammatically*, they are accurate. The scholarship undergirding the translations is superb and devout. But as *prayers* they are not quite right. The Psalms in Hebrew are earthy and rough. They are not genteel. They are not the prayers of nice people, couched in cultured language.

And so in my pastoral work of teaching people to pray, I started paraphrasing the Psalms into the rhythms and idiom of contemporary English. I wanted to provide men and women access to the immense range and the terrific energies of prayer in the kind of language that is most immediate to them, which also happens to be the language in which these psalm prayers were first expressed and written by David and his successors.

I continue to want to do that, convinced that only as we develop raw honesty and detailed thoroughness in our praying do we become whole, truly human in Jesus Christ, who also prayed the Psalms.

# PSALMS

## 1

How well God must like you—
    you don't hang out at Sin Saloon,
    you don't slink along Dead-End Road,
    you don't go to Smart-Mouth College.

Instead you thrill to GOD's Word,
    you chew on Scripture day and night.
You're a tree replanted in Eden,
    bearing fresh fruit every month,
Never dropping a leaf,
    always in blossom.

You're not at all like the wicked,
    who are mere windblown dust—
Without defense in court,
    unfit company for innocent people.

GOD charts the road you take.
The road *they* take is Skid Row.

## 2

Why the big noise, nations?
Why the mean plots, peoples?
Earth-leaders push for position,
Demagogues and delegates meet for summit talks,
The God-deniers, the Messiah-defiers:
"Let's get free of God!
Cast loose from Messiah!"
Heaven-throned God breaks out laughing.
At first he's amused at their presumption;
Then he gets good and angry.
Furiously, he shuts them up:
"Don't you know there's a King in Zion? A coronation banquet
Is spread for him on the holy summit."

Let me tell you what GOD said next.
He said, "You're my son,
And today is your birthday.
What do you want? Name it:
Nations as a present? continents as a prize?
You can command them all to dance for you,
Or throw them out with tomorrow's trash."

So, rebel-kings, use your heads;
Upstart-judges, learn your lesson:
Worship GOD in adoring embrace,
Celebrate in trembling awe. Kiss Messiah!
Your very lives are in danger, you know;
His anger is about to explode,
But if you make a run for God—you won't regret it!

# 3

A DAVID PSALM, WHEN HE ESCAPED FOR HIS LIFE FROM ABSALOM, HIS SON.

GOD! Look! Enemies past counting!
Enemies sprouting like mushrooms,
Mobs of them all around me, roaring their mockery:
"Hah! No help for *him* from God!"

But you, GOD, shield me on all sides;
You ground my feet, you lift my head high;
With all my might I shout up to GOD,
His answers thunder from the holy mountain.

I stretch myself out. I sleep.
Then I'm up again—rested, tall and steady,
Fearless before the enemy mobs
Coming at me from all sides.

Up, GOD! My God, help me!
Slap their faces,
First this cheek, then the other,
Your fist hard in their teeth!

Real help comes from GOD.
Your blessing clothes your people!

# 4

A DAVID PSALM

When I call, give me answers. God, take my side!
Once, in a tight place, you gave me room;
Now I'm in trouble again: grace me! hear me!

You rabble—how long do I put up with your scorn?
How long will you lust after lies?
How long will you live crazed by illusion?

Look at this: look
Who got picked by GOD!
He listens the split second I call to him.

Complain if you must, but don't lash out.
Keep your mouth shut, and let your heart do the talking.
Build your case before God and wait for his verdict.

Why is everyone hungry for *more*? "More, more," they say.
"More, more."
I have God's more-than-enough,
More joy in one ordinary day

Than they get in all their shopping sprees.
At day's end I'm ready for sound sleep,
For you, GOD, have put my life back together.

# 5

A DAVID PSALM

Listen, GOD! Please, pay attention!
    Can you make sense of these ramblings,
    my groans and cries?
    King-God, I need your help.
Every morning
    you'll hear me at it again.

Every morning
    I lay out the pieces of my life
    on your altar
    and watch for fire to descend.

You don't socialize with Wicked,
    or invite Evil over as your houseguest.
Hot-Air-Boaster collapses in front of you;
    you shake your head over Mischief-Maker.
GOD destroys Lie-Speaker;
    Blood-Thirsty and Truth-Bender disgust you.

And here I am, your invited guest—
    it's incredible!
I enter your house; here I am,
    prostrate in your inner sanctum,
Waiting for directions
    to get me safely through enemy lines.

Every word they speak is a land mine;
    their lungs breathe out poison gas.
Their throats are gaping graves,
    their tongues slick as mud slides.
Pile on the guilt, God!
    Let their so-called wisdom wreck them.
Kick them out! They've had their chance.

But you'll welcome us with open arms
    when we run for cover to you.
Let the party last all night!
    Stand guard over our celebration.
You are famous, GOD, for welcoming God-seekers,
    for decking us out in delight.

# 6

A DAVID PSALM

Please, GOD, no more yelling,
    no more trips to the woodshed.

Treat me nice for a change;
    I'm so starved for affection.

Can't you see I'm black and blue,
    beat up badly in bones and soul?
GOD, how long will it take
    for you to let up?

Break in, GOD, and break up this fight;
    if you love me at all, get me out of here.
I'm no good to you dead, am I?
    I can't sing in your choir if I'm buried in some tomb!

I'm tired of all this—so tired. My bed
    has been floating forty days and nights
On the flood of my tears.
    My mattress is soaked, soggy with tears.
The sockets of my eyes are black holes;
    nearly blind, I squint and grope.

Get out of here, you Devil's crew:
    at last GOD has heard my sobs.
My requests have all been granted,
    my prayers are answered.

Cowards, my enemies disappear.
Disgraced, they turn tail and run.

# 7

A DAVID PSALM

GOD! God! I am running to you for dear life;
    the chase is wild.
If they catch me, I'm finished:
    ripped to shreds by foes fierce as lions,
    dragged into the forest and left
    unlooked for, unremembered.

GOD, if I've done what they say—
    betrayed my friends,
    ripped off my enemies—
If my hands are really that dirty,
    let them get me, walk all over me,
    leave me flat on my face in the dirt.

Stand up, GOD; pit your holy fury
    against my furious enemies.
Wake up, God. My accusers have packed
    the courtroom; it's judgment time.
Take your place on the bench, reach for your gavel,
    throw out the false charges against me.
I'm ready, confident in your verdict:
    "Innocent."

Close the book on Evil, GOD,
    but publish your mandate for us.
You get us ready for life:
    you probe for our soft spots,
    you knock off our rough edges.
And I'm feeling so fit, so safe:
    made right, kept right.
God in solemn honor does things right,
    but his nerves are sandpapered raw.

Nobody gets by with anything.
    God is already in action—
Sword honed on his whetstone,
    bow strung, arrow on the string,
Lethal weapons in hand,
    each arrow a flaming missile.

Look at that guy!
    He had sex with sin,
    he's pregnant with evil.
Oh, look! He's having
    the baby—a Lie-Baby!

See that man shoveling day after day,
    digging, then concealing, his man-trap
    down that lonely stretch of road?
Go back and look again—you'll see him in it headfirst,
    legs waving in the breeze.
That's what happens:
    mischief backfires;
    violence boomerangs.

I'm thanking God, who makes things right.
I'm singing the fame of heaven-high GOD.

# 8

A DAVID PSALM

GOD, brilliant Lord,
    yours is a household name.

Nursing infants gurgle choruses about you;
    toddlers shout the songs
That drown out enemy talk,
    and silence atheist babble.

I look up at your macro-skies, dark and enormous,
    your handmade sky-jewelry,
Moon and stars mounted in their settings.
    Then I look at my micro-self and wonder,
Why do you bother with us?
    Why take a second look our way?

Yet we've so narrowly missed being gods,
    bright with Eden's dawn light.
You put us in charge of your handcrafted world,
    repeated to us your Genesis-charge,
Made us lords of sheep and cattle,
    even animals out in the wild,
Birds flying and fish swimming,
    whales singing in the ocean deeps.

God, brilliant Lord,
>    your name echoes around the world.

# 9

A David psalm

I'm thanking you, God, from a full heart,
>    I'm writing the book on your wonders.
I'm whistling, laughing, and jumping for joy;
>    I'm singing your song, High God.

The day my enemies turned tail and ran,
>    they stumbled on you and fell on their faces.
You took over and set everything right;
>    when I needed you, you were there, taking charge.

You blow the whistle on godless nations;
>    you throw dirty players out of the game,
>    wipe their names right off the roster.
Enemies disappear from the sidelines,
>    their reputation trashed,
>    their names erased from the halls of fame.

God holds the high center,
>    he sees and sets the world's mess right.
He decides what is right for us earthlings,
>    gives people their just deserts.

God's a safe-house for the battered,
>    a sanctuary during bad times.
The moment you arrive, you relax;
>    you're never sorry you knocked.

Sing your songs to Zion-dwelling God,
>    tell his stories to everyone you meet:
How he tracks down killers
>    yet keeps his eye on us,
>    registers every whimper and moan.

Be kind to me, GOD;
  I've been kicked around long enough.
Once you've pulled me back
  from the gates of death,
I'll write the book on Hallelujahs;
    on the corner of Main and First
    I'll hold a street meeting;
I'll be the song leader; we'll fill the air
  with salvation songs.

They're trapped, those godless countries,
  in the very snares they set,
Their feet all tangled
  in the net they spread.
They have no excuse;
  the way God works is well-known.
The cunning machinery made by the wicked
  has maimed their own hands.

The wicked bought a one-way
  ticket to hell.
No longer will the poor be nameless—
  no more humiliation for the humble.
Up, GOD! Aren't you fed up with their empty strutting?
  Expose these grand pretensions!
Shake them up, GOD!
  Show them how silly they look.

# 10

GOD, are you avoiding me?
  Where are you when I need you?
Full of hot air, the wicked
  are hot on the trail of the poor.
Trip them up, tangle them up
  in their fine-tuned plots.

The wicked are windbags,
  the swindlers have foul breath.

The wicked snub GOD,
    their noses stuck high in the air.
Their graffiti are scrawled on the walls:
    "Catch us if you can!" "God is dead."

They care nothing for what you think;
    if you get in their way, they blow you off.
They live (they think) a charmed life:
    "We can't go wrong. This is our lucky year!"

They carry a mouthful of hexes,
    their tongues spit venom like adders.
They hide behind ordinary people,
    then pounce on their victims.

They mark the luckless,
    then wait like a hunter in a blind;
When the poor wretch wanders too close,
    they stab him in the back.

The hapless fool is kicked to the ground,
    the unlucky victim is brutally axed.
He thinks God has dumped him,
    he's sure that God is indifferent to his plight.

Time to get up, GOD—get moving.
    The luckless think they're Godforsaken.
They wonder why the wicked scorn God
    and get away with it,
Why the wicked are so cocksure
    they'll never come up for audit.

But you know all about it—
    the contempt, the abuse.
I dare to believe that the luckless
    will get lucky someday in you.
You won't let them down:
    orphans won't be orphans forever.

Break the wicked right arms,
    break all the evil left arms.
Search and destroy
    every sign of crime.
GOD's grace and order wins;
    godlessness loses.

The victim's faint pulse picks up;
    the hearts of the hopeless pump red blood
    as you put your ear to their lips.
Orphans get parents,
    the homeless get homes.
The reign of terror is over,
    the rule of the gang lords is ended.

# 11

A DAVID PSALM

I've already run for dear life
    straight to the arms of GOD.
So why would I run away now
    when you say,

"Run to the mountains; the evil
    bows are bent, the wicked arrows
Aimed to shoot under cover of darkness
    at every heart open to God.
The bottom's dropped out of the country;
    good people don't have a chance"?

But GOD hasn't moved to the mountains;
    his holy address hasn't changed.
He's in charge, as always, his eyes
    taking everything in, his eyelids
Unblinking, examining Adam's unruly brood
    inside and out, not missing a thing.
He tests the good and the bad alike;
    if anyone cheats, God's outraged.
Fail the test and you're out,
    out in a hail of firestones,

Drinking from a canteen
  filled with hot desert wind.

GOD's business is putting things right;
  he loves getting the lines straight,
Setting us straight. Once we're standing tall,
  we can look him straight in the eye.

# 12

A DAVID PSALM

Quick, GOD, I need your helping hand!
The last decent person just went down,
All the friends I depended on gone.
Everyone talks in lie language;
Lies slide off their oily lips.
They doubletalk with forked tongues.

Slice their lips off their faces! Pull
The braggart tongues from their mouths!
I'm tired of hearing, "We can talk anyone into anything!
Our lips manage the world."

Into the hovels of the poor,
Into the dark streets where the homeless groan, God speaks:
"I've had enough; I'm on my way
To heal the ache in the heart of the wretched."

God's words are pure words,
Pure silver words refined seven times
In the fires of his word-kiln,
Pure on earth as well as in heaven.
GOD, keep us safe from their lies,
From the wicked who stalk us with lies,
From the wicked who collect honors
For their wonderful lies.

# 13

A DAVID PSALM

Long enough, GOD—
    you've ignored me long enough.
I've looked at the back of your head
    long enough. Long enough
I've carried this ton of trouble,
    lived with a stomach full of pain.
Long enough my arrogant enemies
    have looked down their noses at me.

Take a good look at me, GOD, my God;
    I want to look life in the eye,
So no enemy can get the best of me
    or laugh when I fall on my face.

I've thrown myself headlong into your arms—
    I'm celebrating your rescue.
I'm singing at the top of my lungs,
    I'm so full of answered prayers.

# 14

A DAVID PSALM

Bilious and bloated, they gas,
    "God is gone."
Their words are poison gas,
    fouling the air; they poison
Rivers and skies;
    thistles are their cash crop.

GOD sticks his head out of heaven.
    He looks around.
He's looking for someone not stupid—
    one man, even, God-expectant,
    just one God-ready woman.

100

He comes up empty. A string
    of zeros. Useless, unshepherded
Sheep, taking turns pretending
    to be Shepherd.
The ninety and nine
    follow their fellow.

Don't they know anything,
    all these impostors?
Don't they know
    they can't get away with this—
Treating people like a fast-food meal
    over which they're too busy to pray?

Night is coming for them, and nightmares,
    for God takes the side of victims.
Do you think you can mess
    with the dreams of the poor?
You can't, for God
    makes their dreams come true.

Is there anyone around to save Israel?
    Yes. God is around; GOD turns life around.
Turned-around Jacob skips rope,
    turned-around Israel sings laughter.

# 15

A DAVID PSALM

GOD, who gets invited
to dinner at your place?
How do we get on your guest list?

"Walk straight,
    act right,
        tell the truth.

"Don't hurt your friend,
     don't blame your neighbor;
          despise the despicable.

"Keep your word even when it costs you,
     make an honest living,
          never take a bribe.

"You'll never get
blacklisted
if you live like this."


# 16

A DAVID SONG

Keep me safe, O God,
     I've run for dear life to you.
I say to GOD, "Be my Lord!"
     Without you, nothing makes sense.

And these God-chosen lives all around—
     what splendid friends they make!

Don't just go shopping for a god.
     Gods are not for sale.
I swear I'll never treat god-names
     like brand-names.

My choice is you, GOD, first and only.
     And now I find I'm *your* choice!
You set me up with a house and yard.
     And then you made me your heir!

The wise counsel GOD gives when I'm awake
     is confirmed by my sleeping heart.
Day and night I'll stick with GOD;
     I've got a good thing going and I'm not letting go.

I'm happy from the inside out,
  and from the outside in, I'm firmly formed.
You canceled my ticket to hell—
  that's not my destination!

Now you've got my feet on the life path,
  all radiant from the shining of your face.
Ever since you took my hand,
  I'm on the right way.

# 17

A DAVID PRAYER

Listen while I build my case, GOD,
  the most honest prayer you'll ever hear.
Show the world I'm innocent—
  in your heart you know I am.

Go ahead, examine me from inside out,
  surprise me in the middle of the night—
You'll find I'm just what I say I am.
  My words don't run loose.

I'm not trying to get my way
  in the world's way.
I'm trying to get *your* way,
  your Word's way.
I'm staying on your trail;
  I'm putting one foot
In front of the other.
  I'm not giving up.

I call to you, God, because I'm sure of an answer.
  So—answer! bend your ear! listen sharp!
Paint grace-graffiti on the fences;
  take in your frightened children who
Are running from the neighborhood bullies
  straight to you.

Keep your eye on me;
    hide me under your cool wing feathers
From the wicked who are out to get me,
    from mortal enemies closing in.

Their hearts are hard as nails,
    their mouths blast hot air.
They are after me, nipping my heels,
    determined to bring me down,
Lions ready to rip me apart,
    young lions poised to pounce.
Up, GOD: beard them! break them!
    By your sword, free me from their clutches;
Barehanded, GOD, break these mortals,
    these flat-earth people who can't think beyond today.

I'd like to see their bellies
    swollen with famine food,
The weeds they've sown
    harvested and baked into famine bread,
With second helpings for their children
    and crusts for their babies to chew on.

And me? I plan on looking
    you full in the face. When I get up,
I'll see your full stature
    and live heaven on earth.

# 18

A DAVID SONG, WHICH HE SANG TO GOD AFTER BEING SAVED FROM ALL HIS ENEMIES AND FROM SAUL.

I love you, GOD—
    you make me strong.
GOD is bedrock under my feet,
    the castle in which I live,
    my rescuing knight.
My God—the high crag
    where I run for dear life,
    hiding behind the boulders,
    safe in the granite hideout.

I sing to GOD, the Praise-Lofty,
  and find myself safe and saved.

The hangman's noose was tight at my throat;
  devil waters rushed over me.
Hell's ropes cinched me tight;
  death traps barred every exit.

A hostile world! I call to GOD,
  I cry to God to help me.
From his palace he hears my call;
  my cry brings me right into his presence—
  a private audience!

Earth wobbles and lurches;
  huge mountains shake like leaves,
Quake like aspen leaves
  because of his rage.
His nostrils flare, bellowing smoke;
  his mouth spits fire.
Tongues of fire dart in and out;
  he lowers the sky.
He steps down;
  under his feet an abyss opens up.
He's riding a winged creature,
  swift on wind-wings.
Now he's wrapped himself
  in a trenchcoat of black-cloud darkness.
But his cloud-brightness bursts through,
  spraying hailstones and fireballs.
Then GOD thundered out of heaven;
  the High God gave a great shout,
  spraying hailstones and fireballs.
God shoots his arrows—pandemonium!
  He hurls his lightnings—a rout!
The secret sources of ocean are exposed,
  the hidden depths of earth lie uncovered
The moment you roar in protest,
  let loose your hurricane anger.

105

But me he caught—reached all the way
    from sky to sea; he pulled me out
Of that ocean of hate, that enemy chaos,
    the void in which I was drowning.
They hit me when I was down,
    but GOD stuck by me.
He stood me up on a wide-open field;
    I stood there saved—surprised to be loved!

GOD made my life complete
    when I placed all the pieces before him.
When I got my act together,
    he gave me a fresh start.
Now I'm alert to GOD's ways;
    I don't take God for granted.
Every day I review the ways he works;
    I try not to miss a trick.
I feel put back together,
    and I'm watching my step.
GOD rewrote the text of my life
    when I opened the book of my heart to his eyes.

The good people taste your goodness,
The whole people taste your health,
The true people taste your truth,
The bad ones can't figure you out.
You take the side of the down-and-out,
But the stuck-up you take down a peg.

Suddenly, GOD, you floodlight my life;
    I'm blazing with glory, God's glory!
I smash the bands of marauders,
    I vault the highest fences.

What a God! His road
    stretches straight and smooth.
Every GOD-direction is road-tested.
    Everyone who runs toward him
Makes it.

Is there any god like GOD?
    Are we not at bedrock?
Is not this the God who armed me,
    then aimed me in the right direction?
Now I run like a deer;
    I'm king of the mountain.
He shows me how to fight;
    I can bend a bronze bow!
You protect me with salvation-armor;
    you hold me up with a firm hand,
    caress me with your gentle ways.
You cleared the ground under me
    so my footing was firm.
When I chased my enemies I caught them;
    I didn't let go till they were dead men.
I nailed them; they were down for good;
    then I walked all over them.
You armed me well for this fight,
    you smashed the upstarts.
You made my enemies turn tail,
    and I wiped out the haters.
They cried "uncle"
    but Uncle didn't come;
They yelled for GOD
    and got no for an answer.
I ground them to dust; they gusted in the wind.
    I threw them out, like garbage in the gutter.

You rescued me from a squabbling people;
    you made me a leader of nations.
People I'd never heard of served me;
    the moment they got wind of me they listened.
The foreign devils gave up; they came
    on their bellies, crawling from their hideouts.

Live, GOD! Blessings from my Rock,
    my free and freeing God, towering!
This God set things right for me
    and shut up the people who talked back.

He rescued me from enemy anger,
    he pulled me from the grip of upstarts,
He saved me from the bullies.

That's why I'm thanking you, GOD,
    all over the world.
That's why I'm singing songs
    that rhyme your name.
God's king takes the trophy;
    God's chosen is beloved.
I mean David and all his children—
    always.

# 19

A DAVID PSALM

God's glory is on tour in the skies,
    God-craft on exhibit across the horizon.
Madame Day holds classes every morning,
    Professor Night lectures each evening.

Their words aren't heard,
    their voices aren't recorded,
But their silence fills the earth:
    unspoken truth is spoken everywhere.

God makes a huge dome
    for the sun—a superdome!
The morning sun's a new husband
    leaping from his honeymoon bed,
The daybreaking sun an athlete
    racing to the tape.

That's how God's Word vaults across the skies
    from sunrise to sunset,
Melting ice, scorching deserts,
    warming hearts to faith.

The revelation of GOD is whole
    and pulls our lives together.
The signposts of GOD are clear
    and point out the right road.
The life-maps of GOD are right,
    showing the way to joy.
The directions of GOD are plain
    and easy on the eyes.
GOD's reputation is twenty-four carat gold,
    with a lifetime guarantee.
The decisions of GOD are accurate
    down to the nth degree.

God's Word is better than a diamond,
    better than a diamond set between emeralds.
You'll like it better than strawberries in spring,
    better than red, ripe strawberries.

There's more: God's Word warns us of danger
    and directs us to hidden treasure.
Otherwise how will we find our way?
    Or know when we play the fool?
Clean the slate, God, so we can start the day fresh!
    Keep me from stupid sins,
    from thinking I can take over your work;
Then I can start this day sun-washed,
    scrubbed clean of the grime of sin.
These are the words in my mouth;
    these are what I chew on and pray.
Accept them when I place them
    on the morning altar,
O God, my Altar-Rock,
    God, Priest-of-My-Altar.

# 20

A DAVID PSALM

GOD answer you on the day you crash,
The name God-of-Jacob put you out of harm's reach,

Send reinforcements from Holy Hill,
Dispatch from Zion fresh supplies,
Exclaim over your offerings,
Celebrate your sacrifices,
Give you what your heart desires,
Accomplish your plans.

When you win, we plan to raise the roof
    and lead the parade with our banners.
May all your wishes come true!

That clinches it—help's coming,
    an answer's on the way,
        everything's going to work out.

See those people polishing their chariots,
    and those others grooming their horses?
    But we're making garlands for GOD our God.
The chariots will rust,
    those horses pull up lame—
    and we'll be on our feet, standing tall.

Make the king a winner, GOD;
    the day we call, give us your answer.

# 21

A DAVID PSALM

Your strength, GOD, is the king's strength.
    Helped, he's hollering Hosannas.
You gave him exactly what he wanted;
    you didn't hold back.
You filled his arms with gifts;
    you gave him a right royal welcome.
He wanted a good life; you gave it to him,
    and then made it a *long* life as a bonus.
You lifted him high and bright as a cumulus cloud,
    then dressed him in rainbow colors.

You pile blessings on him;
    you make him glad when you smile.
Is it any wonder the king loves GOD?
    that he's sticking with the Best?

With a fistful of enemies in one hand
    and a fistful of haters in the other,
You radiate with such brilliance
    that they cringe as before a furnace.
Now the furnace swallows them whole,
    the fire eats them alive!
You purge the earth of their progeny,
    you wipe the slate clean.
All their evil schemes, the plots they cook up,
    have fizzled—every one.
You sent them packing;
    they couldn't face you.

Show your strength, GOD, so no one can miss it.
    We are out singing the good news!

# 22

A DAVID PSALM

God, God . . . my God!
    Why did you dump me
    miles from nowhere?
Doubled up with pain, I call to God
    all the day long. No answer. Nothing.
I keep at it all night, tossing and turning.

And you! Are you indifferent, above it all,
    leaning back on the cushions of Israel's praise?
We know you were there for our parents:
    they cried for your help and you gave it;
    they trusted and lived a good life.

And here I am, a nothing—an earthworm,
    something to step on, to squash.

Everyone pokes fun at me;
    they make faces at me, they shake their heads:
"Let's see how GOD handles this one;
    since God likes him so much, let *him* help him!"

And to think you were midwife at my birth,
    setting me at my mother's breasts!
When I left the womb you cradled me;
    since the moment of birth you've been my God.
Then you moved far away
    and trouble moved in next-door.
I need a neighbor.

Herds of bulls come at me,
    the raging bulls stampede,
Horns lowered, nostrils flaring,
    like a herd of buffalo on the move.

I'm a bucket kicked over and spilled,
    every joint in my body has been pulled apart.
My heart is a blob
    of melted wax in my gut.
I'm dry as a bone,
    my tongue black and swollen.
They have laid me out for burial
    in the dirt.

Now packs of wild dogs come at me;
    thugs gang up on me.
They pin me down hand and foot,
    and lock me in a cage—a bag
Of bones in a cage, stared at
    by every passerby.
They take my wallet and the shirt off my back,
    and then throw dice for my clothes.

You, GOD—don't put off my rescue!
    Hurry and help me!
Don't let them cut my throat;
    don't let those mongrels devour me.

If you don't show up soon,
    I'm done for—gored by the bulls,
    meat for the lions.

Here's the story I'll tell my friends when they come to worship,
    and punctuate it with Hallelujahs:
Shout Hallelujah, you God-worshipers;
    give glory, you sons of Jacob;
    adore him, you daughters of Israel.
He has never let you down,
    never looked the other way
    when you were being kicked around.
He has never wandered off to do his own thing;
    he has been right there, listening.

Here in this great gathering for worship
    I have discovered this praise-life.
And I'll do what I promised right here
    in front of the God-worshipers.
Down-and-outers sit at GOD's table
    and eat their fill.
Everyone on the hunt for God
    is here, praising him.
"Live it up, from head to toe.
    Don't ever quit!"

From the four corners of the earth
    people are coming to their senses,
    are running back to GOD.
Long-lost families
    are falling on their faces before him.
GOD has taken charge;
    from now on he has the last word.

All the power-mongers are before him
    —worshiping!
All the poor and powerless, too
    —worshiping!
Along with those who never got it together
    —worshiping!

Our children and their children
    will get in on this
As the word is passed along
    from parent to child.
Babies not yet conceived
    will hear the good news—
    that God does what he says.

# 23

A DAVID PSALM

GOD, my shepherd!
    I don't need a thing.
You have bedded me down in lush meadows,
    you find me quiet pools to drink from.
True to your word,
    you let me catch my breath
    and send me in the right direction.

Even when the way goes through
    Death Valley,
I'm not afraid
    when you walk at my side.
Your trusty shepherd's crook
    makes me feel secure.

You serve me a six-course dinner
    right in front of my enemies.
You revive my drooping head;
    my cup brims with blessing.

Your beauty and love chase after me
    every day of my life.
I'm back home in the house of GOD
    for the rest of my life.

# 24

A David psalm

God claims Earth and everything in it,
    God claims World and all who live on it.
He built it on Ocean foundations,
    laid it out on River girders.

Who can climb Mount God?
    Who can scale the holy north-face?
Only the clean-handed,
    only the pure-hearted;
Men who won't cheat,
    women who won't seduce.

God is at their side;
    with God's help they make it.
This, Jacob, is what happens
    to God-seekers, God-questers.

Wake up, you sleepyhead city!
Wake up, you sleepyhead people!
    King-Glory is ready to enter.

Who is this King-Glory?
    God, armed
    and battle-ready.

Wake up, you sleepyhead city!
Wake up, you sleepyhead people!
    King-Glory is ready to enter.

Who is this King-Glory?
    God of the angel armies:
    he is King-Glory.

# 25

A DAVID PSALM

My head is high, GOD, held high;
I'm looking to you, GOD;
No hangdog skulking for me.

I've thrown in my lot with you;
You won't embarrass me, will you?
Or let my enemies get the best of me?

Don't embarrass any of us
Who went out on a limb for you.
It's the traitors who should be humiliated.

Show me how you work, GOD;
School me in your ways.

Take me by the hand;
Lead me down the path of truth.
You are my Savior, aren't you?

Mark the milestones of your mercy and love, GOD;
Rebuild the ancient landmarks!

Forget that I sowed wild oats;
Mark me with your sign of love.
Plan only the best for me, GOD!

GOD is fair and just;
He corrects the misdirected,
Sends them in the right direction.

He gives the rejects his hand,
And leads them step by step.

From now on every road you travel
Will take you to GOD.
Follow the Covenant signs;
Read the charted directions.

Keep up your reputation, GOD;
Forgive my bad life;
It's been a very bad life.

My question: What are God-worshipers like?
Your answer: Arrows aimed at God's bull's-eye.

They settle down in a promising place;
Their kids inherit a prosperous farm.

God-friendship is for God-worshipers;
They are the ones he confides in.

If I keep my eyes on GOD,
I won't trip over my own feet.

Look at me and help me!
I'm all alone and in big trouble.

My heart and kidneys are fighting each other;
Call a truce to this civil war.

Take a hard look at my life of hard labor,
Then lift this ton of sin.

Do you see how many people
Have it in for me?
How viciously they hate me?

Keep watch over me and keep me out of trouble;
Don't let me down when I run to you.

Use all your skill to put me together;
I wait to see your finished product.

GOD, give your people a break
From this run of bad luck.

# 26

A DAVID PSALM

Clear my name, GOD;
    I've kept an honest shop.
I've thrown in my lot with you, GOD, and
    I'm not budging.

Examine me, GOD, from head to foot,
    order your battery of tests.
Make sure I'm fit
    inside and out

So I never lose
    sight of your love,
But keep in step with you,
    never missing a beat.

I don't hang out with tricksters,
    I don't pal around with thugs;
I hate that pack of gangsters,
    I don't deal with double-dealers.

I scrub my hands with purest soap,
    then join hands with the others in the great circle,
    dancing around your altar, GOD,
Singing God-songs at the top of my lungs,
    telling God-stories.

GOD, I love living with you;
    your house glows with your glory.
When it's time for spring cleaning,
    don't sweep me out with the quacks and crooks,
Men with bags of dirty tricks,
    women with purses stuffed with bribe-money.

You know I've been aboveboard with you;
    now be aboveboard with me.
I'm on the level with you, GOD;
    I bless you every chance I get.

# 27

A DAVID PSALM

Light, space, zest—
    that's GOD!
So, with him on my side I'm fearless,
    afraid of no one and nothing.

When vandal hordes ride down
    ready to eat me alive,
Those bullies and toughs
    fall flat on their faces.

When besieged,
    I'm calm as a baby.
When all hell breaks loose,
    I'm collected and cool.

I'm asking GOD for one thing,
    only one thing:
To live with him in his house
    my whole life long.
I'll contemplate his beauty;
    I'll study at his feet.

That's the only quiet, secure place
    in a noisy world,
The perfect getaway,
    far from the buzz of traffic.

God holds me head and shoulders
    above all who try to pull me down.
I'm headed for his place to offer anthems
    that will raise the roof!
Already I'm singing God-songs;
    I'm making music to GOD.

Listen, GOD, I'm calling at the top of my lungs:
    "Be good to me! Answer me!"

When my heart whispered, "Seek God,"
    my whole being replied,
"I'm seeking him!"
    Don't hide from me now!

You've always been right there for me;
    don't turn your back on me now.
Don't throw me out, don't abandon me;
    you've always kept the door open.
My father and mother walked out and left me,
    but GOD took me in.

Point me down your highway, GOD;
        direct me along a well-lighted street;
        show my enemies whose side you're on.
Don't throw me to the dogs,
        those liars who are out to get me,
        filling the air with their threats.

I'm sure now I'll see God's goodness
    in the exuberant earth.
Stay with GOD!
    Take heart. Don't quit.
I'll say it again:
    Stay with GOD.

# 28

A DAVID PSALM

Don't turn a deaf ear
    when I call you, GOD.
If all I get from you is
    deafening silence,
I'd be better off
    in the Black Hole.

I'm letting you know what I need,
    calling out for help

And lifting my arms
    toward your inner sanctum.

Don't shove me into
    the same jail cell with those crooks,
With those who are
    full-time employees of evil.
They talk a good line of "peace,"
    then moonlight for the Devil.

Pay them back for what they've done,
    for how bad they've been.
Pay them back for their long hours
    in the Devil's workshop;
Then cap it with a huge bonus.

Because they have no idea how God works
    or what he is up to,
God will smash them to smithereens
    and walk away from the ruins.

Blessed be GOD—
    he heard me praying.
He proved he's on my side;
    I've thrown my lot in with him.

Now I'm jumping for joy,
    and shouting and singing my thanks to him.

GOD is all strength for his people,
    ample refuge for his chosen leader;
Save your people
    and bless your heritage.
Care for them;
    carry them like a good shepherd.

# 29

A DAVID PSALM

Bravo, GOD, bravo!
    Gods and all angels shout, "Encore!"
In awe before the glory,
    in awe before God's visible power.
Stand at attention!
    Dress your best to honor him!

GOD thunders across the waters,
Brilliant, his voice and his face, streaming brightness—
GOD, across the flood waters.

GOD's thunder tympanic,
GOD's thunder symphonic.

GOD's thunder smashes cedars,
GOD topples the northern cedars.

The mountain ranges skip like spring colts,
The high ridges jump like wild kid goats.

GOD's thunder spits fire.
GOD thunders, the wilderness quakes;
He makes the desert of Kadesh shake.

GOD's thunder sets the oak trees dancing
A wild dance, whirling; the pelting rain strips their branches.
We fall to our knees—we call out, "Glory!"

Above the floodwaters is GOD's throne
    from which his power flows,
    from which he rules the world.

GOD makes his people strong.
GOD gives his people peace.

# 30

A DAVID PSALM

I give you all the credit, GOD—
    you got me out of that mess,
    you didn't let my foes gloat.

GOD, my God, I yelled for help
    and you put me together.
GOD, you pulled me out of the grave,
    gave me another chance at life
    when I was down and out.

All you saints! Sing your hearts out to GOD!
    Thank him to his face!
He gets angry once in a while, but across
    a lifetime there is only love.
The nights of crying your eyes out
    give way to days of laughter.

When things were going great
    I crowed, "I've got it made.
I'm GOD's favorite.
    He made me king of the mountain."
Then you looked the other way
    and I fell to pieces.

I called out to you, GOD;
    I laid my case before you:
"Can you sell me for a profit when I'm dead?
    auction me off at a cemetery yard sale?
When I'm 'dust to dust' my songs
    and stories of you won't sell.
So listen! and be kind!
    Help me out of this!"

You did it: you changed wild lament
    into whirling dance;
You ripped off my black mourning band
    and decked me with wildflowers.

I'm about to burst with song;
>   I can't keep quiet about you.
God, my God,
>   I can't thank you enough.

# 31

A David psalm

I run to you, God; I run for dear life.
>   Don't let me down!
>   Take me seriously this time!
Get down on my level and listen,
>   and please—no procrastination!
Your granite cave a hiding place,
>       your high cliff aerie a place of safety.

You're my cave to hide in,
>   my cliff to climb.
Be my safe leader,
>   be my true mountain guide.
Free me from hidden traps;
>   I want to hide in you.
I've put my life in your hands.
>   You won't drop me,
>       you'll never let me down.

I hate all this silly religion,
>   but you, God, I trust.
I'm leaping and singing in the circle of your love;
>   you saw my pain,
>   you disarmed my tormentors,
You didn't leave me in their clutches
>   but gave me room to breathe.
Be kind to me, God—
>   I'm in deep, deep trouble again.
I've cried my eyes out;
>   I feel hollow inside.
My life leaks away, groan by groan;
>   my years fade out in sighs.

My troubles have worn me out,
    turned my bones to powder.
To my enemies I'm a monster;
    I'm ridiculed by the neighbors.
My friends are horrified;
    they cross the street to avoid me.
They want to blot me from memory,
    forget me like a corpse in a grave,
    discard me like a broken dish in the trash.
The street-talk gossip has me
    "criminally insane"!
Behind locked doors they plot
    how to ruin me for good.


Desperate, I throw myself on you:
    *you* are my God!
Hour by hour I place my days in your hand,
    safe from the hands out to get me.
Warm me, your servant, with a smile;
    save me because you love me.
Don't embarrass me by not showing up;
    I've given you plenty of notice.
Embarrass the wicked, stand them up,
    leave them stupidly shaking their heads
    as they drift down to hell.
Gag those loudmouthed liars
    who heckle me, your follower,
    with jeers and catcalls.


What a stack of blessing you have piled up
    for those who worship you,
Ready and waiting for all who run to you
    to escape an unkind world.
You hide them safely away
    from the opposition.
As you slam the door on those oily, mocking faces,
    you silence the poisonous gossip.

Blessed GOD!
    His love is the wonder of the world.
Trapped by a siege, I panicked.
    "Out of sight, out of mind," I said.
But you heard me say it,
    you heard and listened.

Love GOD, all you saints;
    GOD takes care of all who stay close to him,
But he pays back in full
    those arrogant enough to go it alone.

Be brave. Be strong. Don't give up.
    Expect GOD to get here soon.

# 32

A DAVID PSALM

Count yourself lucky, how happy you must be—
    you get a fresh start,
    your slate's wiped clean.

Count yourself lucky—
    GOD holds nothing against you
    and you're holding nothing back from him.

When I kept it all inside,
    my bones turned to powder,
    my words became daylong groans.

The pressure never let up;
    all the juices of my life dried up.

Then I let it all out;
    I said, "I'll make a clean breast of my failures to GOD."

Suddenly the pressure was gone—
    my guilt dissolved,
    my sin disappeared.

These things add up. Every one of us needs to pray;
  when all hell breaks loose and the dam bursts
  we'll be on high ground, untouched.

GOD's my island hideaway,
  keeps danger far from the shore,
  throws garlands of hosannas around my neck.

Let me give you some good advice;
  I'm looking you in the eye
  and giving it to you straight:

"Don't be ornery like a horse or mule
  that needs bit and bridle
  to stay on track."

God-defiers are always in trouble;
  GOD-affirmers find themselves loved
  every time they turn around.

Celebrate GOD.
  Sing together—everyone!
  All you honest hearts, raise the roof!

# 33

Good people, cheer GOD!
  Right-living people sound best when praising.
Use guitars to reinforce your Hallelujahs!
  Play his praise on a grand piano!
Invent your own new song to him;
  give him a trumpet fanfare.

For GOD's Word is solid to the core;
  everything he makes is sound inside and out.
He loves it when everything fits,
  when his world is in plumb-line true.
Earth is drenched
  in GOD's affectionate satisfaction.

127

The skies were made by GOD's command;
    he breathed the word and the stars popped out.
He scooped Sea into his jug,
    put Ocean in his keg.

Earth-creatures, bow before GOD;
    world-dwellers—down on your knees!
Here's why: he spoke and there it was,
    in place the moment he said so.

GOD takes the wind out of Babel pretense,
    he shoots down the world's power-schemes.
GOD's plan for the world stands up,
    all his designs are made to last.
Blessed is the country with GOD for God;
    blessed are the people he's put in his will.

From high in the skies GOD looks around,
    he sees all Adam's brood.
From where he sits
    he overlooks all us earth-dwellers.
He has shaped each person in turn;
    now he watches everything we do.

No king succeeds with a big army alone,
    no warrior wins by brute strength.
Horsepower is not the answer;
    no one gets by on muscle alone.

Watch this: God's eye is on those who respect him,
    the ones who are looking for his love.
He's ready to come to their rescue in bad times;
    in lean times he keeps body and soul together.

We're depending on GOD;
    he's everything we need.
What's more, our hearts brim with joy
    since we've taken for our own his holy name.
Love us, GOD, with all you've got—
    that's what we're depending on.

# 34

I bless G<small>OD</small> every chance I get;
my lungs expand with his praise.

I live and breathe G<small>OD</small>;
if things aren't going well, hear this and be happy:

Join me in spreading the news;
together let's get the word out.

G<small>OD</small> met me more than halfway,
he freed me from my anxious fears.

Look at him; give him your warmest smile.
Never hide your feelings from him.

When I was desperate, I called out,
and G<small>OD</small> got me out of a tight spot.

G<small>OD</small>'s angel sets up a circle
of protection around us while we pray.

Open your mouth and taste, open your eyes and see—
      how good G<small>OD</small> is.
Blessed are you who run to him.

Worship G<small>OD</small> if you want the best;
worship opens doors to all his goodness.

Young lions on the prowl get hungry,
but G<small>OD</small>-seekers are full of God.

Come, children, listen closely;
I'll give you a lesson in G<small>OD</small> worship.

Who out there has a lust for life?
Can't wait each day to come upon beauty?

Guard your tongue from profanity,
and no more lying through your teeth.

Turn your back on sin; do something good.
Embrace peace—don't let it get away!

GOD keeps an eye on his friends,
his ears pick up every moan and groan.

GOD won't put up with rebels;
he'll cull them from the pack.

Is anyone crying for help? GOD is listening,
ready to rescue you.

If your heart is broken, you'll find GOD right there;
if you're kicked in the gut, he'll help you catch your breath.

Disciples so often get into trouble;
still, GOD is there every time.

He's your bodyguard, shielding every bone;
not even a finger gets broken.

The wicked commit slow suicide;
they waste their lives hating the good.

GOD pays for each slave's freedom;
no one who runs to him loses out.

# 35

A DAVID PSALM

Harass these hecklers, GOD,
    punch these bullies in the nose.
Grab a weapon, anything at hand;
    stand up for me!
Get ready to throw the spear, aim the javelin,
    at the people who are out to get me.

Reassure me; let me hear you say,
    "I'll save you."

When those thugs try to knife me in the back,
    make them look foolish.
Frustrate all those
    who are plotting my downfall.
Make them like cinders in a high wind,
    with GOD's angel workingthe bellows.
Make their road lightless and mud-slick,
    with GOD's angel on their tails.
Out of sheer cussedness they set a trap to catch me;
    for no good reason they dug a ditch to stop me.
Surprise them with your ambush—
    catch them in the very trap they set,
    the disaster they planned for me.

But let me run loose and free,
    celebrating GOD's great work,
Every bone in my body laughing, singing, "GOD,
    there's no one like you.
You put the down-and-out on their feet
    and protect the unprotected from bullies!"

Hostile accusers appear out of nowhere,
    they stand up and badger me.
They pay me back misery for mercy,
    leaving my soul empty.

When they were sick, I dressed in black;
    instead of eating, I prayed.
My prayers were like lead in my gut,
    like I'd lost my best friend, my brother.
I paced, distraught as a motherless child,
    hunched and heavyhearted.

But when I was down
    they threw a party!
All the nameless riffraff of the town came
    chanting insults about me.

Like barbarians desecrating a shrine,
    they destroyed my reputation.

GOD, how long are you going
    to stand there doing nothing?
Save me from their brutalities;
    everything I've got is being thrown to the lions.
I will give you full credit
    when everyone gathers for worship;
When the people turn out in force
    I will say my Hallelujahs.

Don't let these liars, my enemies,
    have a party at my expense,
Those who hate me for no reason,
    winking and rolling their eyes.
No good is going to come
    from that crowd;
They spend all their time cooking up gossip
    against those who mind their own business.
They open their mouths
    in ugly grins,
Mocking, "Ha-ha, ha-ha, thought you'd get away with it?
    We've caught you hands down!"

Don't you see what they're doing, GOD?
    You're not going to let them
Get by with it, are you? Not going to walk off
    without *doing* something, are you?

Please get up—wake up! Tend to my case.
    My God, my Lord—my life is on the line.
Do what you think is right, GOD, my God,
    but don't make me pay for their good time.
Don't let them say to themselves,
    "Ha-ha, we got what we wanted."
Don't let them say,
    "We've chewed him up and spit him out."
Let those who are being hilarious
    at my expense

Be made to look ridiculous.
    Make them wear donkey's ears;
Pin them with the donkey's tail,
    who made themselves so high and mighty!

But those who want
    the best for me,
Let them have the last word—a glad shout!—
    and say, over and over and over,
"GOD is great—everything works
    together for good for his servant."
I'll tell the world how great and good you are,
    I'll shout Hallelujah all day, every day.

# 36

A DAVID PSALM

The God-rebel tunes in to sedition—
    all ears, eager to sin.
He has no regard for God,
    he stands insolent before him.
He has smooth-talked himself
    into believing
That his evil
    will never be noticed.
Words gutter from his mouth,
    dishwater dirty.
Can't remember when he
    did anything decent.
Every time he goes to bed,
    he fathers another evil plot.
When he's loose on the streets,
    nobody's safe.
He plays with fire
    and doesn't care who gets burned.

God's love is meteoric,
    his loyalty astronomic,

133

His purpose titanic,
    his verdicts oceanic.
Yet in his largeness
    nothing gets lost;
Not a man, not a mouse,
    slips through the cracks.

How exquisite your love, O God!
    How eager we are to run under your wings,
To eat our fill at the banquet you spread
    as you fill our tankards with Eden spring water.
You're a fountain of cascading light,
    and you open our eyes to light.

Keep on loving your friends;
    do your work in welcoming hearts.
Don't let the bullies kick me around,
    the moral midgets slap me down.
Send the upstarts sprawling
    flat on their faces in the mud.

# 37

A DAVID PSALM

Don't bother your head with braggarts
    or wish you could succeed like the wicked.
In no time they'll shrivel like grass clippings
    and wilt like cut flowers in the sun.

Get insurance with GOD and do a good deed,
    settle down and stick to your last.
Keep company with GOD,
    get in on the best.

Open up before GOD, keep nothing back;
    he'll do whatever needs to be done:
He'll validate your life in the clear light of day
    and stamp you with approval at high noon.

Quiet down before GOD,
    be prayerful before him.
Don't bother with those who climb the ladder,
    who elbow their way to the top.

Bridle your anger, trash your wrath,
    cool your pipes—it only makes things worse.
Before long the crooks will be bankrupt;
    GOD-investors will soon own the store.

Before you know it, the wicked will have had it;
    you'll stare at his once famous place and—nothing!
Down-to-earth people will move in and take over,
    relishing a huge bonanza.

Bad guys have it in for the good guys,
    obsessed with doing them in.
But GOD isn't losing any sleep; to him
    they're a joke with no punch line.

Bullies brandish their swords,
    pull back on their bows with a flourish.
They're out to beat up on the harmless,
    or mug that nice man out walking his dog.
A banana peel lands them flat on their faces—
    slapstick figures in a moral circus.

Less is more and more is less.
    One righteous will outclass fifty wicked,
For the wicked are moral weaklings
    but the righteous are GOD-strong.

GOD keeps track of the decent folk;
    what they do won't soon be forgotten.
In hard times, they'll hold their heads high;
    when the shelves are bare, they'll be full.

God-despisers have had it;
    GOD's enemies are finished—

Stripped bare like vineyards at harvesttime,
    vanished like smoke in thin air.

Wicked borrows and never returns;
    Righteous gives and gives.
Generous gets it all in the end;
    Stingy is cut off at the pass.

Stalwart walks in step with GOD;
    his path blazed by GOD, he's happy.
If he stumbles, he's not down for long;
    GOD has a grip on his hand.

I once was young, now I'm a graybeard—
    not once have I seen an abandoned believer,
    or his kids out roaming the streets.
Every day he's out giving and lending,
    his children making him proud.

Turn your back on evil,
    work for the good and don't quit.
GOD loves this kind of thing,
    never turns away from his friends.

Live this way and you've got it made,
    but bad eggs will be tossed out.
The good get planted on good land
    and put down healthy roots.

Righteous chews on wisdom like a dog on a bone,
    rolls virtue around on his tongue.
His heart pumps God's Word like blood through his veins;
    his feet are as sure as a cat's.

Wicked sets a watch for Righteous,
    he's out for the kill.
GOD, alert, is also on watch—
    Wicked won't hurt a hair of his head.

Wait passionately for GOD,
    don't leave the path.
He'll give you your place in the sun
    while you watch the wicked lose it.

I saw Wicked bloated like a toad,
    croaking pretentious nonsense.
The next time I looked there was nothing—
    a punctured bladder, vapid and limp.

Keep your eye on the healthy soul,
    scrutinize the straight life;
There's a future
    in strenuous wholeness.
But the willful will soon be discarded;
    insolent souls are on a dead-end street.

The spacious, free life is from GOD,
    it's also protected and safe.
GOD-strengthened, we're delivered from evil—
    when we run to him, he saves us.

# 38

A DAVID PSALM

Take a deep breath, GOD; calm down—
    don't be so hasty with your punishing rod.
Your sharp-pointed arrows of rebuke draw blood;
    my backside smarts from your caning.

I've lost twenty pounds in two months
    because of your accusation.
My bones are brittle as dry sticks
    because of my sin.
I'm swamped by my bad behavior,
    collapsed under gunnysacks of guilt.

The cuts in my flesh stink and grow maggots
    because I've lived so badly.

And now I'm flat on my face
    feeling sorry for myself morning to night.
All my insides are on fire,
    my body is a wreck.
I'm on my last legs; I've had it—
    my life is a vomit of groans.

Lord, my longings are sitting in plain sight,
    my groans an old story to you.
My heart's about to break;
    I'm a burned-out case.
Cataracts blind me to God and good;
    old friends avoid me like the plague.
My cousins never visit,
    my neighbors stab me in the back.
My competitors blacken my name,
    devoutly they pray for my ruin.
But I'm deaf and mute to it all,
    ears shut, mouth shut.
I don't hear a word they say,
    don't speak a word in response.
What I do, GOD, is wait for you,
    wait for my Lord, my God—you *will* answer!
I wait and pray so they won't laugh me off,
    won't smugly strut off when I stumble.

I'm on the edge of losing it—
    the pain in my gut keeps burning.
I'm ready to tell my story of failure,
    I'm no longer smug in my sin.
My enemies are alive and in action,
    a lynch mob after my neck.
I give out good and get back evil
    from God-haters who can't stand a God-lover.

Don't dump me, GOD;
    my God, don't stand me up.
Hurry and help me;
    I want some wide-open space in my life!

# 39

A DAVID PSALM

I'm determined to watch steps and tongue
    so they won't land me in trouble.
I decided to hold my tongue
    as long as Wicked is in the room.
"Mum's the word," I said, and kept quiet.
    But the longer I kept silence
The worse it got—
    my insides got hotter and hotter.
My thoughts boiled over;
    I spilled my guts.

"Tell me, what's going on, GOD?
    How long do I have to live?
    Give me the bad news!
You've kept me on pretty short rations;
    my life is string too short to be saved.
Oh! we're all puffs of air.
    Oh! we're all shadows in a campfire.
Oh! we're just spit in the wind.
    We make our pile, and then we leave it.

"What am I doing in the meantime, Lord?
    *Hoping*, that's what I'm doing—hoping
You'll save me from a rebel life,
    save me from the contempt of dunces.
I'll say no more, I'll shut my mouth,
    since you, Lord, are behind all this.
    But I can't take it much longer.
When you put us through the fire
    to purge us from our sin,
    our dearest idols go up in smoke.
Are we also nothing but smoke?

"Ah, GOD, listen to my prayer, my
    cry—open your ears.

Don't be callous;
>    just look at these tears of mine.
I'm a stranger here. I don't know my way—
>    a migrant like my whole family.
Give me a break, cut me some slack
>    before it's too late and I'm out of here."

# 40

A DAVID PSALM

I waited and waited and waited for GOD.
>    At last he looked; finally he listened.
He lifted me out of the ditch,
>    pulled me from deep mud.
He stood me up on a solid rock
>    to make sure I wouldn't slip.
He taught me how to sing the latest God-song,
>    a praise-song to our God.
More and more people are seeing this:
>    they enter the mystery,
>    abandoning themselves to GOD.

Blessed are you who give yourselves over to GOD,
>    turn your backs on the world's "sure thing,"
>    ignore what the world worships;
The world's a huge stockpile
>    of GOD-wonders and God-thoughts.
Nothing and no one
>    comes close to you!
I start talking about you, telling what I know,
>    and quickly run out of words.
Neither numbers nor words
>    account for you.

Doing something for you, bringing something to you—
>    that's not what you're after.
Being religious, acting pious—
>    that's not what you're asking for.

140

You've opened my ears
    so I can listen.

So I answered, "I'm coming.
    I read in your letter what you wrote about me,
And I'm coming to the party
    you're throwing for me."
That's when God's Word entered my life,
    became part of my very being.

I've preached you to the whole congregation,
    I've kept back nothing, GOD—you know that.
I didn't keep the news of your ways
    a secret, didn't keep it to myself.
I told it all, how dependable you are, how thorough.
    I didn't hold back pieces of love and truth
For myself alone. I told it all,
    let the congregation know the whole story.

Now GOD, don't hold out on me,
    don't hold back your passion.
Your love and truth
    are all that keeps me together.
When troubles ganged up on me,
    a mob of sins past counting,
I was so swamped by guilt
    I couldn't see my way clear.
More guilt in my heart than hair on my head,
    so heavy the guilt that my heart gave out.

Soften up, GOD, and intervene;
    hurry and get me some help,
So those who are trying to kidnap my soul
    will be embarrassed and lose face,
So anyone who gets a kick out of making me miserable
    will be heckled and disgraced,
So those who pray for my ruin
    will be booed and jeered without mercy.

141

But all who are hunting for you—
    oh, let them sing and be happy.
Let those who know what you're all about
    tell the world you're great and not quitting.
And me? I'm a mess. I'm nothing and have nothing:
    make something of me.
You can do it; you've got what it takes—
    but God, don't put it off.

# 41

A DAVID PSALM

Dignify those who are down on their luck;
    you'll feel good—*that's* what GOD does.
GOD looks after us all,
    makes us robust with life—
Lucky to be in the land,
    we're free from enemy worries.
Whenever we're sick and in bed,
    GOD becomes our nurse,
    nurses us back to health.

I said, "GOD, be gracious!
    Put me together again—
    my sins have torn me to pieces."
My enemies are wishing the worst for me;
    they make bets on what day I will die.
If someone comes to see me,
    he mouths empty platitudes,
All the while gathering gossip about me
    to entertain the street-corner crowd.
These "friends" who hate me
    whisper slanders all over town.
They form committees
    to plan misery for me.

The rumor goes out, "He's got some dirty,
    deadly disease. The doctors
    have given up on him."

Even my best friend, the one I always told everything
    —he ate meals at my house all the time!—
  has bitten my hand.

GOD, give grace, get me up on my feet.
  I'll show them a thing or two.

Meanwhile, I'm sure you're on my side—
    no victory shouts yet from the enemy camp!
You know me inside and out, you hold me together,
  you never fail to stand me tall in your presence
  so I can look you in the eye.

Blessed is GOD, Israel's God,
  always, always, always.
  Yes. Yes. Yes.

# 42

A PSALM OF THE SONS OF KORAH

A white-tailed deer drinks
  from the creek;
I want to drink God,
  deep draughts of God.
I'm thirsty for God-alive.
I wonder, "Will I ever make it—
  arrive and drink in God's presence?"
I'm on a diet of tears—
  tears for breakfast, tears for supper.
All day long
  people knock at my door,
Pestering,
  "Where is this God of yours?"

These are the things I go over and over,
  emptying out the pockets of my life.
I was always at the head of the worshiping crowd,
  right out in front,

Leading them all,
 eager to arrive and worship,
Shouting praises, singing thanksgiving—
 celebrating, all of us, God's feast!

Why are you down in the dumps, dear soul?
 Why are you crying the blues?
Fix my eyes on God—
 soon I'll be praising again.
He puts a smile on my face.
 He's my God.

When my soul is in the dumps, I rehearse
 everything I know of you,
From Jordan depths to Hermon heights,
 including Mount Mizar.
Chaos calls to chaos,
 to the tune of whitewater rapids.
Your breaking surf, your thundering breakers
 crash and crush me.
Then GOD promises to love me all day,
 sing songs all through the night!
 My life is God's prayer.

Sometimes I ask God, my rock-solid God,
 "Why did you let me down?
Why am I walking around in tears,
 harassed by enemies?"
They're out for the kill, these
 tormentors with their obscenities,
Taunting day after day,
 "Where is this God of yours?"

Why are you down in the dumps, dear soul?
 Why are you crying the blues?
Fix my eyes on God—
 soon I'll be praising again.
He puts a smile on my face.
 He's my God.

# 43

Clear my name, God; stick up for me
　　against these loveless, immoral people.
Get me out of here, away
　　from these lying degenerates.
I counted on you, God.
　　Why did you walk out on me?
Why am I pacing the floor, wringing my hands
　　over these outrageous people?

Give me your lantern and compass,
　　give me a map,
So I can find my way to the sacred mountain,
　　to the place of your presence,
To enter the place of worship,
　　meet my exuberant God,
Sing my thanks with a harp,
　　magnificent God, my God.

Why are you down in the dumps, dear soul?
　　Why are you crying the blues?
Fix my eyes on God—
　　soon I'll be praising again.
He puts a smile on my face.
　　He's my God.

# 44

A PSALM OF THE SONS OF KORAH

We've been hearing about this, God,
　　all our lives.
Our fathers told us the stories
　　their fathers told them,
How single-handedly you weeded out the godless
　　from the fields and planted us,
How you sent those people packing
　　but gave us a fresh start.

We didn't fight for this land;
    we didn't work for it—it was a gift!
You gave it, smiling as you gave it,
    delighting as you gave it.

You're my King, O God—
    command victories for Jacob!
With your help we'll wipe out our enemies,
    in your name we'll stomp them to dust.
I don't trust in weapons;
    my sword won't save me—
But it's you, you who saved us from the enemy;
    you made those who hate us lose face.
All day we parade God's praise—
    we thank you by name over and over.

But now you've walked off and left us,
    you've disgraced us and won't fight for us.
You made us turn tail and run;
    those who hate us have cleaned us out.
You delivered us as sheep to the butcher,
    you scattered us to the four winds.
You sold your people at a discount—
    you made nothing on the sale.

You made people on the street,
    urchins, poke fun and call us names.
You made us a joke among the godless,
    a cheap joke among the rabble.
Every day I'm up against it,
    my nose rubbed in my shame—
Gossip and ridicule fill the air,
    people out to get me crowd the street.

All this came down on us,
    and we've done nothing to deserve it.
We never betrayed your Covenant: our hearts
    were never false, our feet never left your path.
Do we deserve torture in a den of jackals?
    or lockup in a black hole?

If we had forgotten to pray to our God
    or made fools of ourselves with store-bought gods,
Wouldn't God have figured this out?
    We can't hide things from him.
No, you decided to make us martyrs,
    lambs assigned for sacrifice each day.

Get up, GOD! Are you going to sleep all day?
    Wake up! Don't you care what happens to us?
Why do you bury your face in the pillow?
    Why pretend things are just fine with us?
And here we are—flat on our faces in the dirt,
    held down with a boot on our necks.
Get up and come to our rescue.
    If you love us so much, *Help us!*

# 45

A WEDDING SONG OF THE SONS OF KORAH

My heart bursts its banks,
    spilling beauty and goodness.
I pour it out in a poem to the king,
    shaping the river into words:

☩

"You're the handsomest of men;
    every word from your lips is sheer grace,
    and God has blessed you, blessed you so much.
Strap your sword to your side, warrior!
    Accept praise! Accept due honor!
    Ride majestically! Ride triumphantly!
Ride on the side of truth!
    Ride for the righteous meek!

"Your instructions are glow-in-the-dark;
    you shoot sharp arrows
Into enemy hearts; the king's
    foes lie down in the dust, beaten.

"Your throne is God's throne,
     ever and always;
The scepter of your royal rule
     measures right living.
You love the right
     and hate the wrong.
And that is why God, your very own God,
     poured fragrant oil on your head,
Marking you out as king
     from among your dear companions.

"Your ozone-drenched garments
     are fragrant with mountain breeze.
Chamber music—from the throne room—
     makes you want to dance.
Kings' daughters are maids in your court,
     the Bride glittering with golden jewelry.

✞

"Now listen, daughter, don't miss a word:
     forget your country, put your home behind you.
Be *here*—the king is wild for you.
     Since he's your lord, adore him.
Wedding gifts pour in from Tyre;
     rich guests shower you with presents."

(Her wedding dress is dazzling,
     lined with gold by the weavers;
All her dresses and robes
     are woven with gold.
She is led to the king,
     followed by her virgin companions.
A procession of joy and laughter!
     a grand entrance to the king's palace!)

"Set your mind now on sons—
     don't dote on father and grandfather.
You'll set your sons up as princes
     all over the earth.

I'll make you famous for generations;
>    you'll be the talk of the town
>    for a long, long time."

# 46

A SONG OF THE SONS OF KORAH

God is a safe place to hide,
>    ready to help when we need him.
We stand fearless at the cliff-edge of doom,
>    courageous in seastorm and earthquake,
Before the rush and roar of oceans,
>    the tremors that shift mountains.

>    Jacob-wrestling God fights for us,
>    GOD of angel armies protects us.

River fountains splash joy, cooling God's city,
>    this sacred haunt of the Most High.
God lives here, the streets are safe,
>    God at your service from crack of dawn.
Godless nations rant and rave, kings and kingdoms threaten,
>    but Earth does anything he says.

>    Jacob-wrestling God fights for us,
>    GOD of angel armies protects us.

Attention, all! See the marvels of GOD!
>    He plants flowers and trees all over the earth,
Bans war from pole to pole,
>    breaks all the weapons across his knee.
"Step out of the traffic! Take a long,
>    loving look at me, your High God,
>    above politics, above everything."

>    Jacob-wrestling God fights for us,
>    GOD of angel armies protects us.

# 47

A PSALM OF THE SONS OF KORAH

Applause, everyone. Bravo, bravissimo!
    Shout God-songs at the top of your lungs!
GOD Most High is stunning,
    astride land and ocean.
He crushes hostile people,
    puts nations at our feet.
He set us at the head of the line,
    prize-winning Jacob, his favorite.
Loud cheers as God climbs the mountain,
    a ram's horn blast at the summit.
Sing songs to God, sing out!
    Sing to our King, sing praise!
He's Lord over earth,
    so sing your best songs to God.
God is Lord of godless nations—
    sovereign, he's King of the mountain.
Princes from all over are gathered,
    people of Abraham's God.
The powers of earth are God's—
    he soars over all.

# 48

A PSALM OF THE SONS OF KORAH

GOD majestic,
    praise abounds in our God-city!
His sacred mountain,
    breathtaking in its heights—earth's joy.
Zion Mountain looms in the North,
    city of the world-King.
God in his citadel peaks
    impregnable.

The kings got together,
    they united and came.

They took one look and shook their heads,
     they scattered and ran away.
They doubled up in pain
     like a woman having a baby.

You smashed the ships of Tarshish
     with a storm out of the East.
We heard about it, then we saw it
     with our eyes—
In GOD's city of angel armies,
     in the city our God
Set on firm foundations,
     firm forever.

We pondered your love-in-action, God,
     waiting in your temple:
Your name, God, evokes a train
     of Hallelujahs wherever
It is spoken, near and far;
     your arms are heaped with goodness-in-action.

Be glad, Zion Mountain;
     Dance, Judah's daughters!
     He does what he said he'd do!

Circle Zion, take her measure,
     count her fortress peaks,
Gaze long at her sloping bulwark,
     climb her citadel heights—
Then you can tell the next generation
     detail by detail the story of God,
Our God forever,
     who guides us till the end of time.

# 49

A PSALM OF THE SONS OF KORAH

Listen, everyone, listen—
     earth-dwellers, don't miss this.

All you haves
    and have-nots,
All together now: listen.

I set plainspoken wisdom before you,
    my heart-seasoned understandings of life.
I fine-tuned my ear to the sayings of the wise,
    I solve life's riddle with the help of a harp.

So why should I fear in bad times,
    hemmed in by enemy malice,
Shoved around by bullies,
    demeaned by the arrogant rich?

Really! There's no such thing as self-rescue,
    pulling yourself up by your bootstraps.
The cost of rescue is beyond our means,
    and even then it doesn't guarantee
Life forever, or insurance
    against the Black Hole.

Anyone can see that the brightest and best die,
    wiped out right along with fools and dunces.
They leave all their prowess behind,
    move into their new home, The Coffin,
The cemetery their permanent address.
    And to think they named counties after themselves!

    We aren't immortal. We don't last long.
    Like our dogs, we age and weaken. And die.

This is what happens to those who live for the moment,
    who only look out for themselves:
Death herds them like sheep straight to hell;
    they disappear down the gullet of the grave;
They waste away to nothing—
    nothing left but a marker in a cemetery.
But me? God snatches me from the clutch of death,
    he reaches down and grabs me.

So don't be impressed with those who get rich
and pile up fame and fortune.
They can't take it with them;
fame and fortune all get left behind.
Just when they think they've arrived
and folks praise them because they've made good,
They enter the family burial plot
where they'll never see sunshine again.

We aren't immortal. We don't last long.
Like our dogs, we age and weaken. And die.

# 50

An Asaph psalm

The God of gods—it's GOD!—speaks out, shouts, "Earth!"
welcomes the sun in the east,
farewells the disappearing sun in the west.
From the dazzle of Zion,
God blazes into view.
Our God makes his entrance,
he's not shy in his coming.
Starbursts of fireworks precede him.

He summons heaven and earth as a jury,
he's taking his people to court:
"Round up my saints who swore
on the Bible their loyalty to me."

The whole cosmos attests to the fairness of this court,
that here *God* is judge.

"Are you listening, dear people? I'm getting ready to speak;
Israel, I'm about ready to bring you to trial.
This is God, your God,
speaking to you.
I don't find fault with your acts of worship,
the frequent burnt sacrifices you offer.

But why should I want your blue-ribbon bull,
      or more and more goats from your herds?
Every creature in the forest is mine,
      the wild animals on all the mountains.
I know every mountain bird by name;
      the scampering field mice are my friends.
If I get hungry, do you think I'd tell you?
      All creation and its bounty are mine.
Do you think I feast on venison?
      or drink draughts of goats' blood?
Spread for me a banquet of praise,
      serve High God a feast of kept promises,
And call for help when you're in trouble—
      I'll help you, and you'll honor me."

Next, God calls up the wicked:

"What are you up to, quoting my laws,
      talking like we are good friends?
You never answer the door when I call;
      you treat my words like garbage.
If you find a thief, you make him your buddy;
      adulterers are your friends of choice.
Your mouth drools filth;
      lying is a serious art form with you.
You stab your own brother in the back,
      rip off your little sister.
I kept a quiet patience while you did these things;
      you thought I went along with your game.
I'm calling you on the carpet, *now*,
      laying your wickedness out in plain sight.

"Time's up for playing fast and
      loose with me.
I'm ready to pass sentence,
      and there's no help in sight!
It's the praising life that honors me.
      As soon as you set your foot on the Way,
I'll show you my salvation."

# 51

A DAVID PSALM, AFTER HE WAS CONFRONTED BY NATHAN ABOUT THE AFFAIR WITH BATHSHEBA.

Generous in love—God, give grace!
    Huge in mercy—wipe out my bad record.
Scrub away my guilt,
    soak out my sins in your laundry.
I know how bad I've been;
    my sins are staring me down.

You're the One I've violated, and you've seen
    it all, seen the full extent of my evil.
You have all the facts before you;
    whatever you decide about me is fair.
I've been out of step with you for a long time,
    in the wrong since before I was born.
What you're after is truth from the inside out.
    Enter me, then; conceive a new, true life.

Soak me in your laundry and I'll come out clean,
    scrub me and I'll have a snow-white life.
Tune me in to foot-tapping songs,
    set these once-broken bones to dancing.
Don't look too close for blemishes,
    give me a clean bill of health.
God, make a fresh start in me,
    shape a Genesis week from the chaos of my life.
Don't throw me out with the trash,
    or fail to breathe holiness in me.
Bring me back from gray exile,
    put a fresh wind in my sails!
Give me a job teaching rebels your ways
    so the lost can find their way home.
Commute my death sentence, God, my salvation God,
    and I'll sing anthems to your life-giving ways.
Unbutton my lips, dear God;
    I'll let loose with your praise.

Going through the motions doesn't please you,
    a flawless performance is nothing to you.
I learned God-worship
    when my pride was shattered.
Heart-shattered lives ready for love
    don't for a moment escape God's notice.

Make Zion the place you delight in,
    repair Jerusalem's broken-down walls.
Then you'll get real worship from us,
    acts of worship small and large,
Including all the bulls
    they can heave onto your altar!

# 52

A DAVID PSALM, WHEN DOEG THE EDOMITE REPORTED TO SAUL, "DAVID'S AT AHIMELECH'S HOUSE."

Why do you brag of evil, "Big Man"?
    God's mercy carries the day.
You scheme catastrophe;
    your tongue cuts razor-sharp,
    artisan in lies.
You love evil more than good,
    you call black white.
You love malicious gossip,
    you foul-mouth.

God will tear you limb from limb,
    sweep you up and throw you out,
Pull you up by the roots
    from the land of life.

Good people will watch and
    worship. They'll laugh in relief:
"Big Man bet on the wrong horse,
    trusted in big money,
    made his living from catastrophe."

And I'm an olive tree,
    growing green in God's house.
I trusted in the generous mercy
    of God then and now.

I thank you always
    that you went into action.
And I'll stay right here,
    your good name my hope,
    in company with your faithful friends.

# 53

A DAVID PSALM

Bilious and bloated, they gas,
    "God is gone."
It's poison gas—
    they foul themselves, they poison
Rivers and skies;
    thistles are their cash crop.
God sticks his head out of heaven.
    He looks around.
He's looking for someone not stupid—
    one man, even, God-expectant,
    just one God-ready woman.

He comes up empty. A string
    of zeros. Useless, unshepherded
Sheep, taking turns pretending
    to be Shepherd.
The ninety and nine
    follow the one.

Don't they know anything,
    all these impostors?
Don't they know
    they can't get away with this,
Treating people like a fast-food meal
    over which they're too busy to pray?

Night is coming for them, and nightmare—
    a nightmare they'll never wake up from.
God will make hash of these squatters,
    send them packing for good.

Is there anyone around to save Israel?
    God turns life around.
Turned-around Jacob skips rope,
    turned-around Israel sings laughter.

# 54

A DAVID PSALM, WHEN THE ZIPHITES REPORTED TO SAUL, "DAVID IS HIDING OUT WITH US."

God, for your sake, help me!
    Use your influence to clear me.
Listen, God—I'm desperate.
    Don't be too busy to hear me.

Outlaws are out to get me,
    hit men are trying to kill me.
Nothing will stop them;
    God means nothing to them.

Oh, look! God's right here helping!
    GOD's on my side,
Evil is looping back on my enemies.
    Don't let up! Finish them off!

I'm ready now to worship, so ready.
    I thank you, GOD—you're so good.
You got me out of every scrape,
    and I saw my enemies get it.

# 55

A DAVID PSALM

Open your ears, God, to my prayer;
    don't pretend you don't hear me knocking.

Come close and whisper your answer.
    I really need you.
I shudder at the mean voice,
    quail before the evil eye,
As they pile on the guilt,
    stockpile angry slander.

My insides are turned inside out;
    specters of death have me down.
I shake with fear,
    I shudder from head to foot.
"Who will give me wings," I ask—
    "wings like a dove?"
Get me out of here on dove wings;
    I want some peace and quiet.
I want a walk in the country,
    I want a cabin in the woods.
I'm desperate for a change
    from rage and stormy weather.

Come down hard, Lord—slit their tongues.
    I'm appalled how they've split the city
Into rival gangs
    prowling the alleys
Day and night spoiling for a fight,
    trash piled in the streets,
Even shopkeepers gouging and cheating
    in broad daylight.

This isn't the neighborhood bully
    mocking me—I could take that.
This isn't a foreign devil spitting
    invective—I could tune that out.
It's *you*! We grew up together!
    *You!* My best friend!
Those long hours of leisure as we walked
    arm in arm, God a third party to our conversation.

Haul my betrayers off alive to hell—let them
    experience the horror, let them
    feel every desolate detail of a damned life.

I call to God;
    GOD will help me.
At dusk, dawn, and noon I sigh
    deep sighs—he hears, he rescues.
My life is well and whole, secure
    in the middle of danger
Even while thousands
    are lined up against me.
God hears it all, and from his judge's bench
    puts them in their place.
But, set in their ways, they won't change;
    they pay him no mind.

And this, my best friend, betrayed his best friends;
    his life betrayed his word.
All my life I've been charmed by his speech,
    never dreaming he'd turn on me.
His words, which were music to my ears,
    turned to daggers in my heart.

Pile your troubles on GOD's shoulders—
    he'll carry your load, he'll help you out.
He'll never let good people
    topple into ruin.
But you, God, will throw the others
    into a muddy bog,
Cut the lifespan of assassins
    and traitors in half.

And I trust in you.

# 56

A DAVID PSALM, WHEN HE WAS CAPTURED BY THE PHILISTINES IN GATH.

Take my side, God—I'm getting kicked around,
    stomped on every day.
Not a day goes by
    but somebody beats me up;
They make it their duty
    to beat me up.
When I get really afraid
    I come to you in trust.
I'm proud to praise God;
        fearless now, I trust in God.
        What can mere mortals do?

They don't let up—
    they smear my reputation
    and huddle to plot my collapse.
They gang up,
    sneak together through the alleys
To take me by surprise,
    wait their chance to get me.

Pay them back in evil!
    Get angry, God!
    Down with these people!

You've kept track of my every toss and turn
    through the sleepless nights,
Each tear entered in your ledger,
    each ache written in your book.

If my enemies run away,
    turn tail when I yell at them,
Then I'll know
    that God is on my side.

I'm proud to praise God,
    proud to praise GOD.

Fearless now, I trust in God;
    what can mere mortals do to me?

God, you did everything you promised,
    and I'm thanking you with all my heart.
You pulled me from the brink of death,
    my feet from the cliff-edge of doom.
Now I stroll at leisure with God
    in the sunlit fields of life.

# 57

A DAVID PSALM, WHEN HE HID IN A CAVE FROM SAUL.

Be good to me, God—and now!
    I've run to you for dear life.
I'm hiding out under your wings
    until the hurricane blows over.
I call out to High God,
    the God who holds me together.
He sends orders from heaven and saves me,
    he humiliates those who kick me around.
God delivers generous love,
    he makes good on his word.

I find myself in a pride of lions
    who are wild for a taste of human flesh;
Their teeth are lances and arrows,
    their tongues are sharp daggers.

Soar high in the skies, O God!
    Cover the whole earth with your glory!

They booby-trapped my path;
    I thought I was dead and done for.
They dug a mantrap to catch me,
    and fell in headlong themselves.

I'm ready, God, so ready,
    ready from head to toe,

Ready to sing, ready to raise a tune:
    "Wake up, soul!
Wake up, harp! wake up, lute!
    Wake up, you sleepyhead sun!"

I'm thanking you, GOD, out loud in the streets,
    singing your praises in town and country.
The deeper your love, the higher it goes;
    every cloud is a flag to your faithfulness.

Soar high in the skies, O God!
    Cover the whole earth with your glory!

# 58

A DAVID PSALM

Is this any way to run a country?
    Is there an honest politician in the house?
Behind the scenes you brew cauldrons of evil,
    behind closed doors you make deals with demons.

The wicked crawl from the wrong side of the cradle;
    their first words out of the womb are lies.
Poison, lethal rattlesnake poison,
    drips from their forked tongues—
Deaf to threats, deaf to charm,
    decades of wax built up in their ears.

God, smash their teeth to bits,
    leave them toothless tigers.
Let their lives be buckets of water spilled,
    all that's left, a damp stain in the sand.
Let them be trampled grass
    worn smooth by the traffic.
Let them dissolve into snail slime,
    be a miscarried fetus that never sees sunlight.
Before what they cook up is half-done, God,
    throw it out with the garbage!

The righteous will call up their friends
    when they see the wicked get their reward,
Serve up their blood in goblets
    as they toast one another,
Everyone cheering, "It's worth it to play by the rules!
    God's handing out trophies and tending the earth!"

# 59

A David psalm, when Saul set a watch on David's house in order to kill him.

My God! Rescue me from my enemies,
    defend me from these mutineers.
Rescue me from their dirty tricks,
    save me from their hit men.

Desperadoes have ganged up on me,
    they're hiding in ambush for me.
I did nothing to deserve this, GOD,
    crossed no one, wronged no one.
All the same, they're after me,
    determined to get me.

Wake up and see for yourself! You're GOD,
    God of angel armies, Israel's God!
Get on the job and take care of these pagans,
    don't be soft on these hard cases.

    They return when the sun goes down,
    They howl like coyotes, ringing the city.
    Then suddenly they're all at the gate,
    Snarling invective, drawn daggers in their teeth.
    They think they'll never get caught.

But you, GOD, break out laughing;
    you treat the godless nations like jokes.
Strong God, I'm watching you do it,
    I can always count on you.
God in dependable love shows up on time,
    shows me my enemies in ruin.

Don't make quick work of them, GOD,
    lest my people forget.
Bring them down in slow motion,
    take them apart piece by piece.
Let all their mean-mouthed arrogance
    catch up with them,
Catch them out and bring them down
      —every muttered curse
      —every barefaced lie.
Finish them off in fine style!
    Finish them off for good!
Then all the world will see
    that God rules well in Jacob,
    everywhere that God's in charge.

    They return when the sun goes down,
    They howl like coyotes, ringing the city.
    They scavenge for bones,
    And bite the hand that feeds them.

And me? I'm singing your prowess,
    shouting at cockcrow your largesse,
For you've been a safe place for me,
    a good place to hide.
Strong God, I'm watching you do it,
    I can always count on you—
    God, my dependable love.

# 60

A DAVID PSALM, WHEN HE FOUGHT AGAINST ARAM-NAHARAIM AND ARAM-ZOBAH AND JOAB
KILLED TWELVE THOUSAND EDOMITES AT THE VALLEY OF SALT.

God! you walked off and left us,
    kicked our defenses to bits
And stalked off angry.
    Come back. Oh please, come back!

You shook earth to the foundations,
    ripped open huge crevasses.

Heal the breaks! Everything's
    coming apart at the seams.

You made your people look doom in the face,
    then gave us cheap wine to drown our troubles.
Then you planted a flag to rally your people,
    an unfurled flag to look to for courage.
Now do something quickly, answer right now,
    so the one you love best is saved.

That's when God spoke in holy splendor,
    "Bursting with joy,
I make a present of Shechem,
    I hand out Succoth Valley as a gift.
Gilead's in my pocket,
    to say nothing of Manasseh.
Ephraim's my hard hat,
    Judah my hammer;
Moab's a scrub bucket,
    I mop the floor with Moab,
Spit on Edom,
    rain fireworks all over Philistia."

Who will take me to the thick of the fight?
    Who'll show me the road to Edom?
You aren't giving up on us, are you, God?
    refusing to go out with our troops?

Give us help for the hard task;
    human help is worthless.
In God we'll do our very best;
    he'll flatten the opposition for good.

# 61

A DAVID PSALM

God, listen to me shout,
    bend an ear to my prayer.

When I'm far from anywhere,
     down to my last gasp,
I call out, "Guide me
     up High Rock Mountain!"

You've always given me breathing room,
     a place to get away from it all,
A lifetime pass to your safe-house,
     an open invitation as your guest.
You've always taken me seriously, God,
     made me welcome among those who know and love you.

Let the days of the king add up
     to years and years of good rule.
Set his throne in the full light of God;
     post Steady Love and Good Faith as lookouts,
And I'll be the poet who sings your glory—
     and live what I sing every day.

# 62

A DAVID PSALM

God, the one and only—
     I'll wait as long as he says.
Everything I need comes from him,
     so why not?
He's solid rock under my feet,
     breathing room for my soul,
An impregnable castle:
     I'm set for life.

How long will you gang up on me?
     How long will you run with the bullies?
There's nothing to you, any of you—
     rotten floorboards, worm-eaten rafters,
Anthills plotting to bring down mountains,
     far gone in make-believe.
You talk a good line,
     but every "blessing" breathes a curse.

God, the one and only—
    I'll wait as long as he says.
Everything I hope for comes from him,
    so why not?
He's solid rock under my feet,
    breathing room for my soul,
An impregnable castle:
    I'm set for life.

My help and glory are in God
    —granite-strength and safe-harbor-God—
So trust him absolutely, people;
    lay your lives on the line for him.
    God is a safe place to be.

Man as such is smoke,
    woman as such, a mirage.
Put them together, they're nothing;
    two times nothing is nothing.

And a windfall, if it comes—
    don't make too much of it.

God said this once and for all;
    how many times
Have I heard it repeated?
    "Strength comes
Straight from God."

Love to you, Lord God!
    You pay a fair wage for a good day's work!

# 63

A David psalm, when he was out in the Judean wilderness.

God—you're my God!
    I can't get enough of you!
I've worked up such hunger and thirst for God,
    traveling across dry and weary deserts.

So here I am in the place of worship, eyes open,
    drinking in your strength and glory.
In your generous love I am really living at last!
    My lips brim praises like fountains.
I bless you every time I take a breath;
    My arms wave like banners of praise to you.

I eat my fill of prime rib and gravy;
    I smack my lips. It's time to shout praises!
If I'm sleepless at midnight,
    I spend the hours in grateful reflection.
Because you've always stood up for me,
    I'm free to run and play.
I hold on to you for dear life,
    and you hold me steady as a post.

Those who are out to get me are marked for doom,
    marked for death, bound for hell.
They'll die violent deaths;
    jackals will tear them limb from limb.
But the king is glad in God;
    his true friends spread the joy,
While small-minded gossips
    are gagged for good.

# 64

A DAVID PSALM

Listen and help, O God.
    I'm reduced to a whine
And a whimper, obsessed
    with feelings of doomsday.

Don't let them find me—
    the conspirators out to get me,
Using their tongues as weapons,
    flinging poison words,
    poison-tipped arrow-words.

They shoot from ambush,
    shoot without warning,
    not caring who they hit.
They keep fit doing calisthenics
    of evil purpose,
They keep lists of the traps
    they've secretly set.
They say to each other,
    "No one can catch us,
    no one can detect our perfect crime."
The Detective detects the mystery
    in the dark of the cellar heart.

The God of the Arrow shoots!
    They double up in pain,
Fall flat on their faces
    in full view of the grinning crowd.

Everyone sees it. God's
    work is the talk of the town.
Be glad, good people! Fly to GOD!
    Good-hearted people, make praise your habit.

# 65

A DAVID PSALM

Silence is praise to you,
    Zion-dwelling God,
And also obedience.
    You hear the prayer in it all.

We all arrive at your doorstep sooner
    or later, loaded with guilt,
Our sins too much for us—
    but you get rid of them once and for all.
Blessed are the chosen! Blessed the guest
    at home in your place!
We expect our fill of good things
    in your house, your heavenly manse.

All your salvation wonders
    are on display in your trophy room.
Earth-Tamer, Ocean-Pourer,
    Mountain-Maker, Hill-Dresser,
Muzzler of sea storm and wave crash,
    of mobs in noisy riot—
Far and wide they'll come to a stop,
    they'll stare in awe, in wonder.
Dawn and dusk take turns
    calling, "Come and worship."

Oh, visit the earth,
    ask her to join the dance!
Deck her out in spring showers,
    fill the God-River with living water.
Paint the wheat fields golden.
    Creation was made for this!
Drench the plowed fields,
    soak the dirt clods
With rainfall as harrow and rake
    bring her to blossom and fruit.
Snow-crown the peaks with splendor,
    scatter rose petals down your paths,
All through the wild meadows, rose petals.
    Set the hills to dancing,
Dress the canyon walls with live sheep,
    a drape of flax across the valleys.
Let them shout, and shout, and shout!
    Oh, oh, let them sing!

# 66

All together now—applause for God!
    Sing songs to the tune of his glory,
    set glory to the rhythms of his praise.
Say of God, "We've never seen anything like him!"
    When your enemies see you in action,
    they slink off like scolded dogs.
The whole earth falls to its knees—

171

it worships you, sings to you,
    can't stop enjoying your name and fame.

Take a good look at God's wonders—
    they'll take your breath away.
He converted sea to dry land;
    travelers crossed the river on foot.
    Now isn't that cause for a song?

Ever sovereign in his high tower, he keeps
    his eye on the godless nations.
Rebels don't dare
    raise a finger against him.

Bless our God, oh peoples!
    Give him a thunderous welcome!
Didn't he set us on the road to life?
    Didn't he keep us out of the ditch?
He trained us first,
    passed us like silver through refining fires,
Brought us into hardscrabble country,
    pushed us to our very limit,
Road-tested us inside and out,
    took us to hell and back;
Finally he brought us
    to this well-watered place.

I'm bringing my prizes and presents to your house.
    I'm doing what I said I'd do,
What I solemnly swore I'd do
    that day when I was in so much trouble:
The choicest cuts of meat
    for the sacrificial meal;
Even the fragrance
    of roasted lamb is like a meal!
Or make it an ox
    garnished with goat meat!

All believers, come here and listen,
    let me tell you what God did for me.

I called out to him with my mouth,
    my tongue shaped the sounds of music.
If I had been cozy with evil,
    the Lord would never have listened.
But he most surely *did* listen,
    he came on the double when he heard my prayer.
Blessed be God: he didn't turn a deaf ear,
    he stayed with me, loyal in his love.

# 67

God, mark us with grace
    and blessing! Smile!
The whole country will see how you work,
    all the godless nations see how you save.
God! Let people thank and enjoy you.
    Let all people thank and enjoy you.
Let all far-flung people become happy
    and shout their happiness because
You judge them fair and square,
    you tend the far-flung peoples.
God! Let people thank and enjoy you.
    Let all people thank and enjoy you.
Earth, display your exuberance!
    You mark us with blessing, O God, our God.
You mark us with blessing, O God.
    Earth's four corners—honor him!

# 68

A DAVID PSALM

Up with God!
    Down with his enemies!
        Adversaries, run for the hills!
Gone like a puff of smoke,
    like a blob of wax in the fire—
        one look at God and the wicked vanish.

When the righteous see God in action
    they'll laugh, they'll sing,
        they'll laugh and sing for joy.
Sing hymns to God;
    all heaven, sing out;
        clear the way for the coming of Cloud-Rider.
Enjoy GOD,
    cheer when you see him!

Father of orphans,
    champion of widows,
        is God in his holy house.
God makes homes for the homeless,
    leads prisoners to freedom,
        but leaves rebels to rot in hell.

God, when you took the lead with your people,
    when you marched out into the wild,
Earth shook, sky broke out in a sweat;
    God was on the march.
Even Sinai trembled at the sight of God on the move,
    at the sight of Israel's God.
You pour out rain in buckets, O God;
    thorn and cactus become an oasis
For your people to camp in and enjoy.
    You set them up in business;
    they went from rags to riches.

The Lord gave the word;
    thousands called out the good news:
"Kings of the armies
    are on the run, on the run!"
While housewives, safe and sound back home,
    divide up the plunder,
    the plunder of Canaanite silver and gold.

The day Shaddai scattered the kings,
    snow fell on Black Mountain—
A huge mountain, this dragon mountain,

a mighty mountain, this dragon mountain.
All you mountains not chosen,
    sulk now, and feel sorry for yourselves,
For this is the mountain God has chosen to live on;
    he'll rule from this mountain forever.

The chariots of God, twice ten thousand,
    and thousands more besides,
The Lord in the lead, riding down Sinai—
    straight to the Holy Place!
You climbed to the High Place, captives in tow,
    your arms full of booty from rebels,
And now you sit there in state,
    GOD, sovereign GOD!

Blessed be the Lord—
    day after day he carries us along.
He's our Savior, our God, oh yes!
    He's God-for-us, he's God-who-saves-us.
Lord GOD knows all
    death's ins and outs.
What's more, he made heads roll,
    split the skulls of the enemy
As he marched out of heaven,
    saying, "I tied up the Dragon in knots,
    put a muzzle on the Deep Blue Sea."
You can wade through your enemies' blood,
    and your dogs taste of your enemies from your boots.

See God on parade
    to the sanctuary, my God,
    my King on the march!
Singers out front, the band behind,
    maidens in the middle with castanets.
The whole choir blesses God.
    Like a fountain of praise, Israel blesses GOD.
Look—little Benjamin's out
    front and leading
Princes of Judah in their royal robes,

princes of Zebulon, princes of Naphtali.
Parade your power, O God,
    the power, O God, that made us what we are.
Your temple, High God, is Jerusalem;
    kings bring gifts to you.
Rebuke that old crocodile, Egypt,
    with her herd of wild bulls and calves,
Rapacious in her lust for silver,
    crushing peoples, spoiling for a fight.
Let Egyptian traders bring blue cloth
    and Cush come running to God, her hands outstretched.

Sing, oh kings of the earth!
    Sing praises to the Lord!
There he is: Sky-Rider,
    striding the ancient skies.
Listen—he's calling in thunder,
    rumbling, rolling thunder.
Call out "Bravo!" to God,
    the High God of Israel.
His splendor and strength
    rise huge as thunderheads.

A terrible beauty, O God,
    streams from your sanctuary.
It's Israel's strong God! He gives
    power and might to his people!
Oh you, his people—bless God!

# 69

A DAVID PSALM

God, God, save me!
I'm in over my head,

Quicksand under me, swamp water over me;
I'm going down for the third time.

I'm hoarse from calling for help,
Bleary-eyed from searching the sky for God.

I've got more enemies than hairs on my head;
Sneaks and liars are out to knife me in the back.

What I never stole
Must I now give back?

God, you know every sin I've committed;
My life's a wide-open book before you.

Don't let those who look to you in hope
Be discouraged by what happens to me,
Dear Lord! GOD of the armies!

Don't let those out looking for you
Come to a dead end by following me—
Please, dear God of Israel!

Because of you I look like an idiot,
I walk around ashamed to show my face.

My brothers shun me like a bum off the street;
My family treats me like an unwanted guest.

I love you more than I can say.
Because I'm madly in love with you,
They blame me for everything they dislike about you.

When I poured myself out in prayer and fasting,
All it got me was more contempt.

When I put on a sad face,
They treated me like a clown.

Now drunks and gluttons
Make up drinking songs about me.

And me? I pray.
GOD, it's time for a break!

God, answer in love!
Answer with your sure salvation!

Rescue me from the swamp,
Don't let me go under for good,

Pull me out of the clutch of the enemy;
This whirlpool is sucking me down.

Don't let the swamp be my grave, the Black Hole
Swallow me, its jaws clenched around me.

Now answer me, GOD, because you love me;
Let me see your great mercy full-face.

Don't look the other way; your servant can't take it.
I'm in trouble. Answer right now!

Come close, God; get me out of here.
Rescue me from this deathtrap.

You know how they kick me around—
Pin on me the donkey's ears, the dunce's cap.

I'm broken by their taunts,
Flat on my face, reduced to a nothing.

I looked in vain for one friendly face. Not one.
I couldn't find one shoulder to cry on.

They put poison in my soup,
Vinegar in my drink.

Let their supper be bait in a trap that snaps shut;
May their best friends be trappers who'll skin them alive.

Make them become blind as bats,
Give them the shakes from morning to night.

Let them know what you think of them,
Blast them with your red-hot anger.

Burn down their houses,
Leave them desolate with nobody at home.

They gossiped about the one you disciplined,
Made up stories about anyone wounded by God.

Pile on the guilt,
Don't let them off the hook.

Strike their names from the list of the living;
No rock-carved honor for them among the righteous.

I'm hurt and in pain;
Give me space for healing, and mountain air.

Let me shout God's name with a praising song,
Let me tell his greatness in a prayer of thanks.

For GOD, this is better than oxen on the altar,
Far better than blue-ribbon bulls.

The poor in spirit see and are glad—
Oh, you God-seekers, take heart!

For GOD listens to the poor,
He doesn't walk out on the wretched.

You heavens, praise him; praise him, earth;
Also ocean and all things that swim in it.

For God is out to help Zion,
Rebuilding the wrecked towns of Judah.

Guess who will live there—
The proud owners of the land?

No, the children of his servants will get it,
The lovers of his name will live in it.

# 70

A D<small>AVID</small> PRAYER

God! Please hurry to my rescue!
    G<small>OD</small>, come quickly to my side!
Those who are out to get me—
    let them fall all over themselves.
Those who relish my downfall—
    send them down a blind alley.
Give them a taste of their own medicine,
    those gossips off clucking their tongues.

Let those on the hunt for you
    sing and celebrate.
Let all who love your saving way
    say over and over, "God is mighty!"

But I've lost it. I'm wasted.
    God—quickly, quickly!
Quick to my side, quick to my rescue!
    G<small>OD</small>, don't lose a minute.

# 71

I run for dear life to G<small>OD</small>,
    I'll never live to regret it.
Do what you do so well:
    get me out of this mess and up on my feet.
Put your ear to the ground and listen,
    give me space for salvation.
Be a guest room where I can retreat;
    you said your door was always open!
You're my salvation—my vast, granite fortress.

My God, free me from the grip of Wicked,
    from the clutch of Bad and Bully.

You keep me going when times are tough—
    my bedrock, GOD, since my childhood.
I've hung on you from the day of my birth,
    the day you took me from the cradle;
    I'll never run out of praise.
Many gasp in alarm when they see me,
    but you take me in stride.

Just as each day brims with your beauty,
    my mouth brims with praise.
But don't turn me out to pasture when I'm old
    or put me on the shelf when I can't pull my weight.
My enemies are talking behind my back,
    watching for their chance to knife me.
The gossip is: "God has abandoned him.
    Pounce on him now; no one will help him."

God, don't just watch from the sidelines.
    Come on! Run to my side!
My accusers—make them lose face.
    Those out to get me—make them look
Like idiots, while I stretch out, reaching for you,
    and daily add praise to praise.
I'll write the book on your righteousness,
    talk up your salvation the livelong day,
    never run out of good things to write or say.
I come in the power of the Lord GOD,
    I post signs marking his right-of-way.

You got me when I was an unformed youth,
    God, and taught me everything I know.
Now I'm telling the world your wonders;
    I'll keep at it until I'm old and gray.
God, don't walk off and leave me
    until I get out the news
Of your strong right arm to this world,
    news of your power to the world yet to come,
Your famous and righteous
    ways, O God.

God, you've done it all!
    Who is quite like you?
You, who made me stare trouble in the face,
    Turn me around;
Now let me look life in the face.
    I've been to the bottom;
Bring me up, streaming with honors;
    turn to me, be tender to me,
And I'll take up the lute and thank you
    to the tune of your faithfulness, God.
I'll make music for you on a harp,
    Holy One of Israel.
When I open up in song to you,
    I let out lungsful of praise,
    my rescued life a song.
All day long I'm chanting
    about you and your righteous ways,
While those who tried to do me in
    slink off looking ashamed.

# 72

A SOLOMON PSALM

Give the gift of wise rule to the king, O God,
    the gift of just rule to the crown prince.
May he judge your people rightly,
    be honorable to your meek and lowly.
Let the mountains give exuberant witness;
    shape the hills with the contours of right living.
Please stand up for the poor,
    help the children of the needy,
    come down hard on the cruel tyrants.
Outlast the sun, outlive the moon—
    age after age after age.
Be rainfall on cut grass,
    earth-refreshing rain showers.
Let righteousness burst into blossom
    and peace abound until the moon fades to nothing.

Rule from sea to sea,
    from the River to the Rim.

Foes will fall on their knees before God,
    his enemies lick the dust.
Kings remote and legendary will pay homage,
    kings rich and resplendent will turn over their wealth.
All kings will fall down and worship,
    and godless nations sign up to serve him,
Because he rescues the poor at the first sign of need,
    the destitute who have run out of luck.
He opens a place in his heart for the down-and-out,
    he restores the wretched of the earth.
He frees them from tyranny and torture—
    when they bleed, he bleeds;
    when they die, he dies.

And live! Oh, let him live!
    Deck him out in Sheba gold.
Offer prayers unceasing to him,
    bless him from morning to night.
Fields of golden grain in the land,
    cresting the mountains in wild exuberance,
Cornucopias of praise, praises
    springing from the city like grass from the earth.
May he never be forgotten,
    his fame shine on like sunshine.
May all godless people enter his circle of blessing
    and bless the One who blessed them.

Blessed GOD, Israel's God,
    the one and only wonder-working God!
Blessed always his blazing glory!
    All earth brims with his glory.
Yes and Yes and Yes.

# 73

AN ASAPH PSALM

No doubt about it! God is good—
    good to good people, good to the good-hearted.
But I nearly missed it,
    missed seeing his goodness.
I was looking the other way,
    looking up to the people
At the top,
    envying the wicked who have it made,
Who have nothing to worry about,
    not a care in the whole wide world.

Pretentious with arrogance,
    they wear the latest fashions in violence,
Pampered and overfed,
    decked out in silk bows of silliness.
They jeer, using words to kill;
    they bully their way with words.
They're full of hot air,
    loudmouths disturbing the peace.
People actually listen to them—can you believe it?
    Like thirsty puppies, they lap up their words.

What's going on here? Is God out to lunch?
    Nobody's tending the store.
The wicked get by with everything;
    they have it made, piling up riches.
I've been stupid to play by the rules;
    what has it gotten me?
A long run of bad luck, that's what—
    a slap in the face every time I walk out the door.

If I'd have given in and talked like this,
    I would have betrayed your dear children.
Still, when I tried to figure it out,
    all I got was a splitting headache . . .

Until I entered the sanctuary of God.
    Then I saw the whole picture:
The slippery road you've put them on,
    with a final crash in a ditch of delusions.
In the blink of an eye, disaster!
    A blind curve in the dark, and—nightmare!
We wake up and rub our eyes. . . . Nothing.
    There's nothing to them. And there never was.

When I was beleaguered and bitter,
    totally consumed by envy,
I was totally ignorant, a dumb ox
    in your very presence.
I'm still in your presence,
    but you've taken my hand.
You wisely and tenderly lead me,
    and then you bless me.

You're all I want in heaven!
    You're all I want on earth!
When my skin sags and my bones get brittle,
    GOD is rock-firm and faithful.
Look! Those who left you are falling apart!
    Deserters, they'll never be heard from again.
But I'm in the very presence of God—
    oh, how refreshing it is!
I've made Lord GOD my home.
    God, I'm telling the world what you do!

# 74

AN ASAPH PSALM

You walked off and left us, and never looked back.
    God, how could you do that?
We're your very own sheep;
    how can you stomp off in anger?

Refresh your memory of us—you bought us a long time ago.
    Your most precious tribe—you paid a good price for us!

Your very own Mount Zion—you actually lived here once!
Come and visit the site of disaster,
    see how they've wrecked the sanctuary.

While your people were at worship, your enemies barged in,
    brawling and scrawling graffiti.
They set fire to the porch;
    axes swinging, they chopped up the woodwork,
Beat down the doors with sledgehammers,
    then split them into kindling.
They burned your holy place to the ground,
    violated the place of worship.
They said to themselves, "We'll wipe them all out,"
    and burned down all the places of worship.

There's not a sign or symbol of God in sight,
    nor anyone to speak in his name,
    no one who knows what's going on.
How long, God, will barbarians blaspheme,
    enemies curse and get by with it?
Why don't you do something? How long are you going
    to sit there with your hands folded in your lap?
God is my King from the very start;
    he works salvation in the womb of the earth.
With one blow you split the sea in two,
    you made mincemeat of the dragon Tannin.
You lopped off the heads of Leviathan,
    then served them up in a stew for the animals.
With your finger you opened up springs and creeks,
    and dried up the wild floodwaters.
You own the day, you own the night;
    you put stars and sun in place.
You laid out the four corners of earth,
    shaped the seasons of summer and winter.

Mark and remember, GOD, all the enemy
    taunts, each idiot desecration.
Don't throw your lambs to the wolves;
    after all we've been through, don't forget us.

Remember your promises;
>    the city is in darkness, the countryside violent.
Don't leave the victims to rot in the street;
>    make them a choir that sings your praises.

On your feet, O God—
>    stand up for yourself!
Do you hear what they're saying about you,
>    all the vile obscenities?
Don't tune out their malicious filth,
>    the brawling invective that never lets up.

# 75

AN ASAPH PSALM

We thank you, God, we thank you—
>    your Name is our favorite word;
>    your mighty works are all we talk about.

You say, "I'm calling this meeting to order,
>    I'm ready to set things right.
When the earth goes topsy-turvy
>    And nobody knows which end is up,
I nail it all down,
>    I put everything in place again.
I say to the smart alecks, 'That's enough,'
>    to the bullies, 'Not so fast.'"

Don't raise your fist against High God.
>    Don't raise your voice against Rock of Ages.
He's the One from east to west;
>    from desert to mountains, he's the One.

God rules: he brings this one down to his knees,
>    pulls that one up on her feet.
GOD has a cup in his hand,
>    a bowl of wine, full to the brim.

He draws from it and pours;
     it's drained to the dregs.
Earth's wicked ones drink it all,
     drink it down to the last bitter drop!

And I'm telling the story of God Eternal,
     singing the praises of Jacob's God.
The fists of the wicked
     are bloody stumps,
The arms of the righteous
     are lofty green branches.

# 76

An Asaph psalm

God is well-known in Judah;
     in Israel, he's a household name.
He keeps a house in Salem,
     his own suite of rooms in Zion.
That's where, using arrows for kindling,
     he made a bonfire of weapons of war.

Oh, how bright you shine!
     Outshining their huge piles of loot!
The warriors were plundered
     and left there impotent.
And now there's nothing to them,
     nothing to show for their swagger and threats.
Your sudden roar, God of Jacob,
     knocked the wind out of horse and rider.

Fierce you are, and fearsome!
     Who can stand up to your rising anger?
From heaven you thunder judgment;
     earth falls to her knees and holds her breath.
God stands tall and makes things right,
     he saves all the wretched on earth.
Instead of smoldering rage—God-praise!
     All that sputtering rage—now a garland for God!

Do for GOD what you said you'd do—
    he is, after all, your God.
Let everyone in town bring offerings
    to the One Who Watches our every move.
Nobody gets by with anything,
    no one plays fast and loose with him.

# 77

AN ASAPH PSALM

I yell out to my God, I yell with all my might,
    I yell at the top of my lungs. He listens.

I found myself in trouble and went looking for my Lord;
    my life was an open wound that wouldn't heal.
When friends said, "Everything will turn out all right,"
    I didn't believe a word they said.
I remember God—and shake my head.
    I bow my head—then wring my hands.
I'm awake all night—not a wink of sleep;
    I can't even say what's bothering me.
I go over the days one by one,
    I ponder the years gone by.
I strum my lute all through the night,
    wondering how to get my life together.

Will the Lord walk off and leave us for good?
    Will he never smile again?
Is his love worn threadbare?
    Has his salvation promise burned out?
Has God forgotten his manners?
    Has he angrily stalked off and left us?
"Just my luck," I said. "The High God goes out of business
    just the moment I need him."

Once again I'll go over what GOD has done,
    lay out on the table the ancient wonders;
I'll ponder all the things you've accomplished,
    and give a long, loving look at your acts.

Oh God! Your way is holy!
    No god is great like God!
You're the God who makes things happen;
    you showed everyone what you can do—
You pulled your people out of the worst kind of trouble,
    rescued the children of Jacob and Joseph.

Ocean saw you in action, God,
    saw you and trembled with fear;
    Deep Ocean was scared to death.
Clouds belched buckets of rain,
    Sky exploded with thunder,
    your arrows flashing this way and that.
From Whirlwind came your thundering voice,
    Lightning exposed the world,
    Earth reeled and rocked.
You strode right through Ocean,
    walked straight through roaring Ocean,
    but nobody saw you come or go.

Hidden in the hands of Moses and Aaron,
You led your people like a flock of sheep.

# 78

AN ASAPH PSALM

Listen, dear friends, to God's truth,
    bend your ears to what I tell you.
I'm chewing on the morsel of a proverb;
    I'll let you in on the sweet old truths,
Stories we heard from our fathers,
    counsel we learned at our mother's knee.
We're not keeping this to ourselves,
    we're passing it along to the next generation—
GOD's fame and fortune,
    the marvelous things he has done.

He planted a witness in Jacob,
    set his Word firmly in Israel,

190

Then commanded our parents
    to teach it to their children
So the next generation would know,
    and all the generations to come—
Know the truth and tell the stories
    so their children can trust in God,
Never forget the works of God
    but keep his commands to the letter.
Heaven forbid they should be like their parents,
    bullheaded and bad,
A fickle and faithless bunch
    who never stayed true to God.


The Ephraimites, armed to the teeth,
    ran off when the battle began.
They were cowards to God's Covenant,
    refused to walk by his Word.
They forgot what he had done—
    marvels he'd done right before their eyes.
He performed miracles in plain sight of their parents
    in Egypt, out on the fields of Zoan.
He split the Sea and they walked right through it;
    he piled the waters to the right and the left.
He led them by day with a cloud,
    led them all the night long with a fiery torch.
He split rocks in the wilderness,
    gave them all they could drink from underground springs;
He made creeks flow out from sheer rock,
    and water pour out like a river.


All they did was sin even more,
    rebel in the desert against the High God.
They tried to get their own way with God,
    clamored for favors, for special attention.
They whined like spoiled children,
    "Why can't God give us a decent meal in this desert?
Sure, he struck the rock and the water flowed,
    creeks cascaded from the rock.

191

But how about some fresh-baked bread?
How about a nice cut of meat?"


When GOD heard that, he was furious—
his anger flared against Jacob,
he lost his temper with Israel.
It was clear they didn't believe God,
had no intention of trusting in his help.
But God helped them anyway, commanded the clouds
and gave orders that opened the gates of heaven.
He rained down showers of manna to eat,
he gave them the Bread of Heaven.
They ate the bread of the mighty angels;
he sent them all the food they could eat.
He let East Wind break loose from the skies,
gave a strong push to South Wind.
This time it was birds that rained down—
succulent birds, an abundance of birds.
He aimed them right for the center of their camp;
all round their tents there were birds.
They ate and had their fill;
he handed them everything they craved on a platter.
But their greed knew no bounds;
they stuffed their mouths with more and more.
Finally, God was fed up, his anger erupted—
he cut down their brightest and best,
he laid low Israel's finest young men.


And—can you believe it?—they kept right on sinning;
all those wonders and they still wouldn't believe!
So their lives dribbled off to nothing—
nothing to show for their lives but a ghost town.
When he cut them down, they came running for help;
they turned and pled for mercy.
They gave witness that God was their rock,
that High God was their redeemer,
But they didn't mean a word of it;
they lied through their teeth the whole time.

They could not have cared less about him,
    wanted nothing to do with his Covenant.


And God? Compassionate!
    Forgave the sin! Didn't destroy!
Over and over he reined in his anger,
    restrained his considerable wrath.
He knew what they were made of;
    he knew there wasn't much to them,
How often in the desert they had spurned him,
    tried his patience in those wilderness years.
Time and again they pushed him to the limit,
    provoked Israel's Holy God.
How quickly they forgot what he'd done,
    forgot their day of rescue from the enemy,
When he did miracles in Egypt,
    wonders on the plain of Zoan.
He turned the River and its streams to blood—
    not a drop of water fit to drink.
He sent flies, which ate them alive,
    and frogs, which bedeviled them.
He turned their harvest over to caterpillars,
    everything they had worked for to the locusts.
He flattened their grapevines with hail;
    a killing frost ruined their orchards.
He pounded their cattle with hail,
    let thunderbolts loose on their herds.
His anger flared,
    a wild firestorm of havoc,
An advance guard of disease-carrying angels
    to clear the ground, preparing the way before him.
He didn't spare those people,
    he let the plague rage through their lives.
He killed all the Egyptian firstborns,
    lusty infants, offspring of Ham's virility.
Then he led his people out like sheep,
    took his flock safely through the wilderness.
He took good care of them; they had nothing to fear.
    The Sea took care of their enemies for good.

He brought them into his holy land,
 this mountain he claimed for his own.
He scattered everyone who got in their way;
 he staked out an inheritance for them—
 the tribes of Israel all had their own places.

But they kept on giving him a hard time,
 rebelled against God, the High God,
 refused to do anything he told them.
They were worse, if that's possible, than their parents:
 traitors—crooked as a corkscrew.
Their pagan orgies provoked God's anger,
 their obscene idolatries broke his heart.
When God heard their carryings-on, he was furious;
 he posted a huge No over Israel.
He walked off and left Shiloh empty,
 abandoned the shrine where he had met with Israel.
He let his pride and joy go to the dogs,
 turned his back on the pride of his life.
He turned them loose on fields of battle;
 angry, he let them fend for themselves.
Their young men went to war and never came back;
 their young women waited in vain.
Their priests were massacred,
 and their widows never shed a tear.

Suddenly the Lord was up on his feet
 like someone roused from deep sleep,
 shouting like a drunken warrior.
He hit his enemies hard, sent them running,
 yelping, not daring to look back.
He disqualified Joseph as leader,
 told Ephraim he didn't have what it takes,
And chose the Tribe of Judah instead,
 Mount Zion, which he loves so much.
He built his sanctuary there, resplendent,
 solid and lasting as the earth itself.
Then he chose David, his servant,
 handpicked him from his work in the sheep pens.

One day he was caring for the ewes and their lambs,
     the next day God had him shepherding Jacob,
     his people Israel, his prize possession.
His good heart made him a good shepherd;
     he guided the people wisely and well.

# 79

AN ASAPH PSALM

God! Barbarians have broken into your home,
     violated your holy temple,
     left Jerusalem a pile of rubble!
They've served up the corpses of your servants
     as carrion food for birds of prey,
Threw the bones of your holy people
     out to the wild animals to gnaw on.
They dumped out their blood
     like buckets of water.
All around Jerusalem, their bodies
     were left to rot, unburied.
We're nothing but a joke to our neighbors,
     graffiti scrawled on the city walls.

How long do we have to put up with this, GOD?
     Do you have it in for us for good?
     Will your smoldering rage never cool down?
If you're going to be angry, be angry
     with the pagans who care nothing about you,
     or your rival kingdoms who ignore you.
They're the ones who ruined Jacob,
     who wrecked and looted the place where he lived.

Don't blame us for the sins of our parents.
     Hurry up and help us; we're at the end of our rope.
You're famous for helping; God, give *us* a break.
     Your reputation is on the line.
Pull us out of this mess, forgive us our sins—
     do what you're famous for doing!

Don't let the heathen get by with their sneers:
    "Where's your God? Is he out to lunch?"
Go public and show the godless world
    that they can't kill your servants and get by with it.

Give groaning prisoners a hearing;
    pardon those on death row from their doom—you can do it!
Give our jeering neighbors what they've got coming to them;
    let their God-taunts boomerang and knock them flat.
Then we, your people, the ones you love and care for,
    will thank you over and over and over.
We'll tell everyone we meet
    how wonderful you are, how praiseworthy you are!

# 80

An Asaph psalm

Listen, Shepherd, Israel's Shepherd—
    get all your Joseph sheep together.
Throw beams of light
    from your dazzling throne
So Ephraim, Benjamin, and Manasseh
    can see where they're going.
Get out of bed—you've slept long enough!
    Come on the run before it's too late.

    God, come back!
    Smile your blessing smile:
    *That* will be our salvation.

GOD, God of the angel armies,
    how long will you smolder like a sleeping volcano
    while your people call for fire and brimstone?
You put us on a diet of tears,
    bucket after bucket of salty tears to drink.
You make us look ridiculous to our friends;
    our enemies poke fun day after day.

God of the angel armies, come back!
Smile your blessing smile:
*That* will be our salvation.

Remember how you brought a young vine from Egypt,
    cleared out the brambles and briers
    and planted your very own vineyard?
You prepared the good earth,
    you planted her roots deep;
    the vineyard filled the land.
Your vine soared high and shaded the mountains,
    even dwarfing the giant cedars.
Your vine ranged west to the Sea,
    east to the River.
So why do you no longer protect your vine?
    Trespassers pick its grapes at will;
Wild pigs crash through and crush it,
    and the mice nibble away at what's left.
God of the angel armies, turn our way!
    Take a good look at what's happened
    and attend to this vine.
Care for what you once tenderly planted—
    the vine you raised from a shoot.
And those who dared to set it on fire—
    give them a look that will kill!
Then take the hand of your once-favorite child,
    the child you raised to adulthood.
We will never turn our back on you;
    breathe life into our lungs so we can shout your name!

    GOD, God of the angel armies, come back!
    Smile your blessing smile:
    *That* will be our salvation.

# 81

AN ASAPH PSALM

A song to our strong God!
    a shout to the God of Jacob!

Anthems from the choir, music from the band,
    sweet sounds from lute and harp,
Trumpets and trombones and horns:
    it's festival day, a feast to God!
A day decreed by God,
    solemnly ordered by the God of Jacob.
He commanded Joseph to keep this day
    so we'd never forget what he did in Egypt.

I hear this most gentle whisper from One
I never guessed would speak to me:

"I took the world off your shoulders,
    freed you from a life of hard labor.
You called to me in your pain;
    I got you out of a bad place.
I answered you from where the thunder hides,
    I proved you at Meribah Fountain.

"Listen, dear ones—get this straight;
    oh Israel, don't take this lightly.
Don't take up with strange gods,
    don't worship the latest in gods.
I'm GOD, your God, the very God
    who rescued you from doom in Egypt,
Then fed you all you could eat,
    filled your hungry stomachs.

"But my people didn't listen,
    Israel paid no attention;
So I let go of the reins and told them, 'Run!
    Do it your own way!'

"Oh, dear people, will you listen to me now?
    Israel, will you follow my map?
I'll make short work of your enemies,
    give your foes the back of my hand.
I'll send the GOD-haters cringing like dogs,
    never to be heard from again.

You'll feast on my fresh-baked bread
    spread with butter and rock-pure honey."

# 82

AN ASAPH PSALM

God calls the judges into his courtroom,
    he puts all the judges in the dock.

"Enough! You've corrupted justice long enough,
    you've let the wicked get away with murder.
You're here to defend the defenseless,
    to make sure that underdogs get a fair break;
Your job is to stand up for the powerless,
    and prosecute all those who exploit them."

Ignorant judges! Head-in-the-sand judges!
    They haven't a clue to what's going on.
And now everything's falling apart,
    the world's coming unglued.

"I commissioned you judges, each one of you,
    deputies of the High God,
But you've betrayed your commission
    and now you're stripped of your rank, busted."

O God, give them their just deserts!
    You've got the whole world in your hands!

# 83

AN ASAPH PSALM

GOD, don't shut me out;
    don't give me the silent treatment, O God.
Your enemies are out there whooping it up,
    the God-haters are living it up;
They're plotting to do your people in,
    conspiring to rob you of your precious ones.

"Let's wipe this nation from the face of the earth,"
    they say; "scratch Israel's name off the books."
And now they're putting their heads together,
    making plans to get rid of you.

    Edom and the Ishmaelites,
    Moab and the Hagrites,
    Gebal and Ammon and Amalek,
    Philistia and the Tyrians,
    And now Assyria has joined up,
    Giving muscle to the gang of Lot.

Do to them what you did to Midian,
    to Sisera and Jabin at Kishon Brook;
They came to a bad end at Endor,
    nothing but dung for the garden.
Cut down their leaders as you did Oreb and Zeeb,
    their princes to nothings like Zebah and Zalmunna,
With their empty brags, "We're grabbing it all,
    grabbing God's gardens for ourselves."

My God! I've had it with them!
    Blow them away!
Tumbleweeds in the desert waste,
    charred sticks in the burned-over ground.
Knock the breath right out of them, so they're gasping
    for breath, gasping, "GOD."
Bring them to the end of their rope,
    and leave them there dangling, helpless.
Then they'll learn your name: "GOD,"
    the one and only High God on earth.

# 84

A KORAH PSALM

What a beautiful home, GOD of the Angel Armies!
    I've always longed to live in a place like this,
Always dreamed of a room in your house,
    where I could sing for joy to God-alive!

Birds find nooks and crannies in your house,
　　sparrows and swallows make nests there.
They lay their eggs and raise their young,
　　singing their songs in the place where we worship.
GOD of the Angel Armies! King! God!
　　How blessed they are to live and sing there!

And how blessed all those in whom you live,
　　whose lives become roads you travel;
They wind through lonesome valleys, come upon brooks,
　　discover cool springs and pools brimming with rain!
God-traveled, these roads curve up the mountain, and
　　at the last turn—Zion! God in full view!

God of the Angel Armies, listen:
　　O God of Jacob, open your ears—I'm praying!
Look at our shields, glistening in the sun,
　　our faces, shining with your gracious anointing.

One day spent in your house, this beautiful place of worship,
　　beats thousands spent on Greek island beaches.
I'd rather scrub floors in the house of my God
　　than be honored as a guest in the palace of sin.
All sunshine and sovereign is GOD,
　　generous in gifts and glory.
He doesn't scrimp with his traveling companions.
　　It's smooth sailing all the way with GOD of the Angel Armies.

# 85

A KORAH PSALM

GOD, you smiled on your good earth!
　　You brought good times back to Jacob!
You lifted the cloud of guilt from your people,
　　you put their sins far out of sight.
You took back your sin-provoked threats,
　　you cooled your hot, righteous anger.

Help us again, God of our help;
    don't hold a grudge against us forever.
You aren't going to keep this up, are you?
    scowling and angry, year after year?
Why not help us make a fresh start—a resurrection life?
    *Then* your people will laugh and sing!
Show us how much you love us, GOD!
    Give us the salvation we need!

I can't wait to hear what he'll say.
    GOD's about to pronounce his people well,
The holy people he loves so much,
    so they'll never again live like fools.
See how close his salvation is to those who fear him?
    Our country is home base for Glory!

Love and Truth meet in the street,
    Right Living and Whole Living embrace and kiss!
Truth sprouts green from the ground,
    Right Living pours down from the skies!
Oh yes! GOD gives Goodness and Beauty;
    our land responds with Bounty and Blessing.
Right Living strides out before him,
    and clears a path for his passage.

# 86

A DAVID PSALM

Bend an ear, GOD; answer me.
    I'm one miserable wretch!
Keep me safe—haven't I lived a good life?
    Help your servant—I'm depending on you!
You're my God; have mercy on me.
    I count on you from morning to night.
Give your servant a happy life;
    I put myself in your hands!
You're well-known as good and forgiving,
    bighearted to all who ask for help.

Pay attention, GOD, to my prayer;
    bend down and listen to my cry for help.
Every time I'm in trouble I call on you,
    confident that you'll answer.

There's no one quite like you among the gods, O Lord,
    and nothing to compare with your works.
All the nations you made are on their way,
    ready to give honor to you, O Lord,
Ready to put your beauty on display,
    parading your greatness,
And the great things you do—
    God, you're the one, there's no one but you!

Train me, GOD, to walk straight;
    then I'll follow your true path.
Put me together, one heart and mind;
    then, undivided, I'll worship in joyful fear.
From the bottom of my heart I thank you, dear Lord;
    I've never kept secret what you're up to.
You've always been great toward me—what love!
    You snatched me from the brink of disaster!
God, these bullies have reared their heads!
    A gang of thugs is after me—
    and they don't care a thing about you.
But you, O God, are both tender and kind,
    not easily angered, immense in love,
    and you never, never quit.
So look me in the eye and show kindness,
    give your servant the strength to go on,
    save your dear, dear child!
Make a show of how much you love me
    so the bullies who hate me will stand there slack-jawed,
As you, GOD, gently and powerfully
    put me back on my feet.

# 87

A KORAH PSALM

He founded Zion on the Holy Mountain—
　　and oh, how GOD loves his home!
Loves it far better than all
　　the homes of Jacob put together!
God's hometown—oh!
　　everyone there is talking about you!

I name them off, those among whom I'm famous:
　　Egypt and Babylon,
　　also Philistia,
　　even Tyre, along with Cush.
Word's getting around; they point them out:
　　"This one was born again here!"

The word's getting out on Zion:
　　"Men and women, right and left,
　　get born again in her!"

GOD registers their names in his book:
　　"This one, this one, and this one—
　　born again, right here."

Singers and dancers give credit to Zion:
　　"All my springs are in you!"

# 88

A KORAH PRAYER OF HEMAN

GOD, you're my last chance of the day.
　　I spend the night on my knees before you.
Put me on your salvation agenda;
　　take notes on the trouble I'm in.
I've had my fill of trouble;
　　I'm camped on the edge of hell.

I'm written off as a lost cause,
     one more statistic, a hopeless case.
Abandoned as already dead,
     one more body in a stack of corpses,
And not so much as a gravestone—
     I'm a black hole in oblivion.
You've dropped me into a bottomless pit,
     sunk me in a pitch-black abyss.
I'm battered senseless by your rage,
     relentlessly pounded by your waves of anger.
You turned my friends against me,
     made me horrible to them.
I'm caught in a maze and can't find my way out,
     blinded by tears of pain and frustration.

I call to you, GOD; all day I call.
     I wring my hands, I plead for help.
Are the dead a live audience for your miracles?
     Do ghosts ever join the choirs that praise you?
Does your love make any difference in a graveyard?
     Is your faithful presence noticed in the corridors of hell?
Are your marvelous wonders ever seen in the dark?
     your righteous ways noticed in the Land of No Memory?

I'm standing my ground, GOD, shouting for help,
     at my prayers every morning, on my knees each daybreak.
Why, GOD, do you turn a deaf ear?
     Why do you make yourself scarce?
For as long as I remember I've been hurting;
     I've taken the worst you can hand out, and I've had it.
Your wildfire anger has blazed through my life;
     I'm bleeding, black and blue.
You've attacked me fiercely from every side,
     raining down blows till I'm nearly dead.
You made lover and neighbor alike dump me;
     the only friend I have left is Darkness.

# 89

Your love, GOD, is my song, and I'll sing it!
    I'm forever telling everyone how faithful you are.
I'll never quit telling the story of your love—
    how you built the cosmos
    and guaranteed everything in it.
Your love has always been our lives' foundation,
    your fidelity has been the roof over our world.
You once said, "I joined forces with my chosen leader,
    I pledged my word to my servant, David, saying,
'Everyone descending from you is guaranteed life;
    I'll make your rule as solid and lasting as rock.'"

GOD! Let the cosmos praise your wonderful ways,
    the choir of holy angels sing anthems to your faithful ways!
Search high and low, scan skies and land,
    you'll find nothing and no one quite like GOD.
The holy angels are in awe before him;
    he looms immense and august over everyone around him.
GOD of the Angel Armies, who is like you,
    powerful and faithful from every angle?
You put the arrogant ocean in its place
    and calm its waves when they turn unruly.
You gave that old hag Egypt the back of your hand,
    you brushed off your enemies with a flick of your wrist.
You own the cosmos—you made everything in it,
    everything from atom to archangel.
You positioned the North and South Poles;
    the mountains Tabor and Hermon sing duets to you.
With your well-muscled arm and your grip of steel—
    nobody trifles with you!
The Right and Justice are the roots of your rule;
    Love and Truth are its fruits.
Blessed are the people who know the passwords of praise,
    who shout on parade in the bright presence of GOD.
Delighted, they dance all day long; they know
    who you are, what you do—they can't keep it quiet!

Your vibrant beauty has gotten inside us—
    you've been so good to us! We're walking on air!
All we are and have we owe to GOD,
    Holy God of Israel, our King!

A long time ago you spoke in a vision,
    you spoke to your faithful beloved:
"I've crowned a hero,
    I chose the best I could find;
I found David, my servant,
    poured holy oil on his head,
And I'll keep my hand steadily on him,
    yes, I'll stick with him through thick and thin.
No enemy will get the best of him,
    no scoundrel will do him in.
I'll weed out all who oppose him,
    I'll clean out all who hate him.
I'm with him for good and I'll love him forever;
    I've set him on high—he's riding high!
I've put Ocean in his one hand, River in the other;
    he'll call out, 'Oh, my Father—my God, my Rock of Salvation!'
Yes, I'm setting him apart as the First of the royal line,
    High King over all of earth's kings.
I'll preserve him eternally in my love,
    I'll faithfully do all I so solemnly promised.
I'll guarantee his family tree
    and underwrite his rule.
If his children refuse to do what I tell them,
    if they refuse to walk in the way I show them,
If they spit on the directions I give them
    and tear up the rules I post for them—
I'll rub their faces in the dirt of their rebellion
    and make them face the music.
But I'll never throw them out,
    never abandon or disown them.
Do you think I'd withdraw my holy promise?
    or take back words I'd already spoken?
I've given my word, my whole and holy word;
    do you think I would lie to David?

His family tree is here for good,
    his sovereignty as sure as the sun,
Dependable as the phases of the moon,
    inescapable as weather."

But GOD, you did walk off and leave us,
    you lost your temper with the one you anointed.
You tore up the promise you made to your servant,
    you stomped his crown in the mud.
You blasted his home to kingdom come,
    reduced his city to a pile of rubble
Picked clean by wayfaring strangers,
    a joke to all the neighbors.
You declared a holiday for all his enemies,
    and they're celebrating for all they're worth.
Angry, you opposed him in battle,
    refused to fight on his side;
You robbed him of his splendor, humiliated this warrior,
    ground his kingly honor in the dirt.
You took the best years of his life
    and left him an impotent, ruined husk.
How long do we put up with this, GOD?
    Are you gone for good? Will you hold this grudge forever?
Remember my sorrow and how short life is.
    Did you create men and women for nothing but this?
We'll see death soon enough. Everyone does.
    And there's no back door out of hell.
So where is the love you're so famous for, Lord?
    What happened to your promise to David?
Take a good look at your servant, dear Lord;
    I'm the butt of the jokes of all nations,
The taunting jokes of your enemies, GOD,
    as they dog the steps of your dear anointed.

      Blessed be GOD forever and always!
      Yes. Oh, yes.

# 90

A PRAYER OF MOSES, MAN OF GOD

God, it seems you've been our home forever;
    long before the mountains were born,
Long before you brought earth itself to birth,
    from "once upon a time" to "kingdom come"— you are God.


So don't return us to mud, saying,
    "Back to where you came from!"
Patience! You've got all the time in the world—whether
    a thousand years or a day, it's all the same to you.
Are we no more to you than a wispy dream,
    no more than a blade of grass
That springs up gloriously with the rising sun
    and is cut down without a second thought?
Your anger is far and away too much for us;
    we're at the end of our rope.
You keep track of all our sins; every misdeed
    since we were children is entered in your books.
All we can remember is that frown on your face.
    Is that all we're ever going to get?
We live for seventy years or so
    (with luck we might make it to eighty),
And what do we have to show for it? Trouble.
    Toil and trouble and a marker in the graveyard.
Who can make sense of such rage,
    such anger against the very ones who fear you?


Oh! Teach us to live well!
    Teach us to live wisely and well!
Come back, GOD—how long do we have to wait?—
    and treat your servants with kindness for a change.
Surprise us with love at daybreak;
    then we'll skip and dance all the day long.
Make up for the bad times with some good times;
    we've seen enough evil to last a lifetime.
Let your servants see what you're best at—
    the ways you rule and bless your children.

And let the loveliness of our Lord, our God, rest on us,
    confirming the work that we do.
    Oh, yes. Affirm the work that we do!

# 91

You who sit down in the High God's presence,
    spend the night in Shaddai's shadow,
Say this: "GOD, you're my refuge.
    I trust in you and I'm safe!"
That's right—he rescues you from hidden traps,
    shields you from deadly hazards.
His huge outstretched arms protect you—
    under them you're perfectly safe;
    his arms fend off all harm.
Fear nothing—not wild wolves in the night,
    not flying arrows in the day,
Not disease that prowls through the darkness,
    not disaster that erupts at high noon.
Even though others succumb all around,
    drop like flies right and left,
    no harm will even graze you.
You'll stand untouched, watch it all from a distance,
    watch the wicked turn into corpses.
Yes, because GOD's your refuge,
    the High God your very own home,
Evil can't get close to you,
    harm can't get through the door.
He ordered his angels
    to guard you wherever you go.
If you stumble, they'll catch you;
    their job is to keep you from falling.
You'll walk unharmed among lions and snakes,
    and kick young lions and serpents from the path.

"If you'll hold on to me for dear life," says GOD,
    "I'll get you out of any trouble.
I'll give you the best of care
    if you'll only get to know and trust me.

Call me and I'll answer, be at your side in bad times;
    I'll rescue you, then throw you a party.
I'll give you a long life,
    give you a long drink of salvation!"

# 92

A Sabbath song

What a beautiful thing, God, to give thanks,
    to sing an anthem to you, the High God!
To announce your love each daybreak,
    sing your faithful presence all through the night,
Accompanied by dulcimer and harp,
    the full-bodied music of strings.

You made me so happy, God.
    I saw your work and I shouted for joy.
How magnificent your work, God!
    How profound your thoughts!
Dullards never notice what you do;
    fools never do get it.
When the wicked popped up like weeds
    and all the evil men and women took over,
You mowed them down,
    finished them off once and for all.
You, God, are High and Eternal.
    Look at your enemies, God!
Look at your enemies—ruined!
    Scattered to the winds, all those hirelings of evil!

But you've made me strong as a charging bison,
    you've honored me with a festive parade.
The sight of my critics going down is still fresh,
    the rout of my malicious detractors.
My ears are filled with the sounds of promise:
    "Good people will prosper like palm trees,
Grow tall like Lebanon cedars;
    transplanted to God's courtyard,

They'll grow tall in the presence of God,
    lithe and green, virile still in old age."

Such witnesses to upright GOD!
    My Mountain, my huge, holy Mountain!

# 93

GOD is King, robed and ruling,
GOD is robed and surging with strength.

    And yes, the world is firm, immovable,
    Your throne ever firm—you're Eternal!

Sea storms are up, GOD,
Sea storms wild and roaring,
Sea storms with thunderous breakers.

    Stronger than wild sea storms,
    Mightier than sea-storm breakers,
    Mighty GOD rules from High Heaven.

What you say goes—it always has.
"Beauty" and "Holy" mark your palace rule,
GOD, to the very end of time.

# 94

GOD, put an end to evil;
    avenging God, show your colors!
Judge of the earth, take your stand;
    throw the book at the arrogant.

GOD, the wicked get away with murder—
    how long will you let this go on?
They brag and boast
    and crow about their crimes!

They walk all over your people, GOD,
    exploit and abuse your precious people.

They take out anyone who gets in their way;
    if they can't use them, they kill them.
They think, "GOD isn't looking,
    Jacob's God is out to lunch."

Well, think again, you idiots,
    fools—how long before you get smart?
Do you think Ear-Maker doesn't hear,
    Eye-Shaper doesn't see?
Do you think the trainer of nations doesn't correct,
    the teacher of Adam doesn't know?
GOD knows, all right—
    knows your stupidity,
    sees your shallowness.

How blessed the man you train, GOD,
    the woman you instruct in your Word,
Providing a circle of quiet within the clamor of evil,
    while a jail is being built for the wicked.
GOD will never walk away from his people,
    never desert his precious people.
Rest assured that justice is on its way
    and every good heart put right.

Who stood up for me against the wicked?
    Who took my side against evil workers?
If GOD hadn't been there for me,
    I never would have made it.
The minute I said, "I'm slipping, I'm falling,"
    your love, GOD, took hold and held me fast.
When I was upset and beside myself,
    you calmed me down and cheered me up.

Can Misrule have anything in common with you?
    Can Troublemaker pretend to be on your side?
They ganged up on good people,
    plotted behind the backs of the innocent.
But GOD became my hideout,
    God was my high mountain retreat,

Then boomeranged their evil back on them:
  for their evil ways he wiped them out,
  our GOD cleaned them out for good.

# 95

Come, let's shout praises to GOD,
  raise the roof for the Rock who saved us!
Let's march into his presence singing praises,
  lifting the rafters with our hymns!

And why? Because GOD is the best,
  High King over all the gods.
In one hand he holds deep caves and caverns,
  in the other hand grasps the high mountains.
He made Ocean—he owns it!
  His hands sculpted Earth!

So come, let us worship: bow before him,
  on your knees before GOD, who made us!
Oh yes, he's our God,
  and we're the people he pastures, the flock he feeds.

Drop everything and listen, listen as he speaks:
  "Don't turn a deaf ear as in the Bitter Uprising,
As on the day of the Wilderness Test,
  when your ancestors turned and put *me* to the test.
For forty years they watched me at work among them,
  as over and over they tried my patience.
And I was provoked—oh, was I provoked!
  'Can't they keep their minds on God for five minutes?
  Do they simply refuse to walk down my road?'
Exasperated, I exploded,
  'They'll never get where they're headed,
  never be able to sit down and rest.'"

# 96

Sing GOD a brand-new song!
Earth and everyone in it, sing!
Sing to GOD—*worship* GOD!

Shout the news of his victory from sea to sea,
Take the news of his glory to the lost,
News of his wonders to one and all!

For GOD is great, and worth a thousand Hallelujahs.
His terrible beauty makes the gods look cheap;
Pagan gods are mere tatters and rags.

GOD made the heavens—
Royal splendor radiates from him,
A powerful beauty sets him apart.

Bravo, GOD, Bravo!
Everyone join in the great shout: Encore!
In awe before the beauty, in awe before the might.

Bring gifts and celebrate,
Bow before the beauty of GOD,
Then to your knees—everyone worship!

Get out the message—GOD Rules!
He put the world on a firm foundation;
He treats everyone fair and square.

Let's hear it from Sky,
With Earth joining in,
And a huge round of applause from Sea.

Let Wilderness turn cartwheels,
Animals, come dance,
Put every tree of the forest in the choir—

An extravaganza before GOD as he comes,
As he comes to set everything right on earth,
Set everything right, treat everyone fair.

# 97

GOD rules: *there's* something to shout over!
On the double, mainlands and islands—celebrate!

Bright clouds and storm clouds circle 'round him;
Right and justice anchor his rule.

Fire blazes out before him,
Flaming high up the craggy mountains.

His lightnings light up the world;
Earth, wide-eyed, trembles in fear.

The mountains take one look at GOD
And melt, melt like wax before earth's Lord.

The heavens announce that he'll set everything right,
And everyone will see it happen—glorious!

All who serve handcrafted gods will be sorry—
And they were so proud of their ragamuffin gods!

On your knees, all you gods—worship him!
And Zion, you listen and take heart!

Daughters of Zion, sing your hearts out:
GOD has done it all, has set everything right.

You, GOD, are High God of the cosmos,
Far, far higher than any of the gods.

GOD loves all who hate evil,
And those who love him he keeps safe,
Snatches them from the grip of the wicked.

Light-seeds are planted in the souls of God's people,
Joy-seeds are planted in good heart-soil.

So, God's people, shout praise to GOD,
Give thanks to our Holy God!

# 98

Sing to GOD a brand-new song.
He's made a world of wonders!

He rolled up his sleeves,
He set things right.

GOD made history with salvation,
He showed the world what he could do.

He remembered to love us, a bonus
To his dear family, Israel—indefatigable love.

The whole earth comes to attention.
Look—God's work of salvation!

Shout your praises to GOD, everybody!
Let loose and sing! Strike up the band!

Round up an orchestra to play for GOD,
Add on a hundred-voice choir.

Feature trumpets and big trombones,
Fill the air with praises to King GOD.

Let the sea and its fish give a round of applause,
With everything living on earth joining in.

Let ocean breakers call out, "Encore!"
And mountains harmonize the finale—

A tribute to GOD when he comes,
When he comes to set the earth right.

He'll straighten out the whole world,
He'll put the world right, and everyone in it.

# 99

GOD rules. On your toes, everybody!
He rules from his angel throne—take notice!
GOD looms majestic in Zion,
He towers in splendor over all the big names.
Great and terrible your beauty: let everyone praise you!
    Holy. Yes, holy.

Strong King, lover of justice,
You laid things out fair and square;
You set down the foundations in Jacob,
Foundation stones of just and right ways.
Honor GOD, our God; worship his rule!
    Holy. Yes, holy.

Moses and Aaron were his priests,
Samuel among those who prayed to him.
They prayed to GOD and he answered them;
He spoke from the pillar of cloud.
And they did what he said; they kept the law he gave them.
And then GOD, our God, answered them
(But you were never soft on their sins).
Lift high GOD, our God; worship at his holy mountain.
    Holy. Yes, holy is GOD our God.

# 100

A THANKSGIVING PSALM

On your feet now—applaud GOD!
    Bring a gift of laughter,
        sing yourselves into his presence.

Know this: GOD is God, and God, GOD.
    He made us; we didn't make him.
    We're his people, his well-tended sheep.

Enter with the password: "Thank you!"
　　Make yourselves at home, talking praise.
　　Thank him. Worship him.

For GOD is sheer beauty,
　　all-generous in love,
　　loyal always and ever.

# 101

A DAVID PSALM

My theme song is God's love and justice,
　　and I'm singing it right to you, GOD.
I'm finding my way down the road of right living,
　　but how long before you show up?
I'm doing the very best I can,
　　and I'm doing it at home, where it counts.
I refuse to take a second look
　　at corrupting people and degrading things.
I reject made-in-Canaan gods,
　　stay clear of contamination.
The crooked in heart keep their distance;
　　I refuse to shake hands with those who plan evil.
I put a gag on the gossip
　　who bad-mouths his neighbor;
I can't stand
　　arrogance.
But I have my eye on salt-of-the-earth people—
　　they're the ones I want working with me;
Men and women on the straight and narrow—
　　these are the ones I want at my side.
But no one who traffics in lies
　　gets a job with me; I have no patience with liars.
I've rounded up all the wicked like cattle
　　and herded them right out of the country.
I purged GOD's city
　　of all who make a business of evil.

# 102

A PRAYER OF ONE WHOSE LIFE IS FALLING TO PIECES, AND WHO LETS GOD KNOW JUST HOW BAD IT IS.

GOD, listen! Listen to my prayer,
    listen to the pain in my cries.
Don't turn your back on me
    just when I need you so desperately.
Pay attention! This is a cry for *help*!
    And hurry—this can't wait!

I'm wasting away to nothing,
    I'm burning up with fever.
I'm a ghost of my former self,
    half-consumed already by terminal illness.
My jaws ache from gritting my teeth;
    I'm nothing but skin and bones.
I'm like a buzzard in the desert,
    a crow perched on the rubble.
Insomniac, I twitter away,
    mournful as a sparrow in the gutter.
All day long my enemies taunt me,
    while others just curse.
They bring in meals—casseroles of ashes!
    I draw drink from a barrel of my tears.
And all because of your furious anger;
    you swept me up and threw me out.
There's nothing left of me—
    a withered weed, swept clean from the path.

Yet you, GOD, are sovereign still,
    always and ever sovereign.
You'll get up from your throne and help Zion—
    it's time for compassionate help.
Oh, how your servants love this city's rubble
    and weep with compassion over its dust!
The godless nations will sit up and take notice
    —see your glory, worship your name—
When GOD rebuilds Zion,
    when he shows up in all his glory,

When he attends to the prayer of the wretched.
    He won't dismiss their prayer.

Write this down for the next generation
    so people not yet born will praise GOD:
"GOD looked out from his high holy place;
    from heaven he surveyed the earth.
He listened to the groans of the doomed,
    he opened the doors of their death cells."
Write it so the story can be told in Zion,
    so GOD's praise will be sung in Jerusalem's streets
And wherever people gather together
    along with their rulers to worship him.

GOD sovereignly brought me to my knees,
    he cut me down in my prime.
"Oh, don't," I prayed, "please don't let me die.
    You have more years than you know what to do with!
You laid earth's foundations a long time ago,
    and handcrafted the very heavens;
You'll still be around when they're long gone,
    threadbare and discarded like an old suit of clothes.
You'll throw them away like a worn-out coat,
    but year after year you're as good as new.
Your servants' children will have a good place to live
    and their children will be at home with you."

# 103

A DAVID PSALM

Oh my soul, bless GOD.
    From head to toe, I'll bless his holy name!
Oh my soul, bless GOD,
    don't forget a single blessing!

He forgives your sins—every one.
He heals your diseases—every one.
He redeems you from hell—saves your life!

He crowns you with love and mercy—a paradise crown.
He wraps you in goodness—beauty eternal.
He renews your youth—you're always young in his presence.

GOD makes everything come out right;
    he puts victims back on their feet.
He showed Moses how he went about his work,
    opened up his plans to all Israel.
GOD is sheer mercy and grace;
    not easily angered, he's rich in love.
He doesn't endlessly nag and scold,
    nor hold grudges forever.
He doesn't treat us as our sins deserve,
    nor pay us back in full for our wrongs.
As high as heaven is over the earth,
    so strong is his love to those who fear him.
And as far as sunrise is from sunset,
    he has separated us from our sins.
As parents feel for their children,
    GOD feels for those who fear him.
He knows us inside and out,
    keeps in mind that we're made of mud.
Men and women don't live very long;
    like wildflowers they spring up and blossom,
But a storm snuffs them out just as quickly,
    leaving nothing to show they were here.
GOD's love, though, is ever and always,
    eternally present to all who fear him,
Making everything right for them and their children
    as they follow his Covenant ways
    and remember to do whatever he said.

GOD has set his throne in heaven;
    he rules over us all. He's the King!
So bless GOD, you angels,
    ready and able to fly at his bidding,
    quick to hear and do what he says.
Bless GOD, all you armies of angels,
    alert to respond to whatever he wills.

Bless GOD, all creatures, wherever you are—
    everything and everyone made by GOD.

And you, oh my soul, bless GOD!

# 104

Oh my soul, bless GOD!

GOD, my God, how great you are!
    beautifully, gloriously robed,
Dressed up in sunshine,
    and all heaven stretched out for your tent.
You built your palace on the ocean deeps,
    made a chariot out of clouds and took off on wind-wings.
You commandeered winds as messengers,
    appointed fire and flame as ambassadors.
You set earth on a firm foundation
    so that nothing can shake it, ever.
You blanketed earth with ocean,
    covered the mountains with deep waters;
Then you roared and the water ran away—
    your thunder crash put it to flight.
Mountains pushed up, valleys spread out
    in the places you assigned them.
You set boundaries between earth and sea;
    never again will earth be flooded.
You started the springs and rivers,
    sent them flowing among the hills.
All the wild animals now drink their fill,
    wild donkeys quench their thirst.
Along the riverbanks the birds build nests,
    ravens make their voices heard.
You water the mountains from your heavenly cisterns;
    earth is supplied with plenty of water.
You make grass grow for the livestock,
    hay for the animals that plow the ground.

Oh yes, God brings grain from the land,
    wine to make people happy,

Their faces glowing with health,
    a people well-fed and hearty.
GOD's trees are well-watered—
    the Lebanon cedars he planted.
Birds build their nests in those trees;
    look—the stork at home in the treetop.
Mountain goats climb about the cliffs;
    badgers burrow among the rocks.
The moon keeps track of the seasons,
    the sun is in charge of each day.
When it's dark and night takes over,
    all the forest creatures come out.
The young lions roar for their prey,
    clamoring to God for their supper.
When the sun comes up, they vanish,
    lazily stretched out in their dens.
Meanwhile, men and women go out to work,
    busy at their jobs until evening.

What a wildly wonderful world, GOD!
    You made it all, with Wisdom at your side,
    made earth overflow with your wonderful creations.
Oh, look—the deep, wide sea,
    brimming with fish past counting,
    sardines and sharks and salmon.
Ships plow those waters,
    and Leviathan, your pet dragon, romps in them.
All the creatures look expectantly to you
    to give them their meals on time.
You come, and they gather around;
    you open your hand and they eat from it.
If you turned your back,
    they'd die in a minute—
Take back your Spirit and they die,
    revert to original mud;
Send out your Spirit and they spring to life—
    the whole countryside in bloom and blossom.

The glory of GOD—let it last forever!
    Let GOD enjoy his creation!

He takes one look at earth and triggers an earthquake,
　　points a finger at the mountains, and volcanoes erupt.

Oh, let me sing to GOD all my life long,
　　sing hymns to my God as long as I live!
Oh, let my song please him;
　　I'm so pleased to be singing to GOD.
But clear the ground of sinners—
　　no more godless men and women!

Oh my soul, bless GOD!

# 105
Hallelujah!

Thank GOD! Pray to him by name!
　　Tell everyone you meet what he has done!
Sing him songs, belt out hymns,
　　translate his wonders into music!
Honor his holy name with Hallelujahs,
　　you who seek GOD. Live a happy life!
Keep your eyes open for GOD, watch for his works;
　　be alert for signs of his presence.
Remember the world of wonders he has made,
　　his miracles, and the verdicts he's rendered—
　　　　Oh seed of Abraham, his servant,
　　　　Oh child of Jacob, his chosen.

He's GOD, our God,
　　in charge of the whole earth.
And he remembers, remembers his Covenant—
　　for a thousand generations he's been as good as his word.
It's the Covenant he made with Abraham,
　　the same oath he swore to Isaac,
The very statute he established with Jacob,
　　the eternal Covenant with Israel,
Namely, "I give you the land.
　　Canaan is your hill-country inheritance."

When they didn't count for much,
    a mere handful, and strangers at that,
Wandering from country to country,
    drifting from pillar to post,
He permitted no one to abuse them.
    He told kings to keep their hands off:
"Don't you dare lay a hand on my anointed,
    don't hurt a hair on the heads of my prophets."

Then he called down a famine on the country,
    he broke every last blade of wheat.
But he sent a man on ahead:
    Joseph, sold as a slave.
They put cruel chains on his ankles,
    an iron collar around his neck,
Until God's word came to the Pharaoh,
    and GOD confirmed his promise.
God sent the king to release him.
    The Pharaoh set Joseph free;
He appointed him master of his palace,
    put him in charge of all his business
To personally instruct his princes
    and train his advisors in wisdom.

Then Israel entered Egypt,
    Jacob immigrated to Africa.
God gave his people lots of babies;
    soon their numbers alarmed their foes.
He turned the Egyptians against his people;
    they abused and cheated God's servants.
Then he sent his servant Moses,
    and Aaron, whom he also chose.
They worked marvels in that spiritual wasteland,
    miracles in the Land of Ham.
He spoke, "Darkness!" and it turned dark—
    they couldn't see what they were doing.
He turned all their water to blood
    so that all their fish died;
He made frogs swarm through the land,
    even into the king's bedroom;

He gave the word and flies swarmed,
  gnats filled the air.
He substituted hail for rain,
  he stabbed their land with lightning;
He wasted their vines and fig trees,
  smashed their groves of trees to splinters;
With a word he brought in locusts,
  millions of locusts, armies of locusts;
They consumed every blade of grass in the country
  and picked the ground clean of produce;
He struck down every firstborn in the land,
  the first fruits of their virile powers.
He led Israel out, their arms filled with loot,
  and not one among his tribes even stumbled.
Egypt was glad to have them go—
  they were scared to death of them.
God spread a cloud to keep them cool through the day
  and a fire to light their way through the night;
They prayed and he brought quail,
  filled them with the bread of heaven;
He opened the rock and water poured out;
  it flowed like a river through that desert—
All because he remembered his Covenant,
  his promise to Abraham, his servant.

Remember this! He led his people out singing for joy;
  his chosen people marched, singing their hearts out!
He made them a gift of the country they entered,
  helped them seize the wealth of the nations
So they could do everything he told them—
  could follow his instructions to the letter.

Hallelujah!

# 106

Hallelujah!
Thank GOD! And why?
  Because he's good, because his love lasts.

But who on earth can do it—
    declaim GOD's mighty acts, broadcast all his praises?
You're one happy man when you do what's right,
    one happy woman when you form the habit of justice.

Remember me, GOD, when you enjoy your people;
    include me when you save them;
I want to see your chosen succeed,
    celebrate with your celebrating nation,
    join the Hallelujahs of your pride and joy!

We've sinned a lot, both we and our parents;
    We've fallen short, hurt a lot of people.
After our parents left Egypt,
    they took your wonders for granted,
    forgot your great and wonderful love.
They were barely beyond the Red Sea
    when they defied the High God
    —the very place he saved them!
    —the place he revealed his amazing power!
He rebuked the Red Sea so that it dried up on the spot
    —he paraded them right through!
    —no one so much as got wet feet!
He saved them from a life of oppression,
    pried them loose from the grip of the enemy.
Then the waters flowed back on their oppressors;
    there wasn't a single survivor.
*Then* they believed his words were true
    and broke out in songs of praise.

But it wasn't long before they forgot the whole thing,
    wouldn't wait to be told what to do.
They only cared about pleasing themselves in that desert,
    provoked God with their insistent demands.
He gave them exactly what they asked for—
    but along with it they got an empty heart.
One day in camp some grew jealous of Moses,
    also of Aaron, holy priest of GOD.
The ground opened and swallowed Dathan,
    then buried Abiram's gang.

Fire flared against that rebel crew
  and torched them to a cinder.

They cast in metal a bull calf at Horeb
  and worshiped the statue they'd made.
They traded the Glory
  for a cheap piece of sculpture—a grass-chewing bull!
They forgot God, their very own Savior,
  who turned things around in Egypt,
Who created a world of wonders in Africa,
  who gave that stunning performance at the Red Sea.

Fed up, God decided to get rid of them—
  and except for Moses, his chosen, he would have.
But Moses stood in the gap and deflected God's anger,
  prevented it from destroying them utterly.
They went on to reject the Blessed Land,
  didn't believe a word of what God promised.
They found fault with the life they had
  and turned a deaf ear to GOD's voice.
Exasperated, God swore
  that he'd lay them low in the desert,
Scattering their children hither and yon,
  strewing them all over the earth.

Then they linked up with Baal Peor,
  attending funeral banquets and eating idol food.
That made God so angry
  that a plague spread through their ranks;
Phinehas stood up and pled their case
  and the plague was stopped.
This was counted to his credit;
  his descendants will never forget it.

They angered God again at Meribah Springs;
  this time Moses got mixed up in their evil;
Because they defied GOD yet again,
  Moses exploded and lost his temper.

They didn't wipe out those godless cultures
    as ordered by GOD;
Instead they intermarried with the heathen,
    and in time became just like them.
They worshiped their idols,
    were caught in the trap of idols.
They sacrificed their sons and daughters
    at the altars of demon gods.
They slit the throats of their babies,
    murdered their infant girls and boys.
They offered their babies to Canaan's gods;
    the blood of their babies stained the land.
Their way of life stank to high heaven;
    they lived like whores.

And GOD was furious—a wildfire anger;
    he couldn't stand even to look at his people.
He turned them over to the heathen
    so that the people who hated them ruled them.
Their enemies made life hard for them;
    they were tyrannized under that rule.
Over and over God rescued them, but they never learned—
    until finally their sins destroyed them.

Still, when God saw the trouble they were in
    and heard their cries for help,
He remembered his Covenant with them,
    and, immense with love, took them by the hand.
He poured out his mercy on them
    while their captors looked on, amazed.

Save us, GOD, our God!
    Gather us back out of exile
So we can give thanks to your holy name
    and join in the glory when you are praised!

        Blessed be GOD, Israel's God!
        Bless now, bless always!
        Oh! Let everyone say Amen!
        Hallelujah!

# 107

Oh, thank GOD—he's so good!
    His love never runs out.
All of you set free by GOD, tell the world!
    Tell how he freed you from oppression,
Then rounded you up from all over the place,
    from the four winds, from the seven seas.

Some of you wandered for years in the desert,
    looking but not finding a good place to live,
Half-starved and parched with thirst,
    staggering and stumbling, on the brink of exhaustion.
Then, in your desperate condition, you called out to GOD.
    He got you out in the nick of time;
He put your feet on a wonderful road
    that took you straight to a good place to live.
So thank GOD for his marvelous love,
    for his miracle mercy to the children he loves.
He poured great draughts of water down parched throats;
    the starved and hungry got plenty to eat.

Some of you were locked in a dark cell,
    cruelly confined behind bars,
Punished for defying God's Word,
    for turning your back on the High God's counsel—
A hard sentence, and your hearts so heavy,
    and not a soul in sight to help.
Then you called out to GOD in your desperate condition;
    he got you out in the nick of time.
He led you out of your dark, dark cell,
    broke open the jail and led you out.
So thank GOD for his marvelous love,
    for his miracle mercy to the children he loves;
He shattered the heavy jailhouse doors,
    he snapped the prison bars like matchsticks!

Some of you were sick because you'd lived a bad life,
    your bodies feeling the effects of your sin;

231

You couldn't stand the sight of food,
     so miserable you thought you'd be better off dead.
Then you called out to GOD in your desperate condition;
     he got you out in the nick of time.
He spoke the word that healed you,
     that pulled you back from the brink of death.
So thank GOD for his marvelous love,
     for his miracle mercy to the children he loves;
Offer thanksgiving sacrifices,
     tell the world what he's done—sing it out!

Some of you set sail in big ships;
     you put to sea to do business in faraway ports.
Out at sea you saw GOD in action,
     saw his breathtaking ways with the ocean:
With a word he called up the wind—
     an ocean storm, towering waves!
You shot high in the sky, then the bottom dropped out;
     your hearts were stuck in your throats.
You were spun like a top, you reeled like a drunk,
     you didn't know which end was up.
Then you called out to GOD in your desperate condition;
     he got you out in the nick of time.
He quieted the wind down to a whisper,
     put a muzzle on all the big waves.
And you were so glad when the storm died down,
     and he led you safely back to harbor.
So thank GOD for his marvelous love,
     for his miracle mercy to the children he loves.
Lift high your praises when the people assemble,
     shout Hallelujah when the elders meet!

GOD turned rivers into wasteland,
     springs of water into sunbaked mud;
Luscious orchards became alkali flats
     because of the evil of the people who lived there.
Then he changed wasteland into fresh pools of water,
     arid earth into springs of water,
Brought in the hungry and settled them there;
     they moved in—what a great place to live!

They sowed the fields, they planted vineyards,
    they reaped a bountiful harvest.
He blessed them and they prospered greatly;
    their herds of cattle never decreased.
But abuse and evil and trouble declined
    as he heaped scorn on princes and sent them away.
He gave the poor a safe place to live,
    treated their clans like well-cared-for sheep.

Good people see this and are glad;
    bad people are speechless, stopped in their tracks.
If you are really wise, you'll think this over—
    it's time you appreciated GOD's deep love.

# 108

A DAVID PRAYER

I'm ready, God, so ready,
    ready from head to toe.
Ready to sing,
    ready to raise a God-song:
"Wake, soul! Wake, lute!
    Wake up, you sleepyhead sun!"

I'm thanking you, GOD, out in the streets,
    singing your praises in town and country.
The deeper your love, the higher it goes;
    every cloud's a flag to your faithfulness.
Soar high in the skies, O God!
    Cover the whole earth with your glory!
And for the sake of the one you love so much,
    reach down and help me—answer me!

That's when God spoke in holy splendor:
    "Brimming over with joy,
I make a present of Shechem,
    I hand out Succoth Valley as a gift.
Gilead's in my pocket,
    to say nothing of Manasseh.

Ephraim's my hard hat,
    Judah my hammer.
Moab's a scrub bucket—
    I mop the floor with Moab,
Spit on Edom,
    rain fireworks all over Philistia."

Who will take me to the thick of the fight?
    Who'll show me the road to Edom?
You aren't giving up on us, are you, God?
    refusing to go out with our troops?

Give us help for the hard task;
    human help is worthless.
In God we'll do our very best;
    he'll flatten the opposition for good.

# 109

A DAVID PRAYER

My God, don't turn a deaf ear to my hallelujah prayer.
    Liars are pouring out invective on me;
Their lying tongues are like a pack of dogs out to get me,
    barking their hate, nipping my heels—and for no reason!
I loved them and now they slander me—yes, me!—
    and treat my prayer like a crime;
They return my good with evil,
    they return my love with hate.

Send the Evil One to accuse my accusing judge;
    dispatch Satan to prosecute him.
When he's judged, let the verdict be, "Guilty,"
    and when he prays, let his prayer turn to sin.
Give him a short life,
    and give his job to somebody else.
Make orphans of his children,
    dress his wife in widow's weeds;
Turn his children into begging street urchins,
    evicted from their homes—homeless.

May the bank foreclose and wipe him out,
    and strangers, like vultures, pick him clean.
May there be no one around to help him out,
    no one willing to give his orphans a break.
Chop down his family tree
    so that nobody even remembers his name.
But erect a memorial to the sin of his father,
    and make sure his mother's name is there, too—
Their sins recorded forever before GOD,
    but they themselves sunk in oblivion.
That's all he deserves since he was never once kind,
    hounded the afflicted and heartbroken to their graves.
Since he loved cursing so much,
    let curses rain down;
Since he had no taste for blessing,
    let blessings flee far from him.
He dressed up in curses like a fine suit of clothes;
    he drank curses, took his baths in curses.
So give him a gift—a costume of curses;
    he can wear curses every day of the week!
That's what they'll get, those out to get me—
    an avalanche of just deserts from GOD.


Oh, GOD, my Lord, step in;
    work a miracle for me—you can do it!
Get me out of here—your love is so great!—
    I'm at the end of my rope, my life in ruins.
I'm fading away to nothing, passing away,
    my youth gone, old before my time.
I'm weak from hunger and can hardly stand up,
    my body a rack of skin and bones.
I'm a joke in poor taste to those who see me;
    they take one look and shake their heads.


Help me, oh help me, GOD, my God,
    save me through your wonderful love;
Then they'll know that your hand is in this,
    that you, GOD, have been at work.

Let them curse all they want;
    *you* do the blessing.
Let them be jeered by the crowd when they stand up,
    followed by cheers for me, your servant.
Dress my accusers in clothes dirty with shame,
    discarded and humiliating old ragbag clothes.

My mouth's full of great praise for GOD,
    I'm singing his hallelujahs surrounded by crowds,
For he's always at hand to take the side of the needy,
    to rescue a life from the unjust judge.


# 110

A DAVID PRAYER

The word of GOD to my Lord:
    "Sit alongside me here on my throne
    until I make your enemies a stool for your feet."
You were forged a strong scepter by GOD of Zion;
    now rule, though surrounded by enemies!
Your people will freely join you, resplendent in holy armor
    on the great day of your conquest,
Join you at the fresh break of day,
    join you with all the vigor of youth.

GOD gave his word and he won't take it back:
    you're the permanent priest, the Melchizedek priest.
The Lord stands true at your side,
    crushing kings in his terrible wrath,
Bringing judgment on the nations,
    handing out convictions wholesale,
    crushing opposition across the wide earth.
The King-Maker put his King on the throne;
    the True King rules with head held high!

# 111

Hallelujah!
I give thanks to GOD with everything I've got—
Wherever good people gather, and in the congregation.
GOD's works are so great, worth
A lifetime of study—endless enjoyment!
Splendor and beauty mark his craft;
His generosity never gives out.
His miracles are his memorial—
This GOD of Grace, this GOD of Love.
He gave food to those who fear him,
He remembered to keep his ancient promise.
He proved to his people that he could do what he said:
Hand them the nations on a platter—a gift!
He manufactures truth and justice;
All his products are guaranteed to last—
Never out-of-date, never obsolete, rust-proof.
All that he makes and does is honest and true:
He paid the ransom for his people,
He ordered his Covenant kept forever.
He's so personal and holy, worthy of our respect.
The good life begins in the fear of GOD—
Do that and you'll know the blessing of GOD.
His Hallelujah lasts forever!

# 112

Hallelujah!
Blessed man, blessed woman, who fear GOD,
Who cherish and relish his commandments,
Their children robust on the earth,
And the homes of the upright—how blessed!
Their houses brim with wealth
And a generosity that never runs dry.
Sunrise breaks through the darkness for good people—
God's grace and mercy and justice!
The good person is generous and lends lavishly;
No shuffling or stumbling around for this one,

But a sterling and solid and lasting reputation.
Unfazed by rumor and gossip,
Heart ready, trusting in GOD,
Spirit firm, unperturbed,
Ever blessed, relaxed among enemies,
They lavish gifts on the poor—
A generosity that goes on, and on, and on.
An honored life! A beautiful life!
Someone wicked takes one look and rages,
Blusters away but ends up speechless.
There's nothing to the dreams of the wicked. Nothing.

# 113

Hallelujah!
You who serve GOD, praise GOD!
   Just to speak his name is praise!
Just to remember GOD is a blessing—
   now and tomorrow and always.
From east to west, from dawn to dusk,
   keep lifting all your praises to GOD!

GOD is higher than anything and anyone,
   outshining everything you can see in the skies.
Who can compare with GOD, our God,
   so majestically enthroned,
Surveying his magnificent
   heavens and earth?
He picks up the poor from out of the dirt,
   rescues the wretched who've been thrown out with the trash,
Seats them among the honored guests,
   a place of honor among the brightest and best.
He gives childless couples a family,
   gives them joy as the parents of children.
Hallelujah!

# 114

After Israel left Egypt,
    the clan of Jacob left those barbarians behind;
Judah became holy land for him,
    Israel the place of holy rule.
Sea took one look and ran the other way;
    River Jordan turned around and ran off.
The mountains turned playful and skipped like rams,
    the hills frolicked like spring lambs.
What's wrong with you, Sea, that you ran away?
    and you, River Jordan, that you turned and ran off?
And mountains, why did you skip like rams?
    and you, hills, frolic like spring lambs?
Tremble, Earth! You're in the Lord's presence!
    in the presence of Jacob's God.
He turned the rock into a pool of cool water,
    turned flint into fresh spring water.

# 115

Not for our sake, GOD, no, not for our sake,
    but for your name's sake, show your glory.
Do it on account of your merciful love,
    do it on account of your faithful ways.
Do it so none of the nations can say,
    "Where now, oh where is their God?"

Our God is in heaven
    doing whatever he wants to do.
Their gods are metal and wood,
    handmade in a basement shop:
Carved mouths that can't talk,
    painted eyes that can't see,
Tin ears that can't hear,
    molded noses that can't smell,
Hands that can't grasp, feet that can't walk or run,
    throats that never utter a sound.

Those who make them have become just like them,
>    have become just like the gods they trust.

But you, Israel: put your trust in GOD!
>    —trust your Helper! trust your Ruler!
Clan of Aaron, trust in GOD!
>    —trust your Helper! trust your Ruler!
You who fear GOD, trust in GOD!
>    —trust your Helper! trust your Ruler!

O GOD, remember us and bless us,
>    bless the families of Israel and Aaron.
And let GOD bless all who fear GOD—
>    bless the small, bless the great.
Oh, let GOD enlarge your families—
>    giving growth to you, growth to your children.
May you be blessed by GOD,
>    by GOD, who made heaven and earth.
The heaven of heavens is for GOD,
>    but he put us in charge of the earth.

Dead people can't praise GOD—
>    not a word to be heard from those buried in the ground.
But we bless GOD, oh yes—
>    we bless him now, we bless him always!
Hallelujah!

# 116

I love GOD because he listened to me,
>    listened as I begged for mercy.
He listened so intently
>    as I laid out my case before him.
Death stared me in the face,
>    hell was hard on my heels.
Up against it, I didn't know which way to turn;
>    then I called out to GOD for help:
"Please, GOD!" I cried out.
>    "Save my life!"

GOD is gracious—it is he who makes things right,
    our most compassionate God.
GOD takes the side of the helpless;
    when I was at the end of my rope, he saved me.

I said to myself, "Relax and rest.
GOD has showered you with blessings.
Soul, you've been rescued from death;
Eye, you've been rescued from tears;
And you, Foot, were kept from stumbling."

I'm striding in the presence of GOD,
    alive in the land of the living!
I stayed faithful, though bedeviled,
    and despite a ton of bad luck,
Despite giving up on the human race,
    saying, "They're all liars and cheats."

What can I give back to GOD
    for the blessings he's poured out on me?
I'll lift high the cup of salvation—a toast to GOD!
    I'll pray in the name of GOD;
I'll complete what I promised GOD I'd do,
    and I'll do it together with his people.
When they arrive at the gates of death,
    GOD welcomes those who love him.
Oh, GOD, here I am, your servant,
    your faithful servant: set me free for your service!
I'm ready to offer the thanksgiving sacrifice
    and pray in the name of GOD.
I'll complete what I promised GOD I'd do,
    and I'll do it in company with his people,
In the place of worship, in GOD's house,
    in Jerusalem, GOD's city.
Hallelujah!

# 117

Praise GOD, everybody!
Applaud GOD, all people!
His love has taken over our lives;
GOD's faithful ways are eternal.
    Hallelujah!

# 118

Thank GOD because he's good,
    because his love never quits.
Tell the world, Israel,
    "His love never quits."
And you, clan of Aaron, tell the world,
    "His love never quits."
And you who fear GOD, join in,
    "His love never quits."

Pushed to the wall, I called to GOD;
    from the wide open spaces, he answered.
GOD's now at my side and I'm not afraid;
    who would dare lay a hand on me?
GOD's my strong champion;
    I flick off my enemies like flies.
Far better to take refuge in GOD
    than trust in people;
Far better to take refuge in GOD
    than trust in celebrities.
Hemmed in by barbarians,
    in GOD's name I rubbed their faces in the dirt;
Hemmed in and with no way out,
    in GOD's name I rubbed their faces in the dirt;
Like swarming bees, like wild prairie fire, they hemmed me in;
    in GOD's name I rubbed their faces in the dirt.
I was right on the cliff-edge, ready to fall,
    when GOD grabbed and held me.
GOD's my strength, he's also my song,
    and now he's my salvation.

Hear the shouts, hear the triumph songs
    in the camp of the saved?
        "The hand of GOD has turned the tide!
        The hand of GOD is raised in victory!
        The hand of GOD has turned the tide!"

I didn't die. I *lived*!
    And now I'm telling the world what GOD did.
GOD tested me, he pushed me hard,
    but he didn't hand me over to Death.
Swing wide the city gates—the *righteous* gates!
    I'll walk right through and thank GOD!
This Temple Gate belongs to GOD,
    so the victors can enter and praise.

Thank you for responding to me;
    you've truly become my salvation!
The stone the masons discarded as flawed
    is now the capstone!
This is GOD's work.
    We rub our eyes—we can hardly believe it!
This is the very day GOD acted—
    let's celebrate and be festive!
Salvation now, GOD. Salvation now!
    Oh yes, GOD—a free and full life!

Blessed are you who enter in GOD's name—
    from GOD's house we bless you!
GOD is God,
    he has bathed us in light.
Festoon the shrine with garlands,
    hang colored banners above the altar!
You're my God, and I thank you.
    Oh my God, I lift high your praise.
Thank GOD—he's so good.
    His love never quits!

# 119

You're blessed when you stay on course,
  walking steadily on the road revealed by GOD.
You're blessed when you follow his directions,
  doing your best to find him.
That's right—you don't go off on your own;
  you walk straight along the road he set.
You, GOD, prescribed the right way to live;
  now you expect us to live it.
Oh, that my steps might be steady,
  keeping to the course you set;
Then I'd never have any regrets
  in comparing my life with your counsel.
I thank you for speaking straight from your heart;
  I learn the pattern of your righteous ways.
I'm going to do what you tell me to do;
  don't ever walk off and leave me.

✝

How can a young person live a clean life?
  By carefully reading the map of your Word.
I'm single-minded in pursuit of you;
  don't let me miss the road signs you've posted.
I've banked your promises in the vault of my heart
  so I won't sin myself bankrupt.
Be blessed, GOD;
  train me in your ways of wise living.
I'll transfer to my lips
  all the counsel that comes from your mouth;
I delight far more in what you tell me about living
  than in gathering a pile of riches.
I ponder every morsel of wisdom from you,
  I attentively watch how you've done it.
I relish everything you've told me of life,
  I won't forget a word of it.

✝

Be generous with me and I'll live a full life;
    not for a minute will I take my eyes off your road.
Open my eyes so I can see
    what you show me of your miracle-wonders.
I'm a stranger in these parts;
    give me clear directions.
My soul is starved and hungry, ravenous!—
    insatiable for your nourishing commands.
And those who think they know so much,
    ignoring everything you tell them—let them have it!
Don't let them mock and humiliate me;
    I've been careful to do just what you said.
While bad neighbors maliciously gossip about me,
    I'm absorbed in pondering your wise counsel.
Yes, your sayings on life are what give me delight;
    I listen to them as to good neighbors!

✝

I'm feeling terrible—I couldn't feel worse!
    Get me on my feet again. You promised, remember?
When I told my story, you responded;
    train me well in your deep wisdom.
Help me understand these things inside and out
    so I can ponder your miracle-wonders.
My sad life's dilapidated, a falling-down barn;
    build me up again by your Word.
Barricade the road that goes Nowhere;
    grace me with your clear revelation.
I choose the true road to Somewhere,
    I post your road signs at every curve and corner.
I grasp and cling to whatever you tell me;
    GOD, don't let me down!
I'll run the course you lay out for me
    if you'll just show me how.

✝

GOD, teach me lessons for living
    so I can stay the course.

Give me insight so I can do what you tell me—
    my whole life one long, obedient response.
Guide me down the road of your commandments;
    I love traveling this freeway!
Give me a bent for your words of wisdom,
    and not for piling up loot.
Divert my eyes from toys and trinkets,
    invigorate me on the pilgrim way.
Affirm your promises to me—
    promises made to all who fear you.
Deflect the harsh words of my critics—
    but what you say is always so good.
See how hungry I am for your counsel;
    preserve my life through your righteous ways!

☩

Let your love, GOD, shape my life
    with salvation, exactly as you promised;
Then I'll be able to stand up to mockery
    because I trusted your Word.
Don't ever deprive me of truth, not ever—
    your commandments are what I depend on.
Oh, I'll guard with my life what you've revealed to me,
    guard it now, guard it ever;
And I'll stride freely through wide open spaces
    as I look for your truth and your wisdom;
Then I'll tell the world what I find,
    speak out boldly in public, unembarrassed.
I cherish your commandments—oh, how I love them!—
    relishing every fragment of your counsel.

☩

Remember what you said to me, your servant—
    I hang on to these words for dear life!
These words hold me up in bad times;
    yes, your promises rejuvenate me.
The insolent ridicule me without mercy,
    but I don't budge from your revelation.

246

I watch for your ancient landmark words,
    and know I'm on the right track.
But when I see the wicked ignore your directions,
    I'm beside myself with anger.
I set your instructions to music
    and sing them as I walk this pilgrim way.
I meditate on your name all night, GOD,
    treasuring your revelation, O GOD.
Still, I walk through a rain of derision
    because I live by your Word and counsel.

☩

Because you have satisfied me, GOD, I promise
    to do everything you say.
I beg you from the bottom of my heart: smile,
    be gracious to me just as you promised.
When I took a long, careful look at your ways,
    I got my feet back on the trail you blazed.
I was up at once, didn't drag my feet,
    was quick to follow your orders.
The wicked hemmed me in—there was no way out—
    but not for a minute did I forget your plan for me.
I get up in the middle of the night to thank you;
    your decisions are so right, so true—I can't wait till morning!
I'm a friend and companion of all who fear you,
    of those committed to living by your rules.
Your love, GOD, fills the earth!
    Train me to live by your counsel.

☩

Be good to your servant, GOD;
    be as good as your Word.
Train me in good common sense;
    I'm thoroughly committed to living your way.
Before I learned to answer you, I wandered all over the place,
    but now I'm in step with your Word.
You are good, and the source of good;
    train me in your goodness.

The godless spread lies about me,
    but I focus my attention on what you are saying;
They're bland as a bucket of lard,
    while I dance to the tune of your revelation.
My troubles turned out all for the best—
    they forced me to learn from your textbook.
Truth from your mouth means more to me
    than striking it rich in a gold mine.

✛

With your very own hands you formed me;
    now breathe your wisdom over me so I can understand you.
When they see me waiting, expecting your Word,
    those who fear you will take heart and be glad.
I can see now, GOD, that your decisions are right;
    your testing has taught me what's true and right.
Oh, love me—and right now!—hold me tight!
    just the way you promised.
Now comfort me so I can live, really live;
    your revelation is the tune I dance to.
Let the fast-talking tricksters be exposed as frauds;
        they tried to sell me a bill of goods,
    but I kept my mind fixed on your counsel.
Let those who fear you turn to me
    for evidence of your wise guidance.
And let me live whole and holy, soul and body,
    so I can always walk with my head held high.

✛

I'm homesick—longing for your salvation;
    I'm waiting for your word of hope.
My eyes grow heavy watching for some sign of your promise;
    how long must I wait for your comfort?
There's smoke in my eyes—they burn and water,
    but I keep a steady gaze on the instructions you post.
How long do I have to put up with all this?
    How long till you haul my tormentors into court?
The arrogant godless try to throw me off track,
    ignorant as they are of God and his ways.

Everything you command is a sure thing,
    but they harass me with lies. Help!
They've pushed and pushed—they never let up—
    but I haven't relaxed my grip on your counsel.
In your great love revive me
    so I can alertly obey your every word.

✛

What you say goes, GOD,
    and *stays*, as permanent as the heavens.
Your truth never goes out of fashion;
    it's as up-to-date as the earth when the sun comes up.
Your Word and truth are dependable as ever;
    that's what you ordered—you set the earth going.
If your revelation hadn't delighted me so,
    I would have given up when the hard times came.
But I'll never forget the advice you gave me;
    you saved my life with those wise words.
Save me! I'm all yours.
    I look high and low for your words of wisdom.
The wicked lie in ambush to destroy me,
    but I'm only concerned with your plans for me.
I see the limits to everything human,
    but the horizons can't contain your commands!

✛

Oh, how I love all you've revealed;
    I reverently ponder it all the day long.
Your commands give me an edge on my enemies;
    they never become obsolete.
I've even become smarter than my teachers
    since I've pondered and absorbed your counsel.
I've become wiser than the wise old sages
    simply by doing what you tell me.
I watch my step, avoiding the ditches and ruts of evil
    so I can spend all my time keeping your Word.
I never make detours from the route you laid out;
    you gave me such good directions.

Your words are so choice, so tasty;
    I prefer them to the best home cooking.
With your instruction, I understand life;
    that's why I hate false propaganda.

✠

By your words I can see where I'm going;
    they throw a beam of light on my dark path.
I've committed myself and I'll never turn back
    from living by your righteous order.
Everything's falling apart on me, GOD;
    put me together again with your Word.
Festoon me with your finest sayings, GOD;
    teach me your holy rules.
My life is as close as my own hands,
    but I don't forget what you have revealed.
The wicked do their best to throw me off track,
    but I don't swerve an inch from your course.
I inherited your book on living; it's mine forever—
    what a gift! And how happy it makes me!
I concentrate on doing exactly what you say—
    I always have and always will.

✠

I hate the two-faced,
    but I love your clear-cut revelation.
You're my place of quiet retreat;
    I wait for your Word to renew me.
Get out of my life, evil-doers,
    so I can keep my God's commands.
Take my side as you promised; I'll live then for sure.
    Don't disappoint all my grand hopes.
Stick with me and I'll be all right;
    I'll give total allegiance to your definitions of life.
Expose all who drift away from your sayings;
    their casual idolatry is lethal.
You reject earth's wicked as so much rubbish;
    therefore I lovingly embrace everything you say.

I shiver in awe before you;
>your decisions leave me speechless with reverence.

✛

I stood up for justice and the right;
>don't leave me to the mercy of my oppressors.
Take the side of your servant, good God;
>don't let the godless take advantage of me.
I can't keep my eyes open any longer, waiting for you
>to keep your promise to set everything right.
Let your love dictate how you deal with me;
>teach me from your textbook on life.
I'm your servant—help me understand what that means,
>the inner meaning of your instructions.
It's time to act, GOD;
>they've made a shambles of your revelation!
Yea-Saying God, I love what you command,
>I love it better than gold and gemstones;
Yea-Saying God, I honor everything you tell me,
>I despise every deceitful detour.

✛

Every word you give me is a miracle word—
>how could I help but obey?
Break open your words, let the light shine out,
>let ordinary people see the meaning.
Mouth open and panting,
>I wanted your commands more than anything.
Turn my way, look kindly on me,
>as you always do to those who personally love you.
Steady my steps with your Word of promise
>so nothing malign gets the better of me.
Rescue me from the grip of bad men and women
>so I can live life your way.
Smile on me, your servant;
>teach me the right way to live.
I cry rivers of tears
>because nobody's living by your book!

✠

You *are* right and you *do* right, GOD;
    your decisions are right on target.
You rightly instruct us in how to live
    ever faithful to you.
My rivals nearly did me in,
    they persistently ignored your commandments.
Your promise has been tested through and through,
    and I, your servant, love it dearly.
I'm too young to be important,
    but I don't forget what you tell me.
Your righteousness is eternally right,
    your revelation is the only truth.
Even though troubles came down on me hard,
    your commands always gave me delight.
The way you tell me to live is always right;
    help me understand it so I can live to the fullest.

✠

I call out at the top of my lungs,
    "GOD! Answer! I'll do whatever you say."
I called to you, "Save me
    so I can carry out all your instructions."
I was up before sunrise,
    crying for help, hoping for a word from you.
I stayed awake all night,
    prayerfully pondering your promise.
In your love, listen to me;
    in your justice, GOD, keep me alive.
As those out to get me come closer and closer,
    they go farther and farther from the truth you reveal;
But you're the closest of all to me, GOD,
    and all your judgments true.
I've known all along from the evidence of your words
    that you meant them to last forever.

✠

Take a good look at my trouble, and help me—
    I haven't forgotten your revelation.

Take my side and get me out of this;
    give me back my life, just as you promised.
"Salvation" is only gibberish to the wicked
    because they've never looked it up in your dictionary.
Your mercies, GOD, run into the billions;
    following your guidelines, revive me.
My antagonists are too many to count,
    but I don't swerve from the directions you gave.
I took one look at the quitters and was filled with loathing;
    they walked away from your promises so casually!
Take note of how I love what you tell me;
    out of your life of love, prolong my life.
Your words all add up to the sum total: Truth.
    Your righteous decisions are eternal.

✝

I've been slandered unmercifully by the politicians,
    but my awe at your words keeps me stable.
I'm ecstatic over what you say,
    like one who strikes it rich.
I hate lies—can't stand them!—
    but I love what you have revealed.
Seven times each day I stop and shout praises
    for the way you keep everything running right.
For those who love what you reveal, everything fits—
    no stumbling around in the dark for them.
I wait expectantly for your salvation;
    GOD, I do what you tell me.
My soul guards and keeps all your instructions—
    oh, how much I love them!
I follow your directions, abide by your counsel;
    my life's an open book before you.

✝

Let my cry come right into your presence, GOD;
    provide me with the insight that comes only from your Word.
Give my request your personal attention,
    rescue me on the terms of your promise.

Let praise cascade off my lips;
    after all, you've taught me the truth about life!
And let your promises ring from my tongue;
    every order you've given is right.
Put your hand out and steady me
    since I've chosen to live by your counsel.
I'm homesick, GOD, for your salvation;
    I love it when you show yourself!
Invigorate my soul so I can praise you well,
    use your decrees to put iron in my soul.
And should I wander off like a lost sheep—seek me!
    I'll recognize the sound of your voice.

# 120

A PILGRIM SONG

I'm in trouble. I cry to GOD,
    desperate for an answer:
"Deliver me from the liars, GOD!
    They smile so sweetly but lie through their teeth."

Do you know what's next, can you see what's coming,
    all you barefaced liars?
Pointed arrows and burning coals
    will be your reward.

I'm doomed to live in Meshech,
    cursed with a home in Kedar,
My whole life lived camping
    among quarreling neighbors.
I'm all for peace, but the minute
    I tell them so, they go to war!

# 121

A PILGRIM SONG

I look up to the mountains;
    does my strength come from mountains?

No, my strength comes from GOD,
    who made heaven, and earth, and mountains.

He won't let you stumble,
    your Guardian God won't fall asleep.
Not on your life! Israel's
    Guardian will never doze or sleep.

GOD's your Guardian,
    right at your side to protect you—
Shielding you from sunstroke,
    sheltering you from moonstroke.

GOD guards you from every evil,
    he guards your very life.
He guards you when you leave and when you return,
    he guards you now, he guards you always.

# 122

A PILGRIM SONG OF DAVID

When they said, "Let's go to the house of GOD,"
    my heart leaped for joy.
And now we're here, oh Jerusalem,
    inside Jerusalem's walls!

Jerusalem, well-built city,
    built as a place for worship!
The city to which the tribes ascend,
    all GOD's tribes go up to worship,
To give thanks to the name of GOD—
    *this* is what it means to be Israel.
Thrones for righteous judgment
    are set there, famous David-thrones.

Pray for Jerusalem's peace!
    Prosperity to all you Jerusalem-lovers!

Friendly insiders, get along!
    Hostile outsiders, keep your distance!
For the sake of my family and friends,
    I say it again: live in peace!
For the sake of the house of our God, GOD,
    I'll do my very best for you.

# 123

A PILGRIM SONG

I look to you, heaven-dwelling God,
    look up to you for help.
Like servants, alert to their master's commands,
    like a maiden attending her lady,
We're watching and waiting, holding our breath,
    awaiting your word of mercy.
Mercy, GOD, mercy!
    We've been kicked around long enough,
Kicked in the teeth by complacent rich men,
    kicked when we're down by arrogant brutes.

# 124

A PILGRIM SONG OF DAVID

If GOD hadn't been for us
    —all together now, Israel, sing out!—
If GOD hadn't been for us
    when everyone went against us,
We would have been swallowed alive
    by their violent anger,
Swept away by the flood of rage,
    drowned in the torrent;
We would have lost our lives
    in the wild, raging water.

Oh, blessed be GOD!
    He didn't go off and leave us.

He didn't abandon us defenseless,
    helpless as a rabbit in a pack of snarling dogs.

We've flown free from their fangs,
    free of their traps, free as a bird.
Their grip is broken;
    we're free as a bird in flight.

GOD's strong name is our help,
    the same GOD who made heaven and earth.

# 125

A PILGRIM SONG

Those who trust in GOD
    are like Zion Mountain:
Nothing can move it, a rock-solid mountain
    you can always depend on.
Mountains encircle Jerusalem,
    and GOD encircles his people—
    always has and always will.
The fist of the wicked
    will never violate
What is due the righteous,
    provoking wrongful violence.
Be good to your good people, GOD,
    to those whose hearts are right!
GOD will round up the backsliders,
    corral them with the incorrigibles.
Peace over Israel!

# 126

A PILGRIM SONG

It seemed like a dream, too good to be true,
    when GOD returned Zion's exiles.
We laughed, we sang,
    we couldn't believe our good fortune.

We were the talk of the nations—
   "GOD was wonderful to them!"
GOD *was* wonderful to us;
   we are one happy people.

And now, GOD, do it again—
   bring rains to our drought-stricken lives
So those who planted their crops in despair
   will shout hurrahs at the harvest,
So those who went off with heavy hearts
   will come home laughing, with armloads of blessing.

# 127

A PILGRIM SONG OF SOLOMON

If GOD doesn't build the house,
   the builders only build shacks.
If GOD doesn't guard the city,
   the night watchman might as well nap.
It's useless to rise early and go to bed late,
   and work your worried fingers to the bone.
Don't you know he enjoys
   giving rest to those he loves?

Don't you see that children are GOD's best gift?
   the fruit of the womb his generous legacy?
Like a warrior's fistful of arrows
   are the children of a vigorous youth.
Oh, how blessed are you parents,
   with your quivers full of children!
Your enemies don't stand a chance against you;
   you'll sweep them right off your doorstep.

# 128

A PILGRIM SONG

All you who fear GOD, how blessed you are!
   how happily you walk on his smooth straight road!

You worked hard and deserve all you've got coming.
     Enjoy the blessing!  Revel in the goodness!

Your wife will bear children as a vine bears grapes,
     your household lush as a vineyard,
The children around your table
     as fresh and promising as young olive shoots.
Stand in awe of God's Yes.
     Oh, how he blesses the one who fears GOD!

Enjoy the good life in Jerusalem
     every day of your life.
And enjoy your grandchildren.
     Peace to Israel!

# 129

A PILGRIM SONG

"They've kicked me around ever since I was young"
     —this is how Israel tells it—
"They've kicked me around ever since I was young,
     but they never could keep me down.
Their plowmen plowed long furrows
     up and down my back;
Then GOD ripped the harnesses
     of the evil plowmen to shreds."

Oh, let all those who hate Zion
     grovel in humiliation;
Let them be like grass in shallow ground
     that withers before the harvest,
Before the farmhands can gather it in,
     the harvesters get in the crop,
Before the neighbors have a chance to call out,
     "Congratulations on your wonderful crop!
     We bless you in GOD's name!"

# 130

A PILGRIM SONG

Help, GOD—the bottom has fallen out of my life!
    Master, hear my cry for help!
Listen hard! Open your ears!
    Listen to my cries for mercy.

If you, GOD, kept records on wrongdoings,
    who would stand a chance?
As it turns out, forgiveness is your habit,
    and that's why you're worshiped.

I pray to GOD—my life a prayer—
    and wait for what he'll say and do.
My life's on the line before God, my Lord,
    waiting and watching till morning,
    waiting and watching till morning.

Oh Israel, wait and watch for GOD—
    with GOD's arrival comes love,
    with GOD's arrival comes generous redemption.
No doubt about it—he'll redeem Israel,
    buy back Israel from captivity to sin.

# 131

A PILGRIM SONG

GOD, I'm not trying to rule the roost,
    I don't want to be king of the mountain.
I haven't meddled where I have no business
    or fantasized grandiose plans.

I've kept my feet on the ground,
    I've cultivated a quiet heart.
Like a baby content in its mother's arms,
    my soul is a baby content.

Wait, Israel, for GOD. Wait with hope.
    Hope now; hope always!

# 132

A PILGRIM SONG

O GOD, remember David,
    remember all his troubles!
And remember how he promised GOD,
    made a vow to the Strong God of Jacob,
"I'm not going home,
    and I'm not going to bed,
I'm not going to sleep,
    not even take time to rest,
Until I find a home for GOD,
    a house for the Strong God of Jacob."

Remember how we got the news in Ephrathah,
    learned all about it at Jaar Meadows?
We shouted, "Let's go to the shrine dedication!
    Let's worship at God's own footstool!"

Up, GOD, enjoy your new place of quiet repose,
    you and your mighty covenant ark;
Get your priests all dressed up in justice;
    prompt your worshipers to sing this prayer:
"Honor your servant David;
    don't disdain your anointed one."

GOD gave David his word,
    he won't back out on this promise:
"One of your sons
    I will set on your throne;
If your sons stay true to my Covenant
    and learn to live the way I teach them,
Their sons will continue the line—
    always a son to sit on your throne.
Yes—I, GOD, chose Zion,
    the place I wanted for my shrine;

261

This will always be my home;
    this is what I want, and I'm here for good.
I'll shower blessings on the pilgrims who come here,
    and give supper to those who arrive hungry;
I'll dress my priests in salvation clothes;
    the holy people will sing their hearts out!
Oh, I'll make the place radiant for David!
    I'll fill it with light for my anointed!
I'll dress his enemies in dirty rags,
    but I'll make his crown sparkle with splendor."

# 133

A PILGRIM SONG OF DAVID

How wonderful, how beautiful,
    when brothers and sisters get along!
It's like costly anointing oil
    flowing down head and beard,
Flowing down Aaron's beard,
    flowing down the collar of his priestly robes.
It's like the dew on Mount Hermon
    flowing down the slopes of Zion.
Yes, that's where GOD commands the blessing,
    ordains eternal life.

# 134

A PILGRIM SONG

Come, bless GOD,
    all you servants of GOD!
You priests of GOD, posted to the nightwatch
    in GOD's shrine,
Lift your praising hands to the Holy Place,
    and bless GOD.
In turn, may GOD of Zion bless you—
    GOD who made heaven and earth!

# 135

Hallelujah!
Praise the name of GOD,
 praise the works of GOD.
All you priests on duty in GOD's temple,
 serving in the sacred halls of our God,
Shout "Hallelujah!" because GOD's so good,
 sing anthems to his beautiful name.
And why? Because GOD chose Jacob,
 embraced Israel as a prize possession.

I too give witness to the greatness of GOD,
 our Lord, high above all other gods.
He does just as he pleases—
 however, wherever, whenever.
He makes the weather—clouds and thunder,
 lightning and rain, wind pouring out of the north.
He struck down the Egyptian firstborn,
 both human and animal firstborn.
He made Egypt sit up and take notice,
 confronted Pharaoh and his servants with miracles.
Yes, he struck down great nations,
 he slew mighty kings—
Sihon king of the Amorites, also Og of Bashan—
 every last one of the Canaanite kings!
Then he turned their land over to Israel,
 a gift of good land to his people.

GOD, your name is eternal,
 GOD, you'll never be out-of-date.
GOD stands up for his people,
 GOD holds the hands of his people.
The gods of the godless nations are mere trinkets,
 made for quick sale in the markets:
Chiseled mouths that can't talk,
 painted eyes that can't see,
Carved ears that can't hear—
 dead wood! cold metal!

Those who make and trust them
 become like them.

Family of Israel, bless GOD!
 Family of Aaron, bless GOD!
Family of Levi, bless GOD!
 You who fear GOD, bless GOD!
Oh, blessed be GOD of Zion,
 First Citizen of Jerusalem!
Hallelujah!

# 136

Thank GOD! He deserves your thanks.
 *His love never quits.*
Thank the God of all gods,
 *His love never quits.*
Thank the Lord of all lords.
 *His love never quits.*

Thank the miracle-working God,
 *His love never quits.*
The God whose skill formed the cosmos,
 *His love never quits.*
The God who laid out earth on ocean foundations,
 *His love never quits.*
The God who filled the skies with light,
 *His love never quits.*
The sun to watch over the day,
 *His love never quits.*
Moon and stars as guardians of the night,
 *His love never quits.*
The God who struck down the Egyptian firstborn,
 *His love never quits.*
And rescued Israel from Egypt's oppression,
 *His love never quits.*
Took Israel in hand with his powerful hand,
 *His love never quits.*
Split the Red Sea right in half,

*His love never quits.*
Led Israel right through the middle,
*His love never quits.*
Dumped Pharaoh and his army in the sea,
*His love never quits.*
The God who marched his people through the desert,
*His love never quits.*
Smashed huge kingdoms right and left,
*His love never quits.*
Struck down the famous kings,
*His love never quits.*
Struck Sihon the Amorite king,
*His love never quits.*
Struck Og the Bashanite king,
*His love never quits.*
Then distributed their land as booty,
*His love never quits.*
Handed the land over to Israel.
*His love never quits.*

God remembered us when we were down,
*His love never quits.*
Rescued us from the trampling boot,
*His love never quits.*
Takes care of everyone in time of need.
*His love never quits.*
Thank God, who did it all!
*His love never quits!*

# 137

Alongside Babylon's rivers
    we sat on the banks; we cried and cried,
    remembering the good old days in Zion.
Alongside the quaking aspens
    we stacked our unplayed harps;
That's where our captors demanded songs,
    sarcastic and mocking:
    "Sing us a happy Zion song!"

Oh, how could we ever sing GOD's song
    in this wasteland?
If I ever forget you, Jerusalem,
    let my fingers wither and fall off like leaves.
Let my tongue swell and turn black
    if I fail to remember you,
If I fail, oh dear Jerusalem,
    to honor you as my greatest.

GOD, remember those Edomites,
    and remember the ruin of Jerusalem,
That day they yelled out,
    "Wreck it, smash it to bits!"
And you, Babylonians—ravagers!
    A reward to whoever gets back at you
    for all you've done to us;
Yes, a reward to the one who grabs your babies
    and smashes their heads on the rocks!

# 138

A DAVID PSALM

Thank you! Everything in me says "Thank you!"
    Angels listen as I sing my thanks.
I kneel in worship facing your holy temple
    and say it again: "Thank you!"
Thank you for your love,
    thank you for your faithfulness;
Most holy is your name,
    most holy is your Word.
The moment I called out, you stepped in;
    you made my life large with strength.

When they hear what you have to say, GOD,
    all earth's kings will say "Thank you."
They'll sing of what you've done:
    "How great the glory of GOD!"
And here's why: GOD, high above, sees far below;
    no matter the distance, he knows everything about us.

When I walk into the thick of trouble,
    keep me alive in the angry turmoil.
With one hand
    strike my foes,
With your other hand
    save me.
Finish what you started in me, GOD.
    Your love is eternal—don't quit on me now.

# 139

A DAVID PSALM

GOD, investigate my life;
    get all the facts firsthand.
I'm an open book to you;
    even from a distance, you know what I'm thinking.
You know when I leave and when I get back;
    I'm never out of your sight.
You know everything I'm going to say
    before I start the first sentence.
I look behind me and you're there,
    then up ahead and you're there, too—
    your reassuring presence, coming and going.
This is too much, too wonderful—
    I can't take it all in!

Is there anyplace I can go to avoid your Spirit?
    to be out of your sight?
If I climb to the sky, you're there!
    If I go underground, you're there!
If I flew on morning's wings
    to the far western horizon,
You'd find me in a minute—
    you're already there waiting!
Then I said to myself, "Oh, he even sees me in the dark!
    At night I'm immersed in the light!"
It's a fact: darkness isn't dark to you;
    night and day, darkness and light, they're all the same to you.

Oh yes, you shaped me first inside, then out;
    you formed me in my mother's womb.
I thank you, High God—you're breathtaking!
    Body and soul, I am marvelously made!
    I worship in adoration—what a creation!
You know me inside and out,
    you know every bone in my body;
You know exactly how I was made, bit by bit,
    how I was sculpted from nothing into something.
Like an open book, you watched me grow from conception
      to birth;
    all the stages of my life were spread out before you,
The days of my life all prepared
    before I'd even lived one day.

Your thoughts—how rare, how beautiful!
    God, I'll never comprehend them!
I couldn't even begin to count them—
    any more than I could count the sand of the sea.
Oh, let me rise in the morning and live always with you!
    And please, God, do away with wickedness for good!
And you murderers—out of here!—
    all the men and women who belittle you, God,
    infatuated with cheap god-imitations.
See how I hate those who hate you, GOD,
    see how I loathe all this godless arrogance;
I hate it with pure, unadulterated hatred.
    Your enemies are my enemies!

Investigate my life, O God,
    find out everything about me;
Cross-examine and test me,
    get a clear picture of what I'm about;
See for yourself whether I've done anything wrong—
    then guide me on the road to eternal life.

# 140

A DAVID PSALM

GOD, get me out of here, away from this evil;
    protect me from these vicious people.
All they do is think up new ways to be bad;
    they spend their days plotting war games.
They practice the sharp rhetoric of hate and hurt,
    speak venomous words that maim and kill.
GOD, keep me out of the clutch of these wicked ones,
    protect me from these vicious people;
Stuffed with self-importance, they plot ways to trip me up,
    determined to bring me down.
These crooks invent traps to catch me
    and do their best to incriminate me.

I prayed, "GOD, you're my God!
    Listen, GOD! Mercy!
GOD, my Lord, Strong Savior,
    protect me when the fighting breaks out!
Don't let the wicked have their way, GOD,
    don't give them an inch!"

These troublemakers all around me—
    let them drown in their own verbal poison.
Let God pile hellfire on them,
    let him bury them alive in crevasses!
These loudmouths—
    don't let them be taken seriously;
These savages—
    let the Devil hunt them down!

I know that you, GOD, are on the side of victims,
    that you care for the rights of the poor.
And I know that the righteous personally thank you,
    that good people are secure in your presence.

# 141

A DAVID PSALM

GOD, come close. Come quickly!
    Open your ears—it's my voice you're hearing!
Treat my prayer as sweet incense rising;
    my raised hands are my evening prayers.

Post a guard at my mouth, GOD,
    set a watch at the door of my lips.
Don't let me so much as dream of evil
    or thoughtlessly fall into bad company.
And these people who only do wrong—
    don't let them lure me with their sweet talk!
May the Just One set me straight,
    may the Kind One correct me,
Don't let sin anoint my head.
    I'm praying hard against their evil ways!
Oh, let their leaders be pushed off a high rock cliff;
    make them face the music.
Like a rock pulverized by a maul,
    let their bones be scattered at the gates of hell.

But GOD, dear Lord,
    I only have eyes for you.
Since I've run for dear life to you,
    take good care of me.
Protect me from their evil scheming,
    from all their demonic subterfuge.
Let the wicked fall flat on their faces,
    while I walk off without a scratch.

# 142

A DAVID PRAYER—WHEN HE WAS IN THE CAVE.

I cry out loudly to GOD,
    loudly I plead with GOD for mercy.
I spill out all my complaints before him,
    and spell out my troubles in detail:

270

"As I sink in despair, my spirit ebbing away,
    you know how I'm feeling,
Know the danger I'm in,
    the traps hidden in my path.
Look right, look left—
    there's not a soul who cares what happens!
I'm up against it, with no exit—
    bereft, left alone.
I cry out, GOD, call out:
    'You're my last chance, my only hope for life!'
Oh listen, please listen;
    I've never been this low.
Rescue me from those who are hunting me down;
    I'm no match for them.
Get me out of this dungeon
    so I can thank you in public.
Your people will form a circle around me
    and you'll bring me showers of blessing!"

# 143

A DAVID PSALM

Listen to this prayer of mine, GOD;
    pay attention to what I'm asking.
Answer me—you're famous for your answers!
    Do what's right for me.
But don't, please don't, haul me into court;
    not a person alive would be acquitted there.

The enemy hunted me down;
    he kicked me and stomped me within an inch of my life.
He put me in a black hole,
    buried me like a corpse in that dungeon.
I sat there in despair, my spirit draining away,
    my heart heavy, like lead.
I remembered the old days,
    went over all you've done, pondered the ways you've worked,
Stretched out my hands to you,
    as thirsty for you as a desert thirsty for rain.

Hurry with your answer, GOD!
    I'm nearly at the end of my rope.
Don't turn away; don't ignore me!
    That would be certain death.
If you wake me each morning with the sound of your loving voice,
    I'll go to sleep each night trusting in you.
Point out the road I must travel;
    I'm all ears, all eyes before you.
Save me from my enemies, GOD—
    you're my only hope!
Teach me how to live to please you,
    because you're my God.
Lead me by your blessed Spirit
    into cleared and level pastureland.

Keep up your reputation, God—give me life!
    In your justice, get me out of this trouble!
In your great love, vanquish my enemies;
    make a clean sweep of those who harass me.
And why? Because I'm your servant.

# 144

A DAVID PSALM

Blessed be GOD, my mountain,
    who trains me to fight fair and well.
He's the bedrock on which I stand,
    the castle in which I live,
    my rescuing knight,
The high crag where I run for dear life,
    while he lays my enemies low.

I wonder why you care, GOD—
    why do you bother with us at all?
All we are is a puff of air;
    we're like shadows in a campfire.

Step down out of heaven, GOD;
    ignite volcanoes in the hearts of the mountains.

Hurl your lightnings in every direction;
    shoot your arrows this way and that.
Reach all the way from sky to sea:
    pull me out of the ocean of hate,
    out of the grip of those barbarians
Who lie through their teeth,
    who shake your hand
    then knife you in the back.

O God, let me sing a new song to you,
    let me play it on a twelve-string guitar—
A song to the God who saved the king,
    the God who rescued David, his servant.

Rescue me from the enemy sword,
    release me from the grip of those barbarians
Who lie through their teeth,
    who shake your hand
    then knife you in the back.

Make our sons in their prime
    like sturdy oak trees,
Our daughters as shapely and bright
    as fields of wildflowers.
Fill our barns with great harvest,
    fill our fields with huge flocks;
Protect us from invasion and exile—
    eliminate the crime in our streets.

How blessed the people who have all this!
How blessed the people who have GOD for God!

# 145

DAVID'S PRAISE

I lift you high in praise, my God, O my King!
    and I'll bless your name into eternity.

I'll bless you every day,
    and keep it up from now to eternity.

GOD is magnificent; he can never be praised enough.
    There are no boundaries to his greatness.

Generation after generation stands in awe of your work;
    each one tells stories of your mighty acts.

Your beauty and splendor have everyone talking;
    I compose songs on your wonders.

Your marvelous doings are headline news;
    I could write a book full of the details of your greatness.

The fame of your goodness spreads across the country;
    your righteousness is on everyone's lips.

GOD is all mercy and grace—
    not quick to anger, is rich in love.

GOD is good to one and all;
    everything he does is suffused with grace.

Creation and creatures applaud you, GOD;
    your holy people bless you.

They talk about the glories of your rule,
    they exclaim over your splendor,

Letting the world know of your power for good,
    the lavish splendor of your kingdom.

Your kingdom is a kingdom eternal;
    you never get voted out of office.

GOD always does what he says,
    and is gracious in everything he does.

GOD gives a hand to those down on their luck,
gives a fresh start to those ready to quit.

All eyes are on you, expectant;
you give them their meals on time.

Generous to a fault,
you lavish your favor on all creatures.

Everything GOD does is right—
the trademark on all his works is love.

GOD's there, listening for all who pray,
for all who pray and mean it.

He does what's best for those who fear him—
hears them call out, and saves them.

GOD sticks by all who love him,
but it's all over for those who don't.

My mouth is filled with GOD's praise.
Let everything living bless him,
bless his holy name from now to eternity!

# 146

Hallelujah!
Oh my soul, praise GOD!
All my life long I'll praise GOD,
singing songs to my God as long as I live.

Don't put your life in the hands of experts
who know nothing of life, of *salvation* life.
Mere humans don't have what it takes;
when they die, their projects die with them.
Instead, get help from the God of Jacob,
put your hope in GOD and know real blessing!
GOD made sky and soil,
sea and all the fish in it.

He always does what he says—
    he defends the wronged,
    he feeds the hungry.
GOD frees prisoners—
    he gives sight to the blind,
    he lifts up the fallen.
GOD loves good people, protects strangers,
    takes the side of orphans and widows,
    but makes short work of the wicked.

GOD's in charge—*always.*
    Zion's God is God for good!
    Hallelujah!

# 147

Hallelujah!
It's a good thing to sing praise to our God;
    praise is beautiful, praise is fitting.

GOD's the one who rebuilds Jerusalem,
    who regathers Israel's scattered exiles.
He heals the heartbroken
    and bandages their wounds.
He counts the stars
    and assigns each a name.
Our Lord is great, with limitless strength;
    we'll never comprehend what he knows and does.
GOD puts the fallen on their feet again
    and pushes the wicked into the ditch.

Sing to GOD a thanksgiving hymn,
    play music on your instruments to God,
Who fills the sky with clouds,
    preparing rain for the earth,
Then turning the mountains green with grass,
    feeding both cattle and crows.
He's not impressed with horsepower;
    the size of our muscles means little to him.

Those who fear G<small>OD</small> get G<small>OD</small>'s attention;
  they can depend on his strength.

Jerusalem, worship G<small>OD</small>!
  Zion, praise your God!
He made your city secure,
  he blessed your children among you.
He keeps the peace at your borders,
  he puts the best bread on your tables.
He launches his promises earthward—
  how swift and sure they come!
He spreads snow like a white fleece,
  he scatters frost like ashes,
He broadcasts hail like birdseed—
  who can survive his winter?
Then he gives the command and it all melts;
  he breathes on winter—suddenly it's spring!

He speaks the same way to Jacob,
  speaks words that work to Israel.
He never did this to the other nations;
  they never heard such commands.
Hallelujah!

# 148

Hallelujah!
Praise G<small>OD</small> from heaven,
  praise him from the mountaintops;
Praise him, all you his angels,
  praise him, all you his warriors,
Praise him, sun and moon,
  praise him, you morning stars;
Praise him, high heaven,
  praise him, heavenly rain clouds;
Praise, oh let them praise the name of G<small>OD</small>—
  he spoke the word, and there they were!

He set them in place
　　from all time to eternity;
He gave his orders,
　　and that's it!

Praise GOD from earth,
　　you sea dragons, you fathomless ocean deeps;
Fire and hail, snow and ice,
　　hurricanes obeying his orders;
Mountains and all hills,
　　apple orchards and cedar forests;
Wild beasts and herds of cattle,
　　snakes, and birds in flight;
Earth's kings and all races,
　　leaders and important people,
Robust men and women in their prime,
　　and yes, graybeards and little children.

Let them praise the name of GOD—
　　it's the only Name worth praising.
His radiance exceeds anything in earth and sky;
　　he's built a monument—his very own people!

Praise from all who love GOD!
　　Israel's children, intimate friends of GOD.
Hallelujah!

# 149

Hallelujah!
Sing to GOD a brand-new song,
　　praise him in the company of all who love him.
Let all Israel celebrate their Sovereign Creator,
　　Zion's children exult in their King.
Let them praise his name in dance;
　　strike up the band and make great music!
And why? Because GOD delights in his people,
　　festoons plain folk with salvation garlands!

Let true lovers break out in praise,
    sing out from wherever they're sitting,
Shout the high praises of God,
    brandish their swords in the wild sword-dance—
A portent of vengeance on the God-defying nations,
    a signal that punishment's coming,
Their kings chained and hauled off to jail,
    their leaders behind bars for good,
The judgment on them carried out to the letter
    —and all who love God in the seat of honor!
Hallelujah!

# 150

Hallelujah!
Praise God in his holy house of worship,
    praise him under the open skies;
Praise him for his acts of power,
    praise him for his magnificent greatness;
Praise with a blast on the trumpet,
    praise by strumming soft strings;
Praise him with castanets and dance,
    praise him with banjo and flute;
Praise him with cymbals and a big bass drum,
    praise him with fiddles and mandolin.
Let every living, breathing creature praise GOD!
    Hallelujah!

# PROVERBS

INTRODUCTION
# PROVERBS

**M**any people think that what's written in the Bible has mostly to do with getting people into heaven—getting right with God, saving their eternal souls. It does have to do with that, of course, but not *mostly*. It is equally concerned with living on this earth—living well, living in robust sanity. In our Scriptures, heaven is not the primary concern, to which earth is a tag-along afterthought. "On earth *as* it is in heaven" is Jesus' prayer.

"Wisdom" is the biblical term for this on-earth-as-it-is-in-heaven everyday living. Wisdom is the art of living skillfully in whatever actual conditions we find ourselves. It has virtually nothing to do with information as such, with knowledge as such. A college degree is no certification of wisdom—nor is it primarily concerned with keeping us out of moral mud puddles, although it does have a profound moral effect upon us.

Wisdom has to do with becoming skillful in honoring our parents and raising our children, handling our money and conducting our sexual lives, going to work and exercising leadership, using words well and treating friends kindly, eating and drinking healthily, cultivating emotions within ourselves and attitudes toward others that make for peace. Threaded through all these items is the insistence that the way we think of and respond to God is the most practical thing we do. In matters of everyday practicality, nothing, absolutely nothing, takes precedence over God.

Proverbs concentrates on these concerns more than any other book in the Bible. Attention to the here and now is everywhere present in the stories and legislation, the prayers and the sermons, that are spread over the thousands of pages of the Bible. Proverbs distills it all into riveting images and aphorisms that keep us connected in holy obedience to the ordinary.

# PROVERBS

## 1

### A Manual for Living

These are the wise sayings of Solomon,
    David's son, Israel's king—
Written down so we'll know how to live well and right,
    to understand what life means and where it's going;
A manual for living,
    for learning what's right and just and fair;
To teach the inexperienced the ropes
    and give our young people a grasp on reality.
There's something here also for seasoned men and women,
    still a thing or two for the experienced to learn—
Fresh wisdom to probe and penetrate,
    the rhymes and reasons of wise men and women.

### Start With God

Start with GOD—the first step in learning is bowing down to GOD;
    only fools thumb their noses at such wisdom and learning.

Pay close attention, friend, to what your father tells you;
    never forget what you learned at your mother's knee.
Wear their counsel like flowers in your hair,
    like rings on your fingers.
Dear friend, if bad companions tempt you,
    don't go along with them.
If they say—"Let's go out and raise some hell.
    Let's beat up some old man, mug some old woman.
Let's pick them clean
    and get them ready for their funerals.
We'll load up on top-quality loot.
    We'll haul it home by the truckload.
Join us for the time of your life!
    With us, it's share and share alike!"—

283

Oh, friend, don't give them a second look;
>    don't listen to them for a minute.
They're racing to a very bad end,
>    hurrying to ruin everything they lay hands on.
Nobody robs a bank
>    with everyone watching,
Yet that's what these people are doing—
>    they're doing themselves in.
When you grab all you can get, that's what happens:
>    the more you get, the less you are.

LADY WISDOM

Lady Wisdom goes out in the street and shouts.
>    At the town center she makes her speech.
In the middle of the traffic she takes her stand.
>    At the busiest corner she calls out:

"Simpletons! How long will you wallow in ignorance?
>    Cynics! How long will you feed your cynicism?
Idiots! How long will you refuse to learn?
>    About face! I can revise your life.
Look, I'm ready to pour out my spirit on you;
>    I'm ready to tell you all I know.
As it is, I've called, but you've turned a deaf ear;
>    I've reached out to you, but you've ignored me.

"Since you laugh at my counsel
>    and make a joke of my advice,
How can I take you seriously?
>    I'll turn the tables and joke about *your* troubles!
What if the roof falls in,
>    and your whole life goes to pieces?
What if catastrophe strikes and there's nothing
>    to show for your life but rubble and ashes?
You'll need me then. You'll call for me, but don't expect
>        an answer.
>    No matter how hard you look, you won't find me.

"Because you hated Knowledge
    and had nothing to do with the Fear-of-GOD,
Because you wouldn't take my advice
    and brushed aside all my offers to train you,
Well, you've made your bed—now lie in it;
    you wanted your own way—now, how do you like it?
Don't you see what happens, you simpletons, you idiots?
    Carelessness kills; complacency is murder.
First pay attention to me, and then relax.
    Now you can take it easy—you're in good hands."

# 2

## MAKE INSIGHT YOUR PRIORITY

Good friend, take to heart what I'm telling you;
    collect my counsels and guard them with your life.
Tune your ears to the world of Wisdom;
    set your heart on a life of Understanding.
That's right—if you make Insight your priority,
    and won't take no for an answer,
Searching for it like a prospector panning for gold,
    like an adventurer on a treasure hunt,
Believe me, before you know it Fear-of-GOD will be yours;
    you'll have come upon the Knowledge of God.

And here's why: GOD gives out Wisdom free,
    is plainspoken in Knowledge and Understanding.
He's a rich mine of Common Sense for those who live well,
    a personal bodyguard to the candid and sincere.
He keeps his eye on all who live honestly,
    and pays special attention to his loyally committed ones.

So now you can pick out what's true and fair,
    find all the good trails!
Lady Wisdom will be your close friend,
    and Brother Knowledge your pleasant companion.
Good Sense will scout ahead for danger,
    Insight will keep an eye out for you.

They'll keep you from making wrong turns,
    or following the bad directions
Of those who are lost themselves
    and can't tell a trail from a tumbleweed,
These losers who make a game of evil
    and throw parties to celebrate perversity,
Traveling paths that go nowhere,
    wandering in a maze of detours and dead ends.

Wise friends will rescue you from the Temptress—
    that smooth-talking Seductress
Who's faithless to the husband she married years ago,
    never gave a second thought to her promises before God.
Her whole way of life is doomed;
    every step she takes brings her closer to hell.
No one who joins her company ever comes back,
    ever sets foot on the path to real living.

So—join the company of good men and women,
    keep your feet on the tried and true paths.
It's the men who walk straight who will settle this land,
    the women with integrity who will last here.
The corrupt will lose their lives;
    the dishonest will be gone for good.

# 3

## Don't Assume You Know It All

Good friend, don't forget all I've taught you;
    take to heart my commands.
They'll help you live a long, long time,
    a long life lived full and well.

Don't lose your grip on Love and Loyalty.
    Tie them around your neck; carve their initials on your heart.
Earn a reputation for living well
    in God's eyes and the eyes of the people.

Trust GOD from the bottom of your heart;
    don't try to figure out everything on your own.
Listen for GOD's voice in everything you do, everywhere you go;
    he's the one who will keep you on track.
Don't assume that you know it all.
    Run to GOD! Run from evil!
Your body will glow with health,
    your very bones will vibrate with life!
Honor GOD with everything you own;
    give him the first and the best.
Your barns will burst,
    your wine vats will brim over.
But don't, dear friend, resent GOD's discipline;
    don't sulk under his loving correction.
It's the child he loves that GOD corrects;
    a father's delight is behind all this.

## THE VERY TREE OF LIFE

You're blessed when you meet Lady Wisdom,
    when you make friends with Madame Insight.
She's worth far more than money in the bank;
    her friendship is better than a big salary.
Her value exceeds all the trappings of wealth;
    nothing you could wish for holds a candle to her.
With one hand she gives long life,
    with the other she confers recognition.
Her manner is beautiful,
    her life wonderfully complete.
She's the very Tree of Life to those who embrace her.
    Hold her tight—and be blessed!

With Lady Wisdom, GOD formed Earth;
    with Madame Insight, he raised Heaven.
They knew when to signal rivers and springs to the surface,
    and dew to descend from the night skies.

## NEVER WALK AWAY

Dear friend, guard Clear Thinking and Common Sense with your life;
    don't for a minute lose sight of them.

They'll keep your soul alive and well,
    they'll keep you fit and attractive.
You'll travel safely,
    you'll neither tire nor trip.
You'll take afternoon naps without a worry,
    you'll enjoy a good night's sleep.
No need to panic over alarms or surprises,
    or predictions that doomsday's just around the corner,
Because GOD will be right there with you;
    he'll keep you safe and sound.

Never walk away from someone who deserves help;
    your hand is *God's* hand for that person.
Don't tell your neighbor, "Maybe some other time,"
    or, "Try me tomorrow,"
    when the money's right there in your pocket.
Don't figure ways of taking advantage of your neighbor
    when he's sitting there trusting and unsuspecting.

Don't walk around with a chip on your shoulder,
    always spoiling for a fight.
Don't try to be like those who shoulder their way through life.
    Why be a bully?
"Why not?" you say. Because GOD can't stand twisted souls.
    It's the straightforward who get his respect.

GOD's curse blights the house of the wicked,
    but he blesses the home of the righteous.
He gives proud skeptics a cold shoulder,
    but if you're down on your luck, he's right there to help.
Wise living gets rewarded with honor;
    stupid living gets the booby prize.

# 4

YOUR LIFE IS AT STAKE

Listen, friends, to some fatherly advice;
    sit up and take notice so you'll know how to live.

I'm giving you good counsel;
    don't let it go in one ear and out the other.

When I was a boy at my father's knee,
    the pride and joy of my mother,
He would sit me down and drill me:
    "Take this to heart. Do what I tell you—live!
Sell everything and buy Wisdom! Forage for Understanding!
    Don't forget one word! Don't deviate an inch!
Never walk away from Wisdom—she guards your life;
    love her—she keeps her eye on you.
Above all and before all, do this: Get Wisdom!
    Write this at the top of your list: Get Understanding!
Throw your arms around her—believe me, you won't regret it;
    never let her go—she'll make your life glorious.
She'll garland your life with grace,
    she'll festoon your days with beauty."

Dear friend, take my advice;
    it will add years to your life.
I'm writing out clear directions to Wisdom Way,
    I'm drawing a map to Righteous Road.
I don't want you ending up in blind alleys,
    or wasting time making wrong turns.
Hold tight to good advice; don't relax your grip.
    Guard it well—your life is at stake!
Don't take Wicked Bypass;
    don't so much as set foot on that road.
Stay clear of it; give it a wide berth.
    Make a detour and be on your way.

Evil people are restless
    unless they're making trouble;
They can't get a good night's sleep
    unless they've made life miserable for somebody.
Perversity is their food and drink,
    violence their drug of choice.

The ways of right-living people glow with light;
    the longer they live, the brighter they shine.

But the road of wrongdoing gets darker and darker—
    travelers can't see a thing; they fall flat on their faces.

LEARN IT BY HEART

Dear friend, listen well to my words;
    tune your ears to my voice.
Keep my message in plain view at all times.
    Concentrate! Learn it by heart!
Those who discover these words live, really live;
    body and soul, they're bursting with health.

Keep vigilant watch over your heart;
    *that's* where life starts.
Don't talk out of both sides of your mouth;
    avoid careless banter, white lies, and gossip.
Keep your eyes straight ahead;
    ignore all sideshow distractions.
Watch your step,
    and the road will stretch out smooth before you.
Look neither right nor left;
    leave evil in the dust.

# 5

NOTHING BUT SIN AND BONES

Dear friend, pay close attention to this, my wisdom;
    listen very closely to the way I see it.
Then you'll acquire a taste for good sense;
    what I tell you will keep you out of trouble.

The lips of a seductive woman are oh so sweet,
    her soft words are oh so smooth.
But it won't be long before she's gravel in your mouth,
    a pain in your gut, a wound in your heart.
She's dancing down the primrose path to Death;
    she's headed straight for Hell and taking you with her.
She hasn't a clue about Real Life,
    about who she is or where she's going.

So, my friend, listen closely;
    don't treat my words casually.
Keep your distance from such a woman;
    absolutely stay out of her neighborhood.
You don't want to squander your wonderful life,
    to waste your precious life among the hardhearted.
Why should you allow strangers to take advantage of you?
    Why be exploited by those who care nothing for you?
You don't want to end your life full of regrets,
    nothing but sin and bones,
Saying, "Oh, why didn't I do what they told me?
    Why did I reject a disciplined life?
Why didn't I listen to my mentors,
    or take my teachers seriously?
My life is ruined!
    I haven't one blessed thing to show for my life!"

## NEVER TAKE LOVE FOR GRANTED

Do you know the saying, "Drink from your own rain barrel,
    draw water from your own spring-fed well"?
It's true. Otherwise, you may one day come home
    and find your barrel empty and your well polluted.

Your spring water is for you and you only,
    not to be passed around among strangers.
Bless your fresh-flowing fountain!
    Enjoy the wife you married as a young man!
Lovely as an angel, beautiful as a rose—
    don't ever quit taking delight in her body.
    Never take her love for granted!
Why would you trade enduring intimacies for cheap thrills with a
        whore?
    for dalliance with a promiscuous stranger?

Mark well that GOD doesn't miss a move you make;
    he's aware of every step you take.
The shadow of your sin will overtake you;
    you'll find yourself stumbling all over yourself in the dark.

Death is the reward of an undisciplined life;
>    your foolish decisions trap you in a dead end.

# 6

## LIKE A DEER FROM THE HUNTER

Dear friend, if you've gone into hock with your neighbor
>    or locked yourself into a deal with a stranger,
If you've impulsively promised the shirt off your back
>    and now find yourself shivering out in the cold,
Friend, don't waste a minute, get yourself out of that mess.
>    You're in that man's clutches!
>    Go, put on a long face; act desperate.
Don't procrastinate—
>    there's no time to lose.
Run like a deer from the hunter,
>    fly like a bird from the trapper!

## A LESSON FROM THE ANT

You lazy fool, look at an ant.
>    Watch it closely; let it teach you a thing or two.
Nobody has to tell it what to do.
>    All summer it stores up food;
>    at harvest it stockpiles provisions.
So how long are you going to laze around doing nothing?
>    How long before you get out of bed?
A nap here, a nap there, a day off here, a day off there,
>    sit back, take it easy—do you know what comes next?
Just this: You can look forward to a dirt-poor life,
>    poverty your permanent houseguest!

## ALWAYS COOKING UP SOMETHING NASTY

Riffraff and rascals
>    talk out of both sides of their mouths.
They wink at each other, they shuffle their feet,
>    they cross their fingers behind their backs.
Their perverse minds are always cooking up something nasty,
>    always stirring up trouble.

Catastrophe is just around the corner for them,
    a total smash-up, their lives ruined beyond repair.

### SEVEN THINGS GOD HATES

Here are six things GOD hates,
    and one more that he loathes with a passion:

> eyes that are arrogant,
> a tongue that lies,
> hands that murder the innocent,
> a heart that hatches evil plots,
> feet that race down a wicked track,
> a mouth that lies under oath,
> a troublemaker in the family.

### WARNING ON ADULTERY

Good friend, follow your father's good advice;
    don't wander off from your mother's teachings.
Wrap yourself in them from head to foot;
    wear them like a scarf around your neck.
Wherever you walk, they'll guide you;
    whenever you rest, they'll guard you;
    when you wake up, they'll tell you what's next.
For sound advice is a beacon,
    good teaching is a light,
    moral discipline is a life path.

They'll protect you from wanton women,
    from the seductive talk of some temptress.
Don't lustfully fantasize on her beauty,
    nor be taken in by her bedroom eyes.
You can buy an hour with a whore for a loaf of bread,
    but a wanton woman may well eat *you* alive.
Can you build a fire in your lap
    and not burn your pants?
Can you walk barefoot on hot coals
    and not get blisters?
It's the same when you have sex with your neighbor's wife:
    Touch her and you'll pay for it. No excuses.

Hunger is no excuse
    for a thief to steal;
When he's caught he has to pay it back,
    even if he has to put his whole house in hock.
Adultery is a brainless act,
    soul-destroying, self-destructive;
Expect a bloody nose, a black eye,
    and a reputation ruined for good.
For jealousy detonates rage in a cheated husband;
    wild for revenge, he won't make allowances.
Nothing you say or pay will make it all right;
    neither bribes nor reason will satisfy him.

# 7

## Dressed to Seduce

Dear friend, do what I tell you;
    treasure my careful instructions.
Do what I say and you'll live well.
    My teaching is as precious as your eyesight—guard it!
Write it out on the back of your hands;
    etch it on the chambers of your heart.
Talk to Wisdom as to a sister.
    Treat Insight as your companion.
They'll be with you to fend off the Temptress—
    that smooth-talking, honey-tongued Seductress.

As I stood at the window of my house
    looking out through the shutters,
Watching the mindless crowd stroll by,
    I spotted a young man without any sense
Arriving at the corner of the street where she lived,
    then turning up the path to her house.
It was dusk, the evening coming on,
    the darkness thickening into night.
Just then, a woman met him—
    she'd been lying in wait for him, dressed to seduce him.
Brazen and brash she was,
    restless and roaming, never at home,

Walking the streets, loitering in the mall,
    hanging out at every corner in town.

She threw her arms around him and kissed him,
    boldly took his arm and said,
"I've got all the makings for a feast—
    today I made my offerings, my vows are all paid,
So now I've come to find you,
    hoping to catch sight of your face—and here you are!
I've spread fresh, clean sheets on my bed,
    colorful imported linens.
My bed is aromatic with spices
    and exotic fragrances.
Come, let's make love all night,
    spend the night in ecstatic lovemaking!
My husband's not home; he's away on business,
    and he won't be back for a month."

Soon she has him eating out of her hand,
    bewitched by her honeyed speech.
Before you know it, he's trotting behind her,
    like a calf led to the butcher shop,
Like a stag lured into ambush
    and then shot with an arrow,
Like a bird flying into a net
    not knowing that its flying life is over.

So, friends, listen to me,
    take these words of mine most seriously.
Don't fool around with a woman like that;
    don't even stroll through her neighborhood.
Countless victims come under her spell;
    she's the death of many a poor man.
She runs a halfway house to hell,
    fits you out with a shroud and a coffin.

# 8

LADY WISDOM CALLS OUT

Do you hear Lady Wisdom calling?
    Can you hear Madame Insight raising her voice?
She's taken her stand at First and Main,
    at the busiest intersection.
Right in the city square
    where the traffic is thickest, she shouts,
"You—I'm talking to all of you,
    everyone out here on the streets!
Listen, you idiots—learn good sense!
    You blockheads—shape up!
Don't miss a word of this—I'm telling you how to live well,
    I'm telling you how to live at your best.
My mouth chews and savors and relishes truth—
    I can't stand the taste of evil!
You'll only hear true and right words from my mouth;
    not one syllable will be twisted or skewed.
You'll recognize this as true—you with open minds;
    truth-ready minds will see it at once.
Prefer my life-disciplines over chasing after money,
    and God-knowledge over a lucrative career.
For Wisdom is better than all the trappings of wealth;
    nothing you could wish for holds a candle to her.

"I am Lady Wisdom, and I live next to Sanity;
    Knowledge and Discretion live just down the street.
The Fear-of-GOD means hating Evil,
    whose ways I hate with a passion—
    pride and arrogance and crooked talk.
Good counsel and common sense are my characteristics;
    I am both Insight and the Virtue to live it out.
With my help, leaders rule,
    and lawmakers legislate fairly;
With my help, governors govern,
    along with all in legitimate authority.
I love those who love me;
    those who look for me find me.

Wealth and Glory accompany me—
    also substantial Honor and a Good Name.
My benefits are worth more than a big salary, even a *very* big salary;
    the returns on me exceed any imaginable bonus.
You can find me on Righteous Road—that's where I walk—
    at the intersection of Justice Avenue,
Handing out life to those who love me,
    filling their arms with life—armloads of life!

"GOD sovereignly made me—the first, the basic—
    before he did anything else.
I was brought into being a long time ago,
    well before Earth got its start.
I arrived on the scene before Ocean,
    yes, even before Springs and Rivers and Lakes.
Before Mountains were sculpted and Hills took shape,
    I was already there, newborn;
Long before GOD stretched out Earth's Horizons,
    and tended to the minute details of Soil and Weather,
And set Sky firmly in place,
    I was there.
When he mapped and gave borders to wild Ocean,
    built the vast vault of Heaven,
    and installed the fountains that fed Ocean,
When he drew a boundary for Sea,
    posted a sign that said, NO TRESPASSING,
And then staked out Earth's foundations,
    I was right there with him, making sure everything fit.
Day after day I was there, with my joyful applause,
    always enjoying his company,
Delighted with the world of things and creatures,
    happily celebrating the human family.

"So, my dear friends, listen carefully;
    those who embrace these my ways are most blessed.
Mark a life of discipline and live wisely;
    don't squander your precious life.
Blessed the man, blessed the woman, who listens to me,
    awake and ready for me each morning,
    alert and responsive as I start my day's work.

When you find me, you find life, real life,
> to say nothing of G OD 's good pleasure.
But if you wrong me, you damage your very soul;
> when you reject me, you're flirting with death."

# 9

L ADY W ISDOM G IVES A D INNER P ARTY

Lady Wisdom has built and furnished her home;
> it's supported by seven hewn timbers.
The banquet meal is ready to be served: lamb roasted,
> wine poured out, table set with silver and flowers.
Having dismissed her serving maids,
>> Lady Wisdom goes to town, stands in a prominent place,
>> and invites everyone within sound of her voice:
"Are you confused about life, don't know what's going on?
> Come with me, oh come, have dinner with me!
I've prepared a wonderful spread—fresh-baked bread,
> roast lamb, carefully selected wines.
Leave your impoverished confusion and *live!*
> Walk up the street to a life with meaning."

✛

If you reason with an arrogant cynic, you'll get slapped in the face;
> confront bad behavior and get a kick in the shins.
So don't waste your time on a scoffer;
> all you'll get for your pains is abuse.
But if you correct those who care about life,
> that's different—they'll love you for it!
Save your breath for the wise—they'll be wiser for it;
> tell good people what you know—they'll profit from it.
Skilled living gets its start in the Fear-of-G OD ,
> insight into life from knowing a Holy God.
It's through me, Lady Wisdom, that your life deepens,
> and the years of your life ripen.
Live wisely and wisdom will permeate your life;
> mock life and life will mock you.

## MADAME WHORE CALLS OUT, TOO

Then there's this other woman, Madame Whore—
    brazen, empty-headed, frivolous.
She sits on the front porch
    of her house on Main Street,
And as people walk by minding
    their own business, calls out,
"Are you confused about life, don't know what's going on?
    Steal off with me, I'll show you a good time!
    No one will ever know—I'll give you the time of your life."
But they don't know about all the skeletons in her closet,
    that all her guests end up in hell.

# 10      THE WISE SAYINGS OF SOLOMON

## AN HONEST LIFE IS IMMORTAL

Wise son, glad father;
    stupid son, sad mother.

Ill-gotten gain gets you nowhere;
    an honest life is immortal.

GOD won't starve an honest soul,
    but he frustrates the appetites of the wicked.

Sloth makes you poor;
    diligence brings wealth.

Make hay while the sun shines—that's smart;
    go fishing during harvest—that's stupid.

Blessings accrue on a good and honest life,
    but the mouth of the wicked is a dark cave of abuse.

A good and honest life is a blessed memorial;
    a wicked life leaves a rotten stench.

A wise heart takes orders;
> an empty head will come unglued.

Honesty lives confident and carefree,
> but Shifty is sure to be exposed.

An evasive eye is a sign of trouble ahead,
> but an open, face-to-face meeting results in peace.

The mouth of a good person is a deep, life-giving well,
> but the mouth of the wicked is a dark cave of abuse.

Hatred starts fights,
> but love pulls a quilt over the bickering.

You'll find wisdom on the lips of a person of insight,
> but the shortsighted needs a slap in the face.

The wise accumulate knowledge—a true treasure;
> know-it-alls talk too much—a sheer waste.

THE ROAD TO LIFE IS A DISCIPLINED LIFE

The wealth of the rich is their bastion;
> the poverty of the indigent is their ruin.

The wage of a good person is exuberant life;
> an evil person ends up with nothing but sin.

The road to life is a disciplined life;
> ignore correction and you're lost for good.

Liars secretly hoard hatred;
> fools openly spread slander.

The more talk, the less truth;
> the wise measure their words.

The speech of a good person is worth waiting for;
> the blabber of the wicked is worthless.

The talk of a good person is rich fare for many,
    but chatterboxes die of an empty heart.

FEAR-OF-GOD EXPANDS YOUR LIFE

GOD's blessing makes life rich;
    nothing we do can improve on God.

An empty-head thinks mischief is fun,
    but a mindful person relishes wisdom.

The nightmares of the wicked come true;
    what the good people desire, they get.

When the storm is over, there's nothing left of the wicked;
    good people, firm on their rock foundation, aren't even fazed.

A lazy employee will give you nothing but trouble;
    it's vinegar in the mouth, smoke in the eyes.

The Fear-of-GOD expands your life;
    a wicked life is a puny life.

The aspirations of good people end in celebration;
    the ambitions of bad people crash.

GOD is solid backing to a well-lived life,
    but he calls into question a shabby performance.

Good people *last*—they can't be moved;
    the wicked are here today, gone tomorrow.

A good person's mouth is a clear fountain of wisdom;
    a foul mouth is a stagnant swamp.

The speech of a good person clears the air;
    the words of the wicked pollute it.

# 11
WITHOUT GOOD DIRECTION, PEOPLE LOSE THEIR WAY

GOD hates cheating in the marketplace;
    he loves it when business is aboveboard.

The stuck-up fall flat on their faces,
    but down-to-earth people stand firm.

The integrity of the honest keeps them on track;
    the deviousness of crooks brings them to ruin.

A thick bankroll is no help when life falls apart,
    but a principled life can stand up to the worst.

Moral character makes for smooth traveling;
    an evil life is a hard life.

Good character is the best insurance;
    crooks get trapped in their sinful lust.

When the wicked die, that's it—
    the story's over, end of hope.

A good person is saved from much trouble;
    a bad person runs straight into it.

The loose tongue of the godless spreads destruction;
    the common sense of the godly preserves them.

When it goes well for good people, the whole town cheers;
    when it goes badly for bad people, the town celebrates.

When right-living people bless the city, it flourishes;
    evil talk turns it into a ghost town in no time.

Mean-spirited slander is heartless;
    quiet discretion accompanies good sense.

A gadabout gossip can't be trusted with a secret,
    but someone of integrity won't violate a confidence.

Without good direction, people lose their way;
    the more wise counsel you follow, the better your chances.

Whoever makes deals with strangers is sure to get burned;
    if you keep a cool head, you'll avoid rash bargains.

A woman of gentle grace gets respect,
    but men of rough violence grab for loot.

## A GOD-SHAPED LIFE

When you're kind to others, you help yourself;
    when you're cruel to others, you hurt yourself.

Bad work gets paid with a bad check;
    good work gets solid pay.

Take your stand with God's loyal community and live,
    or chase after phantoms of evil and die.

GOD can't stand deceivers,
    but oh how he relishes integrity.

Count on this: The wicked won't get off scot-free,
    and God's loyal people will triumph.

Like a gold ring in a pig's snout
    is a beautiful face on an empty head.

The desires of good people lead straight to the best,
    but wicked ambition ends in angry frustration.

The world of the generous gets larger and larger;
    the world of the stingy gets smaller and smaller.

The one who blesses others is abundantly blessed;
    those who help others are helped.

303

Curses on those who drive a hard bargain!
    Blessings on all who play fair and square!

The one who seeks good finds delight;
    the student of evil becomes evil.

A life devoted to things is a dead life, a stump;
    a God-shaped life is a flourishing tree.

Exploit or abuse your family, and end up with a fistful of air;
    common sense tells you it's a stupid way to live.

A good life is a fruit-bearing tree;
    a violent life destroys souls.

If good people barely make it,
    what's in store for the bad!

# 12

## IF YOU LOVE LEARNING

If you love learning, you love the discipline that goes with it—
    how shortsighted to refuse correction!

A good person basks in the delight of GOD,
    and he wants nothing to do with devious schemers.

You can't find firm footing in a swamp,
    but life rooted in God stands firm.

A hearty wife invigorates her husband,
    but a frigid woman is cancer in the bones.

The thinking of principled people makes for justice;
    the plots of degenerates corrupt.

The words of the wicked kill;
    the speech of the upright saves.

Wicked people fall to pieces—there's nothing to them;
   the homes of good people hold together.

A person who talks sense is honored;
   airheads are held in contempt.

Better to be ordinary and work for a living
   than act important and starve in the process.

Good people are good to their animals;
   the "good-hearted" bad people kick and abuse them.

The one who stays on the job has food on the table;
   the witless chase whims and fancies.

What the wicked construct finally falls into ruin,
   while the roots of the righteous give life, and more life.

WISE PEOPLE TAKE ADVICE

The gossip of bad people gets them in trouble;
   the conversation of good people keeps them out of it.

Well-spoken words bring satisfaction;
   well-done work has its own reward.

Fools are headstrong and do what they like;
   wise people take advice.

Fools have short fuses and explode all too quickly;
   the prudent quietly shrug off insults.

Truthful witness by a good person clears the air,
   but liars lay down a smoke screen of deceit.

Rash language cuts and maims,
   but there is healing in the words of the wise.

Truth lasts;
   lies are here today, gone tomorrow.

Evil scheming distorts the schemer;
    peace-planning brings joy to the planner.

No evil can overwhelm a good person,
    but the wicked have their hands full of it.

God can't stomach liars;
    he loves the company of those who keep their word.

Prudent people don't flaunt their knowledge;
    talkative fools broadcast their silliness.

The diligent find freedom in their work;
    the lazy are oppressed by work.

Worry weighs us down;
    a cheerful word picks us up.

A good person survives misfortune,
    but a wicked life invites disaster.

A lazy life is an empty life,
    but "early to rise" gets the job done.

Good men and women travel right into life;
    sin's detours take you straight to hell.

# 13
WALK WITH THE WISE

Intelligent children listen to their parents;
    foolish children do their own thing.

The good acquire a taste for helpful conversation;
    bullies push and shove their way through life.

Careful words make for a careful life;
    careless talk may ruin everything.

Indolence wants it all and gets nothing;
    the energetic have something to show for their lives.

A good person hates false talk;
    a bad person wallows in gibberish.

A God-loyal life keeps you on track;
    sin dumps the wicked in the ditch.

A pretentious, showy life is an empty life;
    a plain and simple life is a full life.

The rich can be sued for everything they have,
    but the poor are free of such threats.

The lives of good people are brightly lit streets;
    the lives of the wicked are dark alleys.

Arrogant know-it-alls stir up discord,
    but wise men and women listen to each other's counsel.

Easy come, easy go,
    but steady diligence pays off.

Unrelenting disappointment leaves you heartsick,
    but a sudden good break can turn life around.

Ignore the Word and suffer;
    honor God's commands and grow rich.

The teaching of the wise is a fountain of life,
    so, no more drinking from death-tainted wells!

Sound thinking makes for gracious living,
    but liars walk a rough road.

A commonsense person *lives* good sense;
    fools litter the country with silliness.

Irresponsible talk makes a real mess of things,
   but a reliable reporter is a healing presence.

Refuse discipline and end up homeless;
   embrace correction and live an honored life.

Souls who follow their hearts thrive;
   fools bent on evil despise matters of soul.

Become wise by walking with the wise;
   hang out with fools and watch your life fall to pieces.

Disaster entraps sinners,
   but God-loyal people get a good life.

A good life gets passed on to the grandchildren;
   ill-gotten wealth ends up with good people.

Banks foreclose on the farms of the poor,
   or else the poor lose their shirts to crooked lawyers.

A refusal to correct is a refusal to love;
   love your children by disciplining them.

An appetite for good brings much satisfaction,
   but the belly of the wicked always wants more.

# 14

A WAY THAT LEADS TO HELL

Lady Wisdom builds a lovely home;
   Sir Fool comes along and tears it down brick by brick.

An honest life shows respect for GOD;
   a degenerate life is a slap in his face.

Frivolous talk provokes a derisive smile;
   wise speech evokes nothing but respect.

No cattle, no crops;
    a good harvest requires a strong ox for the plow.

A true witness never lies;
    a false witness makes a business of it.

Cynics look high and low for wisdom—and never find it;
    the open-minded find it right on their doorstep!

Escape quickly from the company of fools;
    they're a waste of your time, a waste of your words.

The wisdom of the wise keeps life on track;
    the foolishness of fools lands them in the ditch.

The stupid ridicule right and wrong,
    but a moral life is a favored life.

The person who shuns the bitter moments of friends
    will be an outsider at their celebrations.

Lives of careless wrongdoing are tumbledown shacks;
    holy living builds soaring cathedrals.

There's a way of life that looks harmless enough;
    look again—it leads straight to hell.
Sure, those people appear to be having a good time,
    but all that laughter will end in heartbreak.

SIFT AND WEIGH EVERY WORD

A mean person gets paid back in meanness,
    a gracious person in grace.

The gullible believe anything they're told;
    the prudent sift and weigh every word.

The wise watch their steps and avoid evil;
    fools are headstrong and reckless.

The hotheaded do things they'll later regret;
　　the coldhearted get the cold shoulder.

Foolish dreamers live in a world of illusion;
　　wise realists plant their feet on the ground.

Eventually, evil will pay tribute to good;
　　the wicked will respect God-loyal people.

An unlucky loser is shunned by all,
　　but everyone loves a winner.

It's criminal to ignore a neighbor in need,
　　but compassion for the poor—what a blessing!

Isn't it obvious that conspirators lose out,
　　while the thoughtful win love and trust?

Hard work always pays off;
　　mere talk puts no bread on the table.

The wise accumulate wisdom;
　　fools get stupider by the day.

Souls are saved by truthful witness
　　and betrayed by the spread of lies.

The Fear-of-GOD builds up confidence,
　　and makes a world safe for your children.

The Fear-of-GOD is a spring of living water
　　so you won't go off drinking from poisoned wells.

The mark of a good leader is loyal followers;
　　leadership is nothing without a following.

Slowness to anger makes for deep understanding;
　　a quick-tempered person stockpiles stupidity.

A sound mind makes for a robust body,
    but runaway emotions corrode the bones.

You insult your Maker when you exploit the powerless;
    when you're kind to the poor, you honor God.

The evil of bad people leaves them out in the cold;
    the integrity of good people creates a safe place for living.

Lady Wisdom is at home in an understanding heart—
    fools never even get to say hello.

God-devotion makes a country strong;
    God-avoidance leaves people weak.

Diligent work gets a warm commendation;
    shiftless work earns an angry rebuke.

# 15

GOD DOESN'T MISS A THING

A gentle response defuses anger,
    but a sharp tongue kindles a temper-fire.

Knowledge flows like spring water from the wise;
    fools are leaky faucets, dripping nonsense.

GOD doesn't miss a thing—
    he's alert to good and evil alike.

Kind words heal and help;
    cutting words wound and maim.

Moral dropouts won't listen to their elders;
    welcoming correction is a mark of good sense.

The lives of God-loyal people flourish;
    a misspent life is soon bankrupt.

311

Perceptive words spread knowledge;
    fools are hollow—there's nothing to them.

GOD can't stand pious poses,
    but he delights in genuine prayers.

A life frittered away disgusts GOD;
    he loves those who run straight for the finish line.

It's a school of hard knocks for those who leave God's path,
    a dead-end street for those who hate God's rules.

Even hell holds no secrets from GOD—
    do you think he can't read human hearts?

LIFE ASCENDS TO THE HEIGHTS

Know-it-alls don't like being told what to do;
    they avoid the company of wise men and women.

A cheerful heart brings a smile to your face;
    a sad heart makes it hard to get through the day.

An intelligent person is always eager to take in more truth;
    fools feed on fast-food fads and fancies.

A miserable heart means a miserable life;
    a cheerful heart fills the day with song.

A simple life in the Fear-of-GOD
    is better than a rich life with a ton of headaches.

Better a bread crust shared in love
    than a slab of prime rib served in hate.

Hot tempers start fights;
    a calm, cool spirit keeps the peace.

The path of lazy people is overgrown with briers;
    the diligent walk down a smooth road.

Intelligent children make their parents proud;
    lazy students embarrass their parents.

The empty-headed treat life as a plaything;
    the perceptive grasp its meaning and make a go of it.

Refuse good advice and watch your plans fail;
    take good counsel and watch them succeed.

Congenial conversation—what a pleasure!
    The right word at the right time—beautiful!

Life ascends to the heights for the thoughtful—
    it's a clean about-face from descent into hell.

GOD smashes the pretensions of the arrogant;
    he stands with those who have no standing.

GOD can't stand evil scheming,
    but he puts words of grace and beauty on display.

A greedy and grasping person destroys community;
    those who refuse to exploit live and let live.

Prayerful answers come from God-loyal people;
    the wicked are sewers of abuse.

GOD keeps his distance from the wicked;
    he closely attends to the prayers of God-loyal people.

A twinkle in the eye means joy in the heart,
    and good news makes you feel fit as a fiddle.

Listen to good advice if you want to live well,
    an honored guest among wise men and women.

An undisciplined, self-willed life is puny;
    an obedient, God-willed life is spacious.

Fear-of-GOD is a school in skilled living—
> first you learn humility, then you experience glory.

# 16

## EVERYTHING WITH A PLACE AND A PURPOSE

Mortals make elaborate plans,
> but GOD has the last word.

Humans are satisfied with whatever looks good;
> GOD probes for what *is* good.

Put GOD in charge of your work,
> then what you've planned will take place.

GOD made everything with a place and purpose;
> even the wicked are included—but for *judgment.*

GOD can't stomach arrogance or pretense;
> believe me, he'll put those upstarts in their place.

Guilt is banished through love and truth;
> Fear-of-GOD deflects evil.

When GOD approves of your life,
> even your enemies will end up shaking your hand.

Far better to be right and poor
> than to be wrong and rich.

We plan the way we want to live,
> but only GOD makes us able to live it.

## IT PAYS TO TAKE LIFE SERIOUSLY

A good leader motivates,
> doesn't mislead, doesn't exploit.

GOD cares about honesty in the workplace;
> your business is his business.

Good leaders abhor wrongdoing of all kinds;
    sound leadership has a moral foundation.

Good leaders cultivate honest speech;
    they love advisors who tell them the truth.

An intemperate leader wreaks havoc in lives;
    you're smart to stay clear of someone like that.

Good-tempered leaders invigorate lives;
    they're like spring rain and sunshine.

Get wisdom—it's worth more than money;
    choose insight over income every time.

The road of right living bypasses evil;
    watch your step and save your life.

First pride, then the crash—
    the bigger the ego, the harder the fall.

It's better to live humbly among the poor
    than to live it up among the rich and famous.

It pays to take life seriously;
    things work out when you trust in GOD.

A wise person gets known for insight;
    gracious words add to one's reputation.

True intelligence is a spring of fresh water,
    while fools sweat it out the hard way.

They make a lot of sense, these wise folks;
    whenever they speak, their reputation increases.

Gracious speech is like clover honey—
    good taste to the soul, quick energy for the body.

There's a way that looks harmless enough;
    look again—it leads straight to hell.

Appetite is an incentive to work;
    hunger makes you work all the harder.

Mean people spread mean gossip;
    their words smart and burn.

Troublemakers start fights;
    gossips break up friendships.

Calloused climbers betray their very own friends;
    they'd stab their own grandmothers in the back.

A shifty eye betrays an evil intention;
    a clenched jaw signals trouble ahead.

Gray hair is a mark of distinction,
    the award for a God-loyal life.

Moderation is better than muscle,
    self-control better than political power.

Make your motions and cast your votes,
    but GOD has the final say.

# 17

A WHACK ON THE HEAD OF A FOOL

A meal of bread and water in contented peace
    is better than a banquet spiced with quarrels.

A wise servant takes charge of an unruly child
    and is honored as one of the family.

As silver in a crucible and gold in a pan,
    so our lives are assayed by GOD.

Evil people relish malicious conversation;
    the ears of liars itch for dirty gossip.

Whoever mocks poor people, insults their Creator;
    gloating over misfortune is a punishable crime.

Old people are distinguished by grandchildren;
    children take pride in their parents.

We don't expect eloquence from fools,
    nor do we expect lies from our leaders.

Receiving a gift is like getting a rare gemstone;
    any way you look at it, you see beauty refracted.

Overlook an offense and bond a friendship;
    fasten on to a slight and—goodbye, friend!

A quiet rebuke to a person of good sense
    does more than a whack on the head of a fool.

Criminals out looking for nothing but trouble
    won't have to wait long—they'll meet it coming and going!

Better to meet a grizzly robbed of her cubs
    than a fool hellbent on folly.

Those who return evil for good
    will meet their own evil returning.

The start of a quarrel is like a leak in a dam,
    so stop it before it bursts.

Whitewashing bad people and throwing mud on good people
    are equally abhorrent to GOD.

What's this? Fools out shopping for wisdom!
    They wouldn't recognize it if they saw it!

## ONE WHO KNOWS MUCH SAYS LITTLE

Friends love through all kinds of weather,
    and families stick together in all kinds of trouble.

It's stupid to try to get something for nothing,
    or run up huge bills you can never pay.

The person who courts sin, marries trouble;
    build a wall, invite a burglar.

A bad motive can't achieve a good end;
    double-talk brings you double trouble.

Having a fool for a child is misery;
    it's no fun being the parent of a dolt.

A cheerful disposition is good for your health;
    gloom and doom leave you bone-tired.

The wicked take bribes under the table;
    they show nothing but contempt for justice.

The perceptive find wisdom in their own front yard;
    fools look for it everywhere but right here.

A surly, stupid child is sheer pain to a father,
    a bitter pill for a mother to swallow.

It's wrong to penalize good behavior,
    or make good citizens pay for the crimes of others.

The one who knows much says little;
    an understanding person remains calm.

Even dunces who keep quiet are thought to be wise;
    as long as they keep their mouths shut, they're smart.

# 18

WORDS KILL, WORDS GIVE LIFE

Loners who care only for themselves
    spit on the common good.

Fools care nothing for thoughtful discourse;
    all they do is run off at the mouth.

When wickedness arrives, shame's not far behind;
    contempt for life is contemptible.

Many words rush along like rivers in flood,
    but deep wisdom flows up from artesian springs.

It's not right to go easy on the guilty,
    or come down hard on the innocent.

The words of a fool start fights;
    do him a favor and gag him.

Fools are undone by their big mouths;
    their souls are crushed by their words.

Listening to gossip is like eating cheap candy;
    do you really want junk like that in your belly?

Slack habits and sloppy work
    are as bad as vandalism.

GOD's name is a place of protection—
    good people can run there and be safe.

The rich think their wealth protects them;
    they imagine themselves safe behind it.

Pride first, then the crash,
    but humility is precursor to honor.

Answering before listening
    is both stupid and rude.

A healthy spirit conquers adversity,
    but what can you do when the spirit is crushed?

Wise men and women are always learning,
    always listening for fresh insights.

A gift gets attention;
    it buys the attention of eminent people.

The first speech in a court case is always convincing—
    until the cross-examination starts!

You may have to draw straws
    when faced with a tough decision.

Do a favor and win a friend forever;
    nothing can untie that bond.

Words satisfy the mind as much as fruit does the stomach;
    good talk is as gratifying as a good harvest.

Words kill, words give life;
    they're either poison or fruit—you choose.

Find a good spouse, you find a good life—
    and even more: the favor of GOD!

The poor speak in soft supplications;
    the rich bark out answers.

Friends come and friends go,
    but a true friend sticks by you like family.

# 19

IF YOU QUIT LISTENING

Better to be poor and honest
>than a rich person no one can trust.

Ignorant zeal is worthless;
>haste makes waste.

People ruin their lives by their own stupidity,
>so why does GOD always get blamed?

Wealth attracts friends as honey draws flies,
>but poor people are avoided like a plague.

Perjury won't go unpunished.
>Would you let a liar go free?

Lots of people flock around a generous person;
>everyone's a friend to the philanthropist.

When you're down on your luck, even your family avoids you—
>yes, even your best friends wish you'd get lost.
If they see you coming, they look the other way—
>out of sight, out of mind.

Grow a wise heart—you'll do yourself a favor;
>keep a clear head—you'll find a good life.

The person who tells lies gets caught;
>the person who spreads rumors is ruined.

Blockheads shouldn't live on easy street
>any more than workers should give orders to their boss.

Smart people know how to hold their tongue;
>their grandeur is to forgive and forget.

Mean-tempered leaders are like mad dogs;
    the good-natured are like fresh morning dew.

A parent is worn to a frazzle by a stupid child;
    a nagging spouse is a leaky faucet.

House and land are handed down from parents,
    but a congenial spouse comes straight from God.

Life collapses on loafers;
    lazybones go hungry.

Keep the rules and keep your life;
    careless living kills.

Mercy to the needy is a loan to GOD,
    and GOD pays back those loans in full.

Discipline your children while you still have the chance;
    indulging them destroys them.

Let angry people endure the backlash of their own anger;
    if you try to make it better, you'll only make it worse.

Take good counsel and accept correction—
    that's the way to live wisely and well.

We humans keep brainstorming options and plans,
    but GOD's purpose prevails.

It's only human to want to make a buck,
    but it's better to be poor than a liar.

Fear-of-GOD is life itself,
    a full life, and serene—no nasty surprises.

Some people dig a fork into the pie
    but are too lazy to raise it to their mouth.

Punish the insolent—make an example of them.
    Who knows? Somebody might learn a good lesson.

Kids who lash out against their parents
    are an embarrassment and disgrace.

If you quit listening, dear child, and strike off on your own,
    you'll soon be out of your depth.

An unprincipled witness desecrates justice;
    the mouths of the wicked spew malice.

The irreverent have to learn reverence the hard way;
    only a slap in the face brings fools to attention.

# 20

DEEP WATER IN THE HEART

Wine makes you mean, beer makes you quarrelsome—
    a staggering drunk is not much fun.

Quick-tempered leaders are like mad dogs—
    cross them and they bite your head off.

It's a mark of good character to avert quarrels,
    but fools love to pick fights.

A farmer too lazy to plant in the spring
    has nothing to harvest in the fall.

Knowing what is right is like deep water in the heart;
    a wise person draws from the well within.

Lots of people claim to be loyal and loving,
    but where on earth can you find one?

God-loyal people, living honest lives,
    make it much easier for their children.

Leaders who know their business and care
    keep a sharp eye out for the shoddy and cheap,
For who among us can be trusted
    to be always diligent and honest?

Switching price tags and padding the expense account
    are two things GOD hates.

Young people eventually reveal by their actions
    if their motives are on the up and up.

DRINKING FROM THE CHALICE OF KNOWLEDGE

Ears that hear and eyes that see—
    we get our basic equipment from GOD!

Don't be too fond of sleep; you'll end up in the poorhouse.
    Wake up and get up; then there'll be food on the table.

The shopper says, "That's junk—I'll take it off your hands,"
    then goes off boasting of the bargain.

Drinking from the beautiful chalice of knowledge
    is better than adorning oneself with gold and rare gems.

Hold tight to collateral on any loan to a stranger;
    beware of accepting what a transient has pawned.

Stolen bread tastes sweet,
    but soon your mouth is full of gravel.

Form your purpose by asking for counsel,
    then carry it out using all the help you can get.

Gossips can't keep secrets,
    so never confide in blabbermouths.

Anyone who curses father and mother
    extinguishes light and exists benighted.

THE VERY STEPS WE TAKE

A bonanza at the beginning
    is no guarantee of blessing at the end.

Don't ever say, "I'll get you for that!"
    Wait for GOD; he'll settle the score.

GOD hates cheating in the marketplace;
    rigged scales are an outrage.

The very steps we take come from GOD;
    otherwise how would we know where we're going?

An impulsive vow is a trap;
    later you'll wish you could get out of it.

After careful scrutiny, a wise leader
    makes a clean sweep of rebels and dolts.

GOD is in charge of human life,
    watching and examining us inside and out.

Love and truth form a good leader;
    sound leadership is founded on loving integrity.

Youth may be admired for vigor,
    but gray hair gives prestige to old age.

A good thrashing purges evil;
    punishment goes deep within us.

# 21

GOD EXAMINES OUR MOTIVES

Good leadership is a channel of water controlled by God;
    he directs it to whatever ends he chooses.

We justify our actions by appearances;
    GOD examines our motives.

Clean living before God and justice with our neighbors
    mean far more to GOD than religious performance.

Arrogance and pride—distinguishing marks in the wicked—
    are just plain sin.

Careful planning puts you ahead in the long run;
    hurry and scurry puts you further behind.

Make it to the top by lying and cheating;
    get paid with smoke and a promotion—to death!

The wicked get buried alive by their loot
    because they refuse to use it to help others.

Mixed motives twist life into tangles;
    pure motives take you straight down the road.

DO YOUR BEST, PREPARE FOR THE WORST

Better to live alone in a tumbledown shack
    than share a mansion with a nagging spouse.

Wicked souls love to make trouble;
    they feel nothing for friends and neighbors.

Simpletons only learn the hard way,
    but the wise learn by listening.

A God-loyal person will see right through the wicked
    and undo the evil they've planned.

If you stop your ears to the cries of the poor,
    your cries will go unheard, unanswered.

A quietly given gift soothes an irritable person;
    a heartfelt present cools a hot temper.

Good people celebrate when justice triumphs,
    but for the workers of evil it's a bad day.

Whoever wanders off the straight and narrow
    ends up in a congregation of ghosts.

You're addicted to thrills? What an empty life!
    The pursuit of pleasure is never satisfied.

What a bad person plots against the good, boomerangs;
    the plotter gets it in the end.

Better to live in a tent in the wild
    than with a cross and petulant spouse.

Valuables are safe in a wise person's home;
    fools put it all out for yard sales.

Whoever goes hunting for what is right and kind
    finds life itself—*glorious* life!

One sage entered a whole city of armed soldiers—
    their trusted defenses fell to pieces!

Watch your words and hold your tongue;
    you'll save yourself a lot of grief.

You know their names—Brash, Impudent, Blasphemer—
    intemperate hotheads, every one.

Lazy people finally die of hunger
    because they won't get up and go to work.

Sinners are always wanting what they don't have;
    the God-loyal are always giving what they do have.

Religious performance by the wicked stinks;
    it's even worse when they use it to get ahead.

A lying witness is unconvincing;
    a person who speaks truth is respected.

Unscrupulous people fake it a lot;
    honest people are sure of their steps.

Nothing clever, nothing conceived, nothing contrived,
    can get the better of GOD.

Do your best, prepare for the worst—
    then trust GOD to bring victory.

# 22

## THE CURE COMES THROUGH DISCIPLINE

A sterling reputation is better than striking it rich;
    a gracious spirit is better than money in the bank.

The rich and the poor shake hands as equals—
    GOD made them both!

A prudent person sees trouble coming and ducks;
    a simpleton walks in blindly and is clobbered.

The payoff for meekness and Fear-of-GOD
    is plenty and honor and a satisfying life.

The perverse travel a dangerous road, potholed and mud-slick;
    if you know what's good for you, stay clear of it.

Point your kids in the right direction—
    when they're old they won't be lost.

The poor are always ruled over by the rich,
    so don't borrow and put yourself under their power.

Whoever sows sin reaps weeds,
    and bullying anger sputters into nothing.

Generous hands are blessed hands
    because they give bread to the poor.

Kick out the troublemakers and things will quiet down;
    you need a break from bickering and griping!

GOD loves the pure-hearted and well-spoken;
    good leaders also delight in their friendship.

GOD guards knowledge with a passion,
    but he'll have nothing to do with deception.

The loafer says, "There's a lion on the loose!
    If I go out I'll be eaten alive!"

The mouth of a whore is a bottomless pit;
    you'll fall in that pit if you're on the outs with GOD.

Young people are prone to foolishness and fads;
    the cure comes through tough-minded discipline.

Exploit the poor or glad-hand the rich—whichever,
    you'll end up the poorer for it.

## THE THIRTY PRECEPTS OF THE SAGES

### DON'T MOVE BACK THE BOUNDARY LINES

Listen carefully to my wisdom;
    take to heart what I can teach you.
You'll treasure its sweetness deep within;
    you'll give it bold expression in your speech.
I'm giving you thirty sterling principles—
    tested guidelines to live by.
Believe me—these are truths that work,
    and will keep you accountable
    to those who sent you.

329

### 1

Don't walk on the poor just because they're poor,
  and don't use your position to crush the weak,
Because GOD will come to their defense;
  the life you took, he'll take from you and give back to them.

### 2

Don't hang out with angry people;
  don't keep company with hotheads.
Bad temper is contagious—
  don't get infected.

### 3

Don't gamble on the pot of gold at the end of the rainbow,
  hocking your house against a lucky chance.
The time will come when you have to pay up;
  you'll be left with nothing but the shirt on your back.

### 4

Don't stealthily move back the boundary lines
  staked out long ago by your ancestors.

### 5

Observe people who are good at their work—
  skilled workers are always in demand and admired;
  they don't take a back seat to anyone.

# 23

RESTRAIN YOURSELF

### 6

When you go out to dinner with an influential person,
  mind your manners:
Don't gobble your food,
  don't talk with your mouth full.
And don't stuff yourself;
  bridle your appetite.

### 7

Don't wear yourself out trying to get rich;
　　restrain yourself!
Riches disappear in the blink of an eye;
　　wealth sprouts wings
　　　and flies off into the wild blue yonder.

### 8

Don't accept a meal from a tightwad;
　　don't expect anything special.
He'll be as stingy with you as he is with himself;
　　he'll say, "Eat! Drink!" but won't mean a word of it.
His miserly serving will turn your stomach
　　when you realize the meal's a sham.

### 9

Don't bother talking sense to fools;
　　they'll only poke fun at your words.

### 10

Don't stealthily move back the boundary lines
　　or cheat orphans out of their property,
For they have a powerful Advocate
　　who will go to bat for them.

### 11

Give yourselves to disciplined instruction;
　　open your ears to tested knowledge.

### 12

Don't be afraid to correct your young ones;
　　a spanking won't kill them.
A good spanking, in fact, might save them
　　from something worse than death.

### 13

Dear child, if you become wise,
　　I'll be one happy parent.
My heart will dance and sing
　　to the tuneful truth you'll speak.

14

Don't for a minute envy careless rebels;
    soak yourself in the Fear-of-GOD—
*That's* where your future lies.
    *Then* you won't be left with an armload of nothing.

15

Oh listen, dear child—become wise;
    point your life in the right direction.
Don't drink too much wine and get drunk;
    don't eat too much food and get fat.
Drunks and gluttons will end up on skid row,
    in a stupor and dressed in rags.

BUY WISDOM, EDUCATION, INSIGHT

16

Listen with respect to the father who raised you,
    and when your mother grows old, don't neglect her.
Buy truth—don't sell it for love or money;
    buy wisdom, buy education, buy insight.
Parents rejoice when their children turn out well;
    wise children become proud parents.
So make your father happy!
    Make your mother proud!

17

Dear child, I want your full attention;
    please do what I show you.

A whore is a bottomless pit;
    a loose woman can get you in deep trouble fast.
She'll take you for all you've got;
    she's worse than a pack of thieves.

18

Who are the people who are always crying the blues?
    Who do you know who reeks of self-pity?
Who keeps getting beat up for no reason at all?

Whose eyes are bleary and bloodshot?
It's those who spend the night with a bottle,
    for whom drinking is serious business.
Don't judge wine by its label,
    or its bouquet, or its full-bodied flavor.
Judge it rather by the hangover it leaves you with—
    the splitting headache, the queasy stomach.
Do you really prefer seeing double,
    with your speech all slurred,
Reeling and seasick,
    drunk as a sailor?
"They hit me," you'll say, "but it didn't hurt;
    they beat on me, but I didn't feel a thing.
When I'm sober enough to manage it,
    bring me another drink!"

# 24

## INTELLIGENCE OUTRANKS MUSCLE

### 19

Don't envy bad people;
    don't even want to be around them.
All they think about is causing a disturbance;
    all they talk about is making trouble.

### 20

It takes wisdom to build a house,
    and understanding to set it on a firm foundation;
It takes knowledge to furnish its rooms
    with fine furniture and beautiful draperies.

### 21

It's better to be wise than strong;
    intelligence outranks muscle any day.
Strategic planning is the key to warfare;
    to win, you need a lot of good counsel.

22

Wise conversation is way over the head of fools;
in a serious discussion they haven't a clue.

23

The person who's always cooking up some evil
soon gets a reputation as prince of rogues.
Fools incubate sin;
cynics desecrate beauty.

RESCUE THE PERISHING

24

If you fall to pieces in a crisis,
there wasn't much to you in the first place.

25

Rescue the perishing;
don't hesitate to step in and help.
If you say, "Hey, that's none of my business,"
will that get you off the hook?
Someone is watching you closely, you know—
Someone not impressed with weak excuses.

26

Eat honey, dear child—it's good for you—
and delicacies that melt in your mouth.
Likewise knowledge,
and wisdom for your soul—
Get that and your future's secured,
your hope is on solid rock.

27

Don't interfere with good people's lives;
don't try to get the best of them.
No matter how many times you trip them up,
God-loyal people don't stay down long;
Soon they're up on their feet,
while the wicked end up flat on their faces.

28

Don't laugh when your enemy falls;
  don't crow over his collapse.
GOD might see, and become very provoked,
  and then take pity on his plight.

29

Don't bother your head with braggarts
  or wish you could succeed like the wicked.
Those people have no future at all;
  they're headed down a dead-end street.

30

Fear GOD, dear child—respect your leaders;
  don't be defiant or mutinous.
Without warning your life can turn upside-down,
  and who knows how or when it might happen?

## MORE SAYINGS OF THE WISE

### AN HONEST ANSWER

It's wrong, very wrong,
  to go along with injustice.

Whoever whitewashes the wicked
  gets a black mark in the history books,
But whoever exposes the wicked
  will be thanked and rewarded.

An honest answer
  is like a warm hug.

First plant your fields;
  *then* build your barn.

Don't talk about your neighbors behind their backs—
  no slander or gossip, please.
Don't say to anyone, "I'll get back at you for what you did to me.
  I'll make you pay for what you did!"

335

One day I walked by the field of an old lazybones,
    and then passed the vineyard of a lout;
They were overgrown with weeds,
    thick with thistles, all the fences broken down.
I took a long look and pondered what I saw;
    the fields preached me a sermon and I listened:
"A nap here, a nap there, a day off here, a day off there,
    sit back, take it easy—do you know what comes next?
Just this: You can look forward to a dirt-poor life,
    with poverty as your permanent houseguest!"


# 25 FURTHER WISE SAYINGS OF SOLOMON

THE RIGHT WORD AT THE RIGHT TIME

There are also these proverbs of Solomon,
    collected by scribes of Hezekiah, king of Judah.

God delights in concealing things;
    scientists delight in discovering things.

Like the horizons for breadth and the ocean for depth,
    the understanding of a good leader is broad and deep.

Remove impurities from the silver
    and the silversmith can craft a fine chalice;
Remove the wicked from leadership
    and authority will be credible and God-honoring.

Don't work yourself into the spotlight;
    don't push your way into the place of prominence.
It's better to be promoted to a place of honor
    than face humiliation by being demoted.

Don't jump to conclusions—there may be
    a perfectly good explanation for what you just saw.

In the heat of an argument,
    don't betray confidences;

Word is sure to get around,
    and no one will trust you.

The right word at the right time
    is like a custom-made piece of jewelry,
And a wise friend's timely reprimand
    is like a gold ring slipped on your finger.

Reliable friends who do what they say
    are like cool drinks in sweltering heat—refreshing!

Like billowing clouds that bring no rain
    is the person who talks big but never produces.

Patient persistence pierces through indifference;
    gentle speech breaks down rigid defenses.

A PERSON WITHOUT SELF-CONTROL

When you're given a box of candy, don't gulp it all down;
    eat too much chocolate and you'll make yourself sick;
And when you find a friend, don't outwear your welcome;
    show up at all hours and he'll soon get fed up.

Anyone who tells lies against the neighbors
    in court or on the street is a loose cannon.

Trusting a double-crosser when you're in trouble
    is like biting down on an abscessed tooth.

Singing light songs to the heavyhearted
    is like pouring salt in their wounds.

If you see your enemy hungry, go buy him lunch;
    if he's thirsty, bring him a drink.
Your generosity will surprise him with goodness,
    and GOD will look after you.

A north wind brings stormy weather,
    and a gossipy tongue stormy looks.

Better to live alone in a tumbledown shack
 than share a mansion with a nagging spouse.

Like a cool drink of water when you're worn out and weary
 is a letter from a long-lost friend.

A good person who gives in to a bad person
 is a muddied spring, a polluted well.

It's not smart to stuff yourself with sweets,
 nor is glory piled on glory good for you.

A person without self-control
 is like a house with its doors and windows knocked out.

# 26

FOOLS RECYCLE SILLINESS

We no more give honors to fools
 than pray for snow in summer or rain during harvest.

You have as little to fear from an undeserved curse
 as from the dart of a wren or the swoop of a swallow.

A whip for the racehorse, a tiller for the sailboat—
 and a stick for the back of fools!

Don't respond to the stupidity of a fool;
 you'll only look foolish yourself.

Answer a fool in simple terms
 so he doesn't get a swelled head.

You're only asking for trouble
 when you send a message by a fool.

A proverb quoted by fools
 is limp as a wet noodle.

Putting a fool in a place of honor
    is like setting a mud brick on a marble column.

To ask a moron to quote a proverb
    is like putting a scalpel in the hands of a drunk.

Hire a fool or a drunk
    and you shoot yourself in the foot.

As a dog eats its own vomit,
    so fools recycle silliness.

See that man who thinks he's so smart?
    You can expect far more from a fool than from him.

Loafers say, "It's dangerous out there!
    Tigers are prowling the streets!"
    and then pull the covers back over their heads.

Just as a door turns on its hinges,
    so a lazybones turns back over in bed.

A shiftless sluggard puts his fork in the pie,
    but is too lazy to lift it to his mouth.

## LIKE GLAZE ON CRACKED POTTERY

Dreamers fantasize their self-importance;
    they think they are smarter
    than a whole college faculty.

You grab a mad dog by the ears
    when you butt into a quarrel that's none of your business.

People who shrug off deliberate deceptions,
    saying, "I didn't mean it, I was only joking,"
Are worse than careless campers
    who walk away from smoldering campfires.

When you run out of wood, the fire goes out;
    when the gossip ends, the quarrel dies down.

A quarrelsome person in a dispute
    is like kerosene thrown on a fire.

Listening to gossip is like eating cheap candy;
    do you want junk like that in your belly?

Smooth talk from an evil heart
    is like glaze on cracked pottery.

Your enemy shakes hands and greets you like an old friend,
    all the while conniving against you.
When he speaks warmly to you, don't believe him for a minute;
    he's just waiting for the chance to rip you off.
No matter how cunningly he conceals his malice,
    eventually his evil will be exposed in public.

Malice backfires;
    spite boomerangs.

Liars hate their victims;
    flatterers sabotage trust.

# 27

## You Don't Know Tomorrow

Don't brashly announce what you're going to do tomorrow;
    you don't know the first thing about tomorrow.

Don't call attention to yourself;
    let others do that for you.

Carrying a log across your shoulders
    while you're hefting a boulder with your arms
Is nothing compared to the burden
    of putting up with a fool.

We're blasted by anger and swamped by rage,
    but who can survive jealousy?

A spoken reprimand is better
    than approval that's never expressed.

The wounds from a lover are worth it;
    kisses from an enemy do you in.

When you've stuffed yourself, you refuse dessert;
    when you're starved, you could eat a horse.

People who won't settle down, wandering hither and yon,
    are like restless birds, flitting to and fro.

Just as lotions and fragrance give sensual delight,
    a sweet friendship refreshes the soul.

Don't leave your friends or your parents' friends
    and run home to your family when things get rough;
Better a nearby friend
    than a distant family.

Become wise, dear child, and make me happy;
    then nothing the world throws my way will upset me.

A prudent person sees trouble coming and ducks;
    a simpleton walks in blindly and is clobbered.

Hold tight to collateral on any loan to a stranger;
    be wary of accepting what a transient has pawned.

If you wake your friend in the early morning
    by shouting "Rise and shine!"
It will sound to him
    more like a curse than a blessing.

A nagging spouse is like
    the drip, drip, drip of a leaky faucet;

341

You can't turn it off,
    and you can't get away from it.

YOUR FACE MIRRORS YOUR HEART

You use steel to sharpen steel,
    and one friend sharpens another.

If you care for your orchard, you'll enjoy its fruit;
    if you honor your boss, you'll be honored.

Just as water mirrors your face,
    so your face mirrors your heart.

Hell has a voracious appetite,
    and lust just never quits.

The purity of silver and gold is tested
    by putting them in the fire;
The purity of human hearts is tested
    by giving them a little fame.

Pound on a fool all you like—
    you can't pound out foolishness.

Know your sheep by name;
    carefully attend to your flocks;
(Don't take them for granted;
    possessions don't last forever, you know.)
And then, when the crops are in
    and the harvest is stored in the barns,
You can knit sweaters from lambs' wool,
    and sell your goats for a profit;
There will be plenty of milk and meat
    to last your family through the winter.

# 28
IF YOU DESERT GOD'S LAW

The wicked are edgy with guilt, ready to run off
    even when no one's after them;
Honest people are relaxed and confident,
    bold as lions.

When the country is in chaos,
    everybody has a plan to fix it—
But it takes a leader of real understanding
    to straighten things out.

The wicked who oppress the poor
    are like a hailstorm that beats down the harvest.

If you desert God's law, you're free to embrace depravity;
    if you love God's law, you fight for it tooth and nail.

Justice makes no sense to the evilminded;
    those who seek GOD know it inside and out.

It's better to be poor and direct
    than rich and crooked.

Practice God's law—get a reputation for wisdom;
    hang out with a loose crowd—embarrass your family.

Get as rich as you want
    through cheating and extortion,
But eventually some friend of the poor
    is going to give it all back to them.

God has no use for the prayers
    of the people who won't listen to him.

Lead good people down a wrong path
    and you'll come to a bad end;
        do good and you'll be rewarded for it.

The rich think they know it all,
    but the poor can see right through them.

When good people are promoted, everything is great,
    but when the bad are in charge, watch out!

You can't whitewash your sins and get by with it;
    you find mercy by admitting and leaving them.

A tenderhearted person lives a blessed life;
    a hardhearted person lives a hard life.

Lions roar and bears charge—
    and the wicked lord it over the poor.

Among leaders who lack insight, abuse abounds,
    but for one who hates corruption, the future is bright.

A murderer haunted by guilt
    is doomed—there's no helping him.

Walk straight—live well and be saved;
    a devious life is a doomed life.

### DOING GREAT HARM IN SEEMINGLY HARMLESS WAYS

Work your garden—you'll end up with plenty of food;
    play and party—you'll end up with an empty plate.

Committed and persistent work pays off;
    get-rich-quick schemes are ripoffs.

Playing favorites is always a bad thing;
    you can do great harm in seemingly harmless ways.

A miser in a hurry to get rich
    doesn't know that he'll end up broke.

In the end, serious reprimand is appreciated
    far more than bootlicking flattery.

Anyone who robs father and mother
    and says, "So, what's wrong with that?"
    is worse than a pirate.

A grasping person stirs up trouble,
    but trust in GOD brings a sense of well-being.

If you think you know it all, you're a fool for sure;
    real survivors learn wisdom from others.

Be generous to the poor—you'll never go hungry;
    shut your eyes to their needs, and run a gauntlet of curses.

When corruption takes over, good people go underground,
    but when the crooks are thrown out, it's safe to come out.

# 29

## IF PEOPLE CAN'T SEE WHAT GOD IS DOING

For people who hate discipline
    and only get more stubborn,
There'll come a day when life tumbles in and they break,
    but by then it'll be too late to help them.

When good people run things, everyone is glad,
    but when the ruler is bad, everyone groans.

If you love wisdom, you'll delight your parents,
    but you'll destroy their trust if you run with whores.

A leader of good judgment gives stability;
    an exploiting leader leaves a trail of waste.

A flattering neighbor is up to no good;
    he's probably planning to take advantage of you.

Evil people fall into their own traps;
>good people run the other way, glad to escape.

The good-hearted understand what it's like to be poor;
>the hardhearted haven't the faintest idea.

A gang of cynics can upset a whole city;
>a group of sages can calm everyone down.

A sage trying to work things out with a fool
>gets only scorn and sarcasm for his trouble.

Murderers hate honest people;
>moral folks encourage them.

A fool lets it all hang out;
>a sage quietly mulls it over.

When a leader listens to malicious gossip,
>all the workers get infected with evil.

The poor and their abusers have at least something in common:
>they can both *see*—their sight GOD's gift!

Leadership gains authority and respect
>when the voiceless poor are treated fairly.

Wise discipline imparts wisdom;
>spoiled adolescents embarrass their parents.

When degenerates take charge, crime runs wild,
>but the righteous will eventually observe their collapse.

Discipline your children; you'll be glad you did—
>they'll turn out delightful to live with.

If people can't see what God is doing,
>they stumble all over themselves;
But when they attend to what he reveals,
>they are most blessed.

It takes more than talk to keep workers in line;
    mere words go in one ear and out the other.

Observe the people who always talk before they think—
    even simpletons are better off than they are.

If you let people treat you like a doormat,
    you'll be quite forgotten in the end.

Angry people stir up a lot of discord;
    the intemperate stir up trouble.

Pride lands you flat on your face;
    humility prepares you for honors.

Befriend an outlaw
    and become an enemy to yourself.
When the victims cry out,
    you'll be included in their curses
    if you're a coward to their cause in court.

The fear of human opinion disables;
    trusting in GOD protects you from that.

Everyone tries to get help from the leader,
    but only GOD will give us justice.

Good people can't stand the sight of deliberate evil;
    the wicked can't stand the sight of well-chosen goodness.

# 30    THE WORDS OF AGUR BEN YAKEH

## GOD? WHO NEEDS HIM?

The skeptic swore, "There is no God!
    No God!—I can do anything I want!
I'm more animal than human;
    so-called human intelligence escapes me.

I flunked 'wisdom.'
     I see no evidence of a holy God.
Has anyone ever seen Anyone
     climb into Heaven and take charge?
     grab the winds and control them?
     gather the rains in his bucket?
     stake out the ends of the earth?
Just tell me his name, tell me the names of his sons.
     Come on now—tell me!"

The believer replied, "Every promise of God proves true;
     he protects everyone who runs to him for help.
So don't second-guess him;
     he might take you to task and show up your lies."

And then he prayed, "God, I'm asking for two things
     before I die; don't refuse me—
Banish lies from my lips
     and liars from my presence.
Give me enough food to live on,
     neither too much nor too little.
If I'm too full, I might get independent,
     saying, 'God? Who needs him?'
If I'm poor, I might steal
     and dishonor the name of my God."

✢

Don't blow the whistle on your fellow workers
     behind their backs;
They'll accuse you of being underhanded,
     and then *you'll* be the guilty one!

Don't curse your father
     or fail to bless your mother.

Don't imagine yourself to be quite presentable
     when you haven't had a bath in weeks.

Don't be stuck-up
    and think you're better than everyone else.

Don't be greedy,
    merciless and cruel as wolves,
Tearing into the poor and feasting on them,
    shredding the needy to pieces only to discard them.

A leech has twin daughters
    named "Gimme" and "Gimme more."

FOUR INSATIABLES

Three things are never satisfied,
    no, there are four that never say, "That's enough, thank you!"—

        hell,
        a barren womb,
        a parched land,
        a forest fire.

✠

An eye that disdains a father
    and despises a mother—
that eye will be plucked out by wild vultures
    and consumed by young eagles.

FOUR MYSTERIES

Three things amaze me,
    no, four things I'll never understand—

        how an eagle flies so high in the sky,
        how a snake glides over a rock,
        how a ship navigates the ocean,
        why adolescents act the way they do.

✠

Here's how a prostitute operates:
    she has sex with her client,

Takes a bath,
>then asks, "Who's next?"

## Four Intolerables

Three things are too much for even the earth to bear,
>yes, four things shake its foundations—

>>when the janitor becomes the boss,
>>when a fool gets rich,
>>when a whore is voted "woman of the year,"
>>when a "girlfriend" replaces a faithful wife.

## Four Small Wonders

There are four small creatures,
>wisest of the wise they are—

>>ants—frail as they are,
>>>get plenty of food in for the winter;
>>marmots—vulnerable as they are,
>>>manage to arrange for rock-solid homes;
>>locusts—leaderless insects,
>>>yet they strip the field like an army regiment;
>>lizards—easy enough to catch,
>>>but they sneak past vigilant palace guards.

## Four Dignitaries

There are three solemn dignitaries,
>four that are impressive in their bearing—

>>a lion, king of the beasts, deferring to none;
>>a rooster, proud and strutting;
>>a billy goat;
>>a head of state in stately procession.

☩

If you're dumb enough to call attention to yourself
>by offending people and making rude gestures,

Don't be surprised if someone bloodies your nose.
  Churned milk turns into butter;
    riled emotions turn into fist fights.

# 31

## SPEAK OUT FOR JUSTICE

The words of King Lemuel,
  the strong advice his mother gave him:

"Oh, son of mine, what can you be thinking of!
  Child whom I bore! The son I dedicated to God!
Don't dissipate your virility on fortune-hunting women,
  promiscuous women who shipwreck leaders.

"Leaders can't afford to make fools of themselves,
  gulping wine and swilling beer,
Lest, hung over, they don't know right from wrong,
  and the people who depend on them are hurt.
Use wine and beer only as sedatives,
  to kill the pain and dull the ache
Of the terminally ill,
  for whom life is a living death.

"Speak up for the people who have no voice,
  for the rights of all the down-and-outers.
Speak out for justice!
  Stand up for the poor and destitute!"

## HYMN TO A GOOD WIFE

A good woman is hard to find,
  and worth far more than diamonds.
Her husband trusts her without reserve,
  and never has reason to regret it.
Never spiteful, she treats him generously
  all her life long.
She shops around for the best yarns and cottons,
  and enjoys knitting and sewing.

She's like a trading ship that sails to faraway places
    and brings back exotic surprises.
She's up before dawn, preparing breakfast
    for her family and organizing her day.
She looks over a field and buys it,
    then, with money she's put aside, plants a garden.
First thing in the morning, she dresses for work,
    rolls up her sleeves, eager to get started.
She senses the worth of her work,
    is in no hurry to call it quits for the day.
She's skilled in the crafts of home and hearth,
    diligent in homemaking.
She's quick to assist anyone in need,
    reaches out to help the poor.
She doesn't worry about her family when it snows;
    their winter clothes are all mended and ready to wear.
She makes her own clothing,
    and dresses in colorful linens and silks.
Her husband is greatly respected
    when he deliberates with the city fathers.
She designs gowns and sells them,
    brings the sweaters she knits to the dress shops.
Her clothes are well-made and elegant,
    and she always faces tomorrow with a smile.
When she speaks she has something worthwhile to say,
    and she always says it kindly.
She keeps an eye on everyone in her household,
    and keeps them all busy and productive.
Her children respect and bless her;
    her husband joins in with words of praise:
"Many women have done wonderful things,
    but you've outclassed them all!"
Charm can mislead and beauty soon fades.
    The woman to be admired and praised
    is the woman who lives in the Fear-of-God.
Give her everything she deserves!
    Festoon her life with praises!

# ECCLESIASTES

# ECCLESIASTES

U nlike the animals, who seem quite content to simply be themselves, we humans are always looking for ways to be more than or other than what we find ourselves to be. We explore the countryside for excitement, search our souls for meaning, shop the world for pleasure. We try this. Then we try that. The usual fields of endeavor are money, sex, power, adventure, and knowledge.

Everything we try is so promising at first! But nothing ever seems to amount to very much. We intensify our efforts—but the harder we work at it, the less we get out of it. Some people give up early and settle for a humdrum life. Others never seem to learn, and so they flail away through a lifetime, becoming less and less human by the year, until by the time they die there is hardly enough humanity left to compose a corpse.

Ecclesiastes is a famous—maybe the world's most famous—witness to this experience of futility. The acerbic wit catches our attention. The stark honesty compels notice. And people do notice—oh, how they notice! Nonreligious and religious alike notice. Unbelievers and believers notice. More than a few of them are surprised to find this kind of thing in the Bible.

But it is most emphatically and necessarily in the Bible in order to call a halt to our various and futile attempts to make something of our lives, so that we can give our full attention to God—who God is and what he does to make something of us. Ecclesiastes actually doesn't say that much about God; the author leaves that to the other sixty-five books of the Bible. His task is to expose our total incapacity to find the meaning and completion of our lives on our own.

It is our propensity to go off on our own, trying to be human by our own devices and desires, that makes Ecclesiastes necessary reading. Ecclesiastes sweeps our souls clean of all "lifestyle" spiritualities so that we can be ready for God's visitation revealed in Jesus Christ. Ecclesiastes is a John-the-Baptist kind of book. It functions not as a meal but as a bath. It is not nourishment; it is cleansing. It is repentance. It is purging. We read Ecclesiastes to get scrubbed clean from illusion and sentiment, from ideas that are idolatrous and feelings that cloy. It is an exposé and rejection of every arrogant and ignorant expectation that we can live our lives by ourselves on our own terms.

Ecclesiastes challenges the naive optimism that sets a goal that appeals to us and then goes after it with gusto, expecting the result to be a good life. The author's cool skepticism, a refreshing negation to the lush and seductive suggestions swirling around us, promising everything but delivering nothing, clears the air. And once the air is cleared, we are ready for reality—for God.

["Ecclesiastes" is a Greek word that is usually translated "the Preacher" or "the Teacher." Because of the experiential stance of the writing in this book, giving voice to what is so basic among men and women throughout history, I have translated it "the Quester."]

# ECCLESIASTES

## 1

### THE QUESTER

These are the words of the Quester, David's son and king in Jerusalem:

Smoke, nothing but smoke. [That's what the Quester says.]
    There's nothing to anything—it's all smoke.
What's there to show for a lifetime of work,
    a lifetime of working your fingers to the bone?
One generation goes its way, the next one arrives,
    but nothing changes—it's business as usual for old
        planet earth.
The sun comes up and the sun goes down,
    then does it again, and again—the same old round.
The wind blows south, the wind blows north.
    Around and around and around it blows,
    blowing this way, then that—the whirling, erratic wind.
All the rivers flow into the sea,
    but the sea never fills up.
The rivers keep flowing to the same old place,
    and then start all over and do it again.
Everything's boring, utterly boring—
    no one can find any meaning in it.
Boring to the eye,
    boring to the ear.
What was will be again,
    what happened will happen again.
There's nothing new on this earth.
    Year after year it's the same old thing.
Does someone call out, "Hey, *this* is new"?
    Don't get excited—it's the same old story.
Nobody remembers what happened yesterday.
    And the things that will happen tomorrow?
Nobody'll remember them either.
    Don't count on being remembered.

I'VE SEEN IT ALL

Call me "the Quester." I've been king over Israel in Jerusalem. I looked most carefully into everything, searched out all that is done on this earth. And let me tell you, there's not much to write home about. God hasn't made it easy for us. I've seen it all and it's nothing but smoke—smoke, and spitting into the wind.

> Life's a corkscrew that can't be straightened,
> A minus that won't add up.

I said to myself, "I know more and I'm wiser than anyone before me in Jerusalem. I've stockpiled wisdom and knowledge." What I've finally concluded is that so-called wisdom and knowledge are mindless and witless—nothing but spitting into the wind.

> Much learning earns you much trouble.
> The more you know, the more you hurt.

# 2

I said to myself, "Let's go for it—experiment with pleasure, have a good time!" But there was nothing to it, nothing but smoke.

> What do I think of the fun-filled life? Insane! Inane!
> My verdict on the pursuit of happiness? Who needs it?
> With the help of a bottle of wine
> and all the wisdom I could muster,
> I tried my level best
> to penetrate the absurdity of life.
> I wanted to get a handle on anything useful we mortals might do
> during the years we spend on this earth.

I NEVER SAID NO TO MYSELF

> Oh, I did great things:
> built houses,
> planted vineyards,
> designed gardens and parks

357

and planted a variety of fruit trees in them,
made pools of water
to irrigate the groves of trees.
I bought slaves, male and female,
who had children, giving me even more slaves;
then I acquired large herds and flocks,
larger than any before me in Jerusalem.
I piled up silver and gold,
loot from kings and kingdoms.
I gathered a chorus of singers to entertain me with song,
and—most exquisite of all pleasures—
voluptuous maidens for my bed.

Oh, how I prospered! I left all my predecessors in Jerusalem far behind, left them behind in the dust. What's more, I kept a clear head through it all. Everything I wanted I took—I never said no to myself. I gave in to every impulse, held back nothing. I sucked the marrow of pleasure out of every task—my reward to myself for a hard day's work!

I HATE LIFE

Then I took a good look at everything I'd done, looked at all the sweat and hard work. But when I looked, I saw nothing but smoke. Smoke and spitting into the wind. There was nothing to any of it. Nothing.

And then I took a hard look at what's smart and what's stupid. What's left to do after you've been king? That's a hard act to follow. You just do what you can, and that's it. But I did see that it's better to be smart than stupid, just as light is better than darkness. Even so, though the smart ones see where they're going and the stupid ones grope in the dark, they're all the same in the end. One fate for all—and that's it.

When I realized that my fate's the same as the fool's, I had to ask myself, "So why bother being wise?" It's all smoke, nothing but smoke. The smart and the stupid both disappear out of sight. In a day or two they're both forgotten. Yes, both the smart and the stupid die, and that's it.

I hate life. As far as I can see, what happens on earth is a bad business. It's smoke—and spitting into the wind.

And I hated everything I'd accomplished and accumulated on this earth. I can't take it with me—no, I have to leave it to whoever comes after me. Whether they're worthy or worthless—and who's to tell?—they'll take over the earthly results of my intense thinking and hard work. Smoke.

That's when I called it quits, gave up on anything that could be hoped for on this earth. What's the point of working your fingers to the bone if you hand over what you worked for to someone who never lifted a finger for it? Smoke, that's what it is. A bad business from start to finish. So what do you get from a life of hard labor? Pain and grief from dawn to dusk. Never a decent night's rest. Nothing but smoke.

The best you can do with your life is have a good time and get by the best you can. The way I see it, that's it—divine fate. Whether we feast or fast, it's up to God. God may give wisdom and knowledge and joy to his favorites, but sinners are assigned a life of hard labor, and end up turning their wages over to God's favorites. Nothing but smoke—and spitting into the wind.

# 3

THERE'S A RIGHT TIME FOR EVERYTHING

There's an opportune time to do things, a right time for everything on the earth:

> A right time for birth and another for death,
> A right time to plant and another to reap,
> A right time to kill and another to heal,
> A right time to destroy and another to construct,
> A right time to cry and another to laugh,
> A right time to lament and another to cheer,
> A right time to make love and another to abstain,
> A right time to embrace and another to part,
> A right time to search and another to count your losses,
> A right time to hold on and another to let go,
> A right time to rip out and another to mend,
> A right time to shut up and another to speak up,
> A right time to love and another to hate,
> A right time to wage war and another to make peace.

But in the end, does it really make a difference what anyone does?

I've had a good look at what God has given us to do—busywork, mostly. True, God made everything beautiful in itself and in its time—but he's left us in the dark, so we can never know what God is up to, whether he's coming or going. I've decided that there's nothing better to do than go ahead and have a good time and get the most we can out of life. That's it—eat, drink, and make the most of your job. It's God's gift.

I've also concluded that whatever God does, that's the way it's going to be, always. No addition, no subtraction. God's done it and that's it. That's so we'll quit asking questions and simply worship in holy fear.

> Whatever was, is.
> Whatever will be, is.
> That's how it always is with God.

## God's Testing Us

I took another good look at what's going on: The very place of judgment—corrupt! The place of righteousness—corrupt! I said to myself, "God will judge righteous and wicked." There's a right time for every thing, every deed—and there's no getting around it. I said to myself regarding the human race, "God's testing the lot of us, showing us up as nothing but animals."

Humans and animals come to the same end—humans die, animals die. We all breathe the same air. So there's really no advantage in being human. None. Everything's smoke. We all end up in the same place—we all came from dust, we all end up as dust. Nobody knows for sure that the human spirit rises to heaven or that the animal spirit sinks into the earth. So I made up my mind that there's nothing better for us men and women than to have a good time in whatever we do—that's our lot. Who knows if there's anything else to life?

# 4

## Slow Suicide

Next I turned my attention to all the outrageous violence that takes place on this planet—the tears of the victims, no one to comfort them; the iron grip of oppressors, no one to rescue the victims from them. So I congratulated the dead who are already dead instead of the living who are still alive. But luckier than the dead or the living is the person who has never even been, who has never seen the bad business that takes place on this earth.

Then I observed all the work and ambition motivated by envy. What a waste! Smoke. And spitting into the wind.

> The fool sits back and takes it easy,
> His sloth is slow suicide.

> One handful of peaceful repose
> Is better than two fistfuls of worried work—
> More spitting into the wind.

## WHY AM I WORKING LIKE A DOG?

I turned my head and saw yet another wisp of smoke on its way to nothingness: a solitary person, completely alone—no children, no family, no friends—yet working obsessively late into the night, compulsively greedy for more and more, never bothering to ask, "Why am I working like a dog, never having any fun? And who cares?" More smoke. A bad business.

> It's better to have a partner than go it alone.
> Share the work, share the wealth.
> And if one falls down, the other helps,
> But if there's no one to help, tough!

> Two in a bed warm each other.
> Alone, you shiver all night.

> By yourself you're unprotected.
> With a friend you can face the worst.
> Can you round up a third?
> A three-stranded rope isn't easily snapped.

✠

A poor youngster with some wisdom is better off than an old but foolish king who doesn't know which end is up. I saw a youth just like this start with nothing and go from rags to riches, and I saw everyone rally to the rule of this young successor to the king. Even so, the excitement died quickly, the throngs of people soon lost interest. Can't you see it's only smoke? And spitting into the wind?

# 5

## God's In Charge, Not You

Watch your step when you enter God's house.
Enter to learn. That's far better than mindlessly offering
　　　　a sacrifice,
Doing more harm than good.

Don't shoot off your mouth, or speak before you think.
Don't be too quick to tell God what you think he wants to hear.
God's in charge, not you—the less you speak, the better.

Over-work makes for restless sleep.
Over-talk shows you up as a fool.

When you tell God you'll do something, do it—now.
God takes no pleasure in foolish gabble. Vow it, then do it.
Far better not to vow in the first place than to vow and not pay up.

Don't let your mouth make a total sinner of you.
When called to account, you won't get by with
　　　　"Sorry, I didn't mean it."
Why risk provoking God to angry retaliation?

But against all illusion and fantasy and empty talk
There's always this rock foundation: Fear God!

## A Salary of Smoke

Don't be too upset when you see the poor kicked around, and justice and right violated all over the place. Exploitation filters down from one petty official to another. There's no end to it, and nothing can be done about it. But the good earth doesn't cheat anyone—even a bad king is honestly served by a field.

The one who loves money is never satisfied with money,
Nor the one who loves wealth with big profits. More smoke.

The more loot you get, the more looters show up.
And what fun is that—to be robbed in broad daylight?

Hard and honest work earns a good night's sleep,
Whether supper is beans or steak.
But a rich man's belly gives him insomnia.

Here's a piece of bad luck I've seen happen:
A man hoards far more wealth than is good for him
And then loses it all in a bad business deal.
He fathered a child but hasn't a cent left to give him.
He arrived naked from the womb of his mother;
He'll leave in the same condition—with nothing.
This is bad luck, for sure—naked he came, naked he went.
So what was the point of working for a salary of smoke?
All for a miserable life spent in the dark?

## MAKE THE MOST OF WHAT GOD GIVES

After looking at the way things are on this earth, here's what I've decided is the best way to live: Take care of yourself, have a good time, and make the most of whatever job you have for as long as God gives you life. And that's about it. That's the human lot. Yes, we should make the most of what God gives, both the bounty and the capacity to enjoy it, accepting what's given and delighting in the work. It's God's gift! God deals out joy in the present, the *now*. It's useless to brood over how long we might live.

# 6

## THINGS ARE BAD

I looked long and hard at what goes on around here, and let me tell you, things are bad. And people feel it. There are people, for instance, on whom God showers everything—money, property, reputation— all they ever wanted or dreamed of. And then God doesn't let them enjoy it. Some stranger comes along and has all the fun. It's more of what I'm calling *smoke*. A bad business.

Say a couple have scores of children and live a long, long life but never enjoy themselves—even though they end up with a big funeral!

I'd say that a stillborn baby gets the better deal. It gets its start in a mist and ends up in the dark—unnamed. It sees nothing and knows nothing, but is better off by far than anyone living.

Even if someone lived a thousand years—make it two thousand!—but didn't enjoy anything, what's the point? Doesn't everyone end up in the same place?

> We work to feed our appetites;
> Meanwhile our souls go hungry.

So what advantage has a sage over a fool, or over some poor wretch who barely gets by? Just grab whatever you can while you can; don't assume something better might turn up by and by. All it amounts to anyway is smoke. And spitting into the wind.

> Whatever happens, happens. Its destiny is fixed.
> You can't argue with fate.

The more words that are spoken, the more smoke there is in the air. And who is any better off? And who knows what's best for us as we live out our meager smoke-and-shadow lives? And who can tell any of us the next chapter of our lives?

# 7

## Don't Take Anything for Granted

> A good reputation is better than a fat bank account.
> Your death date tells more than your birth date.

> You learn more at a funeral than at a feast—
> After all, that's where we'll end up. We might discover
> something from it.

> Crying is better than laughing.
> It blotches the face but it scours the heart.

> Sages invest themselves in hurt and grieving.
> Fools waste their lives in fun and games.

You'll get more from the rebuke of a sage
Than from the song and dance of fools.

The giggles of fools are like the crackling of twigs
Under the cooking pot. And like smoke.

Brutality stupefies even the wise
And destroys the strongest heart.

Endings are better than beginnings.
Sticking to it is better than standing out.

Don't be quick to fly off the handle.
Anger boomerangs. You can spot a fool by the lumps on his head.

Don't always be asking, "Where are the good old days?"
Wise folks don't ask questions like that.

Wisdom is better when it's paired with money,
Especially if you get both while you're still living.
Double protection: wisdom and wealth!
Plus this bonus: Wisdom energizes its owner.

Take a good look at God's work.
Who could simplify and reduce Creation's curves and angles
To a plain straight line?

On a good day, enjoy yourself;
On a bad day, examine your conscience.
God arranges for both kinds of days
So that we won't take anything for granted.

Stay in Touch With Both Sides

I've seen it all in my brief and pointless life—here a good person cut down in the middle of doing good, there a bad person living a long life of sheer evil. So don't knock yourself out being good, and don't go overboard being wise. Believe me, you won't get anything out of it. But don't press your luck by being bad, either. And don't be reckless. Why die needlessly?

It's best to stay in touch with both sides of an issue. A person who
fears God deals responsibly with all of reality, not just a piece of it.

> Wisdom puts more strength in one wise person
> Than ten strong men give to a city.

> There's not one totally good person on earth,
> Not one who is truly pure and sinless.

> Don't eavesdrop on the conversation of others.
> What if the gossip's about you and you'd rather not hear it?
> You've done that a few times, haven't you—said things
> Behind someone's back you wouldn't say to his face?

## How to Interpret the Meaning of Life

I tested everything in my search for wisdom. I set out to be wise, but
it was beyond me, far beyond me, and deep—oh so deep! Does anyone ever find it? I concentrated with all my might, studying and
exploring and seeking wisdom—the meaning of life. I also wanted to
identify evil and stupidity, foolishness and craziness.

One discovery: A woman can be a bitter pill to swallow, full of
seductive scheming and grasping. The lucky escape her; the undis-
cerning get caught. At least this is my experience—what I, the Quester,
have pieced together as I've tried to make sense of life. But the wisdom I've looked for I haven't found. I didn't find one man or woman
in a thousand worth my while. Yet I did spot one ray of light in this
murk: God made men and women true and upright; *we're* the ones
who've made a mess of things.

# 8

> There's nothing better than being wise,
> Knowing how to interpret the meaning of life.
> Wisdom puts light in the eyes,
> And gives gentleness to words and manners.

## No One Can Control the Wind

Do what your king commands; you gave a sacred oath of obedience.
Don't worryingly second-guess your orders or try to back out when

the task is unpleasant. You're serving his pleasure, not yours. The king has the last word. Who dares say to him, "What are you doing?" Carrying out orders won't hurt you a bit; the wise person obeys promptly and accurately. Yes, there's a right time and way for everything, even though, unfortunately, we miss it for the most part. It's true that no one knows what's going to happen, or when. Who's around to tell us?

> No one can control the wind or lock it in a box.
> No one has any say-so regarding the day of death.
> No one can stop a battle in its tracks.
> No one who does evil can be saved by evil.

All this I observed as I tried my best to understand all that's going on in this world. As long as men and women have the power to hurt each other, this is the way it is.

## ONE FATE FOR EVERYBODY

One time I saw wicked men given a solemn burial in holy ground. When the people returned to the city, they delivered flowery eulogies—and in the very place where wicked acts were done by those very men! More smoke. Indeed.

Because the sentence against evil deeds is so long in coming, people in general think they can get by with murder.

Even though a person sins and gets by with it hundreds of times throughout a long life, I'm still convinced that the good life is reserved for the person who fears God, who lives reverently in his presence, and that the evil person will not experience a "good" life. No matter how many days he lives, they'll all be as flat and colorless as a shadow— because he doesn't fear God.

✠

Here's something that happens all the time and makes no sense at all: Good people get what's coming to the wicked, and bad people get what's coming to the good. I tell you, this makes no sense. It's smoke.

So, I'm all for just going ahead and having a good time—the best possible. The only earthly good men and women can look forward to is to eat and drink well and have a good time—compensation for the struggle for survival these few years God gives us on earth.

When I determined to load up on wisdom and examine everything taking place on earth, I realized that if you keep your eyes open day and night without even blinking, you'll still never figure out the meaning of what God is doing on this earth. Search as hard as you like, you're not going to make sense of it. No matter how smart you are, you won't get to the bottom of it.

# 9

Well, I took all this in and thought it through, inside and out. Here's what I understood: The good, the wise, and all that they do are in God's hands—but, day by day, whether it's love or hate they're dealing with, they don't know.

Anything's possible. It's one fate for everybody—righteous and wicked, good people, bad people, the nice and the nasty, worshipers and non-worshipers, committed and uncommitted. I find this outrageous—the worst thing about living on this earth—that everyone's lumped together in one fate. Is it any wonder that so many people are obsessed with evil? Is it any wonder that people go crazy right and left? Life leads to death. That's it.

Seize Life!

Still, anyone selected out for life has hope, for, as they say, "A living dog is better than a dead lion." The living at least know *something*, even if it's only that they're going to die. But the dead know nothing and get nothing. They're a minus that no one remembers. Their loves, their hates, yes, even their dreams, are long gone. There's not a trace of them left in the affairs of this earth.

> Seize life! Eat bread with gusto,
> Drink wine with a robust heart.
> Oh yes—God takes pleasure in *your* pleasure!
> Dress festively every morning.
> Don't skimp on colors and scarves.
> Relish life with the spouse you love
> Each and every day of your precarious life.
> Each day is God's gift. It's all you get in exchange
> For the hard work of staying alive.

Make the most of each one!
Whatever turns up, grab it and do it. And heartily!
This is your last and only chance at it,
For there's neither work to do nor thoughts to think
In the company of the dead, where you're most certainly headed.

✠

I took another walk around the neighborhood and realized that on
this earth as it is—

The race is not always to the swift,
Nor the battle to the strong,
Nor satisfaction to the wise,
Nor riches to the smart,
Nor grace to the learned.
Sooner or later bad luck hits us all.

No one can predict misfortune.
Like fish caught in a cruel net or birds in a trap,
So men and women are caught
By accidents evil and sudden.

## WISDOM IS BETTER THAN MUSCLE

One day as I was observing how wisdom fares on this earth, I saw
something that made me sit up and take notice. There was a small
town with only a few people in it. A strong king came and mounted
an attack, building trenches and attack posts around it. There was a
poor but wise man in that town whose wisdom saved the town, but
he was promptly forgotten. (He was only a poor man, after all.)

All the same, I still say that wisdom is better than muscle, even
though the wise poor man was treated with contempt and soon forgotten.

The quiet words of the wise are more effective
Than the ranting of a king of fools.

Wisdom is better than warheads,
But one hothead can ruin the good earth.

369

# 10

Dead flies in perfume make it stink,
And a little foolishness decomposes much wisdom.

Wise thinking leads to right living;
Stupid thinking leads to wrong living.

Fools on the road have no sense of direction.
The way they walk tells the story: "There goes the fool again!"

If a ruler loses his temper against you, don't panic;
A calm disposition quiets intemperate rage.

☩

Here's a piece of bad business I've seen on this earth,
An error that can be blamed on whoever is in charge:
Immaturity is given a place of prominence,
While maturity is made to take a back seat.
I've seen unproven upstarts riding in style,
While experienced veterans are put out to pasture.

☩

Caution: The trap you set might catch you.
Warning: Your accomplice in crime might double-cross you.

Safety first: Quarrying stones is dangerous.
Be alert: Felling trees is hazardous.

Remember: The duller the ax the harder the work;
Use your head: The more brains, the less muscle.

If the snake bites before it's been charmed,
What's the point in then sending for the charmer?

☩

The words of a wise person are gracious.
The talk of a fool self-destructs—

370

He starts out talking nonsense
And ends up spouting insanity and evil.

Fools talk way too much,
Chattering stuff they know nothing about.

A decent day's work so fatigues fools
That they can't find their way back to town.

✝

Unlucky the land whose king is a young pup,
And whose princes party all night.
Lucky the land whose king is mature,
Where the princes behave themselves
And don't drink themselves silly.

✝

A shiftless man lives in a tumbledown shack;
A lazy woman ends up with a leaky roof.

Laughter and bread go together,
And wine gives sparkle to life—
But it's money that makes the world go around.

Don't bad-mouth your leaders, not even under your breath,
And don't abuse your betters, even in the privacy of your home.
Loose talk has a way of getting picked up and spread around.
Little birds drop the crumbs of your gossip far and wide.

# 11

Be generous: Invest in acts of charity.
Charity yields high returns.

Don't hoard your goods; spread them around.
Be a blessing to others. This could be your last night.

When the clouds are full of water, it rains.
When the wind blows down a tree, it lies where it falls.

Don't sit there watching the wind. Do your own work.
Don't stare at the clouds. Get on with your life.

Just as you'll never understand
the mystery of life forming in a pregnant woman,
So you'll never understand
the mystery at work in all that God does.

Go to work in the morning
and stick to it until evening without watching the clock.
You never know from moment to moment
how your work will turn out in the end.

BEFORE THE YEARS TAKE THEIR TOLL

Oh, how sweet the light of day,
And how wonderful to live in the sunshine!
Even if you live a long time, don't take a single day for granted.
Take delight in each light-filled hour,
Remembering that there will also be many dark days
And that most of what comes your way is smoke.

You who are young, make the most of your youth.
Relish your youthful vigor.
Follow the impulses of your heart.
If something looks good to you, pursue it.
But know also that not just anything goes;
You have to answer to God for every last bit of it.

Live footloose and fancy free—
You won't be young forever.
Youth lasts about as long as smoke.

# 12

Honor and enjoy your Creator while you're still young,
Before the years take their toll and your vigor wanes,
Before your vision dims and the world blurs
And the winter years keep you close to the fire.

In old age, your body no longer serves you so well.
Muscles slacken, grip weakens, joints stiffen.
The shades are pulled down on the world.
You can't come and go at will. Things grind to a halt.
The hum of the household fades away.
You are wakened now by bird-song.
Hikes to the mountains are a thing of the past.
Even a stroll down the road has its terrors.
Your hair turns apple-blossom white,
Adorning a fragile and impotent matchstick body.
Yes, you're well on your way to eternal rest,
While your friends make plans for your funeral.

Life, lovely while it lasts, is soon over.
Life as we know it, precious and beautiful, ends.
The body is put back in the same ground it came from.
The spirit returns to God, who first breathed it.

It's all smoke, nothing but smoke.
The Quester says that everything's smoke.

## THE FINAL WORD

Besides being wise himself, the Quester also taught others knowledge.
He weighed, examined, and arranged many proverbs. The Quester
did his best to find the right words and write the plain truth.

The words of the wise prod us to live well.
They're like nails hammered home, holding life together.
They are given by God, the one Shepherd.

But regarding anything beyond this, dear friend, go easy. There's
no end to the publishing of books, and constant study wears you out
so you're no good for anything else. The last and final word is this:

Fear God.
Do what he tells you.

And that's it. Eventually God will bring everything that we do out
into the open and judge it according to its hidden intent, whether it's
good or evil.

# SONG OF SONGS

# SONG OF SONGS

We don't read very far in the Song of Songs before we realize two things: one, it contains exquisite love lyrics, and two, it is very explicit sexually. The Song, in other words, makes a connection between conjugal love and sex—a very important and very biblical connection to make. There are some who would eliminate sex when they speak of love, supposing that they are making it more holy. Others, when they think of sex, never think of love. The Song proclaims an integrated wholeness that is at the center of Christian teaching on committed, wedded love for a world that seems to specialize in loveless sex.

The Song is a convincing witness that men and women were created physically, emotionally, and spiritually to live in love. At the outset of Scripture we read, "It is not good for man to live alone." The Song of Songs elaborates on the Genesis story by celebrating the union of two diverse personalities in love.

We read Genesis and learn that this is the created pattern of joy and mutuality. We read the Song and see the goal and ideal toward which we all press for fulfillment. Despite our sordid failures in love, we see here what we are created for, what God intends for us in the ecstasy and fulfillment that is celebrated in the lyricism of the Song.

Christians read the Song on many levels: as the intimacy of marital love between man and woman, God's deep love for his people, Christ's Bridegroom love for his church, the Christian's love for his or her Lord. It is a prism in which all the love of God in all the world, and all the responses of those who love and whom God loves, gathers and then separates into individual colors.

# SONG OF SONGS

# 1

The Song—best of all songs—Solomon's song!

THE WOMAN

Kiss me—full on the mouth!
  Yes! For your love is better than wine,
  headier than your aromatic oils.
The syllables of your name murmur like a meadow brook.
  No wonder everyone loves to say your name!

Take me away with you! Let's run off together!
  An elopement with my King-Lover!
We'll celebrate, we'll sing,
  we'll make great music.
Yes! For your love is better than vintage wine.
  Everyone loves you—of course! And why not?

I am weathered but still elegant,
  oh, dear sisters in Jerusalem,
Weather-darkened like Kedar desert tents,
  time-softened like Solomon's Temple hangings.
Don't look down on me because I'm dark,
  darkened by the sun's harsh rays.
My brothers ridiculed me and sent me to work in the fields.
  They made me care for the face of the earth,
  but I had no time to care for my own face.

Tell me where you're working
  —I love you so much—
Tell me where you're tending your flocks,
  where you let them rest at noontime.
Why should I be the one left out,
  outside the orbit of your tender care?

THE MAN

If you can't find me, loveliest of all women,
    it's all right. Stay with your flocks.
Lead your lambs to good pasture.
    Stay with your shepherd neighbors.

You remind me of Pharaoh's
    well-groomed and satiny mares.
Pendant earrings line the elegance of your cheeks;
    strands of jewels illumine the curve of your throat.
I'm making jewelry for you, gold and silver jewelry
    that will mark and accent your beauty.

THE WOMAN

When my King-Lover lay down beside me,
    my fragrance filled the room.
His head resting between my breasts—
    the head of my lover was a sachet of sweet myrrh.
My beloved is a bouquet of wildflowers
    picked just for me from the fields of Engedi.

THE MAN

Oh, my dear friend! You're so beautiful!
    And your eyes so beautiful—like doves!

THE WOMAN

And you, my dear lover—you're so handsome!
    And the bed we share is like a forest glen.
We enjoy a canopy of cedars
    enclosed by cypresses, fragrant and green.

# 2

I'm just a wildflower picked from the plains of Sharon,
    a lotus blossom from the valley pools.

THE MAN

A lotus blossoming in a swamp of weeds—
    that's my dear friend among the girls in the village.

THE WOMAN

As an apricot tree stands out in the forest,
    my lover stands above the young men in town.
All I want is to sit in his shade,
    to taste and savor his delicious love.
He took me home with him for a festive meal,
    but his eyes feasted on *me*!

Oh! Give me something refreshing to eat—and quickly!
    Apricots, raisins—anything. I'm about to faint with love!
His left hand cradles my head,
    and his right arm encircles my waist!

Oh, let me warn you, sisters in Jerusalem,
    by the gazelles, yes, by all the wild deer:
Don't excite love, don't stir it up,
    until the time is ripe—and you're ready.

Look! Listen! There's my lover!
    Do you see him coming?
Vaulting the mountains,
    leaping the hills.
My lover is like a gazelle, graceful;
    like a young stag, virile.
Look at him there, on tiptoe at the gate,
    all ears, all eyes—ready!
My lover has arrived
    and he's speaking to me!

THE MAN

Get up, my dear friend,
    fair and beautiful lover—come to me!
Look around you: Winter is over;
    the winter rains are over, gone!

379

Spring flowers are in blossom all over.
  The whole world's a choir—and singing!
Spring warblers are filling the forest
  with sweet arpeggios.
Lilacs are exuberantly purple and perfumed,
  and cherry trees fragrant with blossoms.
Oh, get up, dear friend,
  my fair and beautiful lover—come to me!
Come, my shy and modest dove—
  leave your seclusion, come out in the open.
Let me see your face,
  let me hear your voice.
For your voice is soothing
  and your face is ravishing.

THE WOMAN

Then you must protect me from the foxes,
  foxes on the prowl,
Foxes who would like nothing better
  than to get into our flowering garden.

My lover is mine, and I am his.
  Nightly he strolls in our garden,
Delighting in the flowers
  until dawn breathes its light and night slips away.

Turn to me, dear lover.
  Come like a gazelle.
Leap like a wild stag
  on delectable mountains!

# 3

Restless in bed and sleepless through the night,
  I longed for my lover.
  I wanted him desperately. His absence was painful.
So I got up, went out and roved the city,
  hunting through streets and down alleys.

I wanted my lover in the worst way!
    I looked high and low, and didn't find him.
And then the night watchmen found me
    as they patrolled the darkened city.
    "Have you seen my dear lost love?" I asked.
No sooner had I left them than I found him,
    found my dear lost love.
I threw my arms around him and held him tight,
    wouldn't let him go until I had him home again,
    safe at home beside the fire.

Oh, let me warn you, sisters in Jerusalem,
    by the gazelles, yes, by all the wild deer:
Don't excite love, don't stir it up,
    until the time is ripe—and you're ready.

What's this I see, approaching from the desert,
    raising clouds of dust,
Filling the air with sweet smells
    and pungent aromatics?
Look! It's Solomon's carriage,
    carried and guarded by sixty soldiers,
    sixty of Israel's finest,
All of them armed to the teeth,
    trained for battle,
    ready for anything, anytime.
King Solomon once had a carriage built
    from fine-grained Lebanon cedar.
He had it framed with silver and roofed with gold.
    The cushions were covered with a purple fabric,
    the interior lined with tooled leather.

Come and look, sisters in Jerusalem.
    Oh, sisters of Zion, don't miss this!
My King-Lover,
    dressed and garlanded for his wedding,
    his heart full, bursting with joy!

# 4

## THE MAN

You're so beautiful, my darling,
    so beautiful, and your dove eyes are veiled
By your hair as it flows and shimmers,
    like a flock of goats in the distance
    streaming down a hillside in the sunshine.
Your smile is generous and full—
    expressive and strong and clean.
Your lips are jewel red,
    your mouth elegant and inviting,
    your veiled cheeks soft and radiant.
The smooth, lithe lines of your neck
    command notice—all heads turn in awe and admiration!
Your breasts are like fawns,
    twins of a gazelle, grazing among the first spring flowers.

The sweet, fragrant curves of your body,
    the soft, spiced contours of your flesh
Invite me, and I come. I stay
    until dawn breathes its light and night slips away.
You're beautiful from head to toe, my dear love,
    beautiful beyond compare, absolutely flawless.

Come with me from Lebanon, my bride.
    Leave Lebanon behind, and come.
Leave your high mountain hideaway.
    Abandon your wilderness seclusion,
Where you keep company with lions
    and panthers guard your safety.
You've captured my heart, dear friend.
    You looked at me, and I fell in love.
    One look my way and I was hopelessly in love!
How beautiful your love, dear, dear friend—
    far more pleasing than a fine, rare wine,
    your fragrance more exotic than select spices.
The kisses of your lips are honey, my love,
    every syllable you speak a delicacy to savor.

Your clothes smell like the wild outdoors,
    the ozone scent of high mountains.
Dear lover and friend, you're a secret garden,
    a private and pure fountain.
Body and soul, you are paradise,
    a whole orchard of succulent fruits—
Ripe apricots and peaches,
    oranges and pears;
Nut trees and cinnamon,
    and all scented woods;
Mint and lavender,
    and all herbs aromatic;
A garden fountain, sparkling and splashing,
    fed by spring waters from the Lebanon mountains.

THE WOMAN

Wake up, North Wind,
    get moving, South Wind!
Breathe on my garden,
    fill the air with spice fragrance.

Oh, let my lover enter his garden!
    Yes, let him eat the fine, ripe fruits.

THE MAN

I went to my garden, dear friend, best lover!
    breathed the sweet fragrance.
I ate the fruit and honey,
    I drank the nectar and wine.

# 5

Celebrate with me, friends!
    Raise your glasses—"To life! To love!"

THE WOMAN

I was sound asleep, but in my dreams I was wide awake.
Oh, listen! It's the sound of my lover knocking, calling!

THE MAN

"Let me in, dear companion, dearest friend,
 my dove, consummate lover!
I'm soaked with the dampness of the night,
 drenched with dew, shivering and cold."

THE WOMAN

"But I'm in my nightgown—do you expect me to get dressed?
 I'm bathed and in bed—do you want me to get dirty?"

But my lover wouldn't take no for an answer,
 and the longer he knocked, the more excited I became.
I got up to open the door to my lover,
 sweetly ready to receive him,
Desiring and expectant
 as I turned the door handle.
But when I opened the door he was gone.
 My loved one had tired of waiting and left.
And I died inside—oh, I felt so bad!
 I ran out looking for him
But he was nowhere to be found.
 I called into the darkness—but no answer.
The night watchmen found me
 as they patrolled the streets of the city.
They slapped and beat and bruised me,
 ripping off my clothes,
These watchmen,
 who were supposed to be guarding the city.

I beg you, sisters in Jerusalem—
 if you find my lover,
Please tell him I want him,
 that I'm heartsick with love for him.

THE CHORUS

What's so great about your lover, fair lady?
What's so special about him that you beg for our help?

## THE WOMAN

My dear lover glows with health—
  red-blooded, radiant!
He's one in a million.
  There's no one quite like him!
My golden one, pure and untarnished,
  with raven black curls tumbling across his shoulders.
His eyes are like doves, soft and bright,
  but deep-set, brimming with meaning, like wells of water.
His face is rugged, his beard smells like sage,
  His voice, his words, warm and reassuring.
Fine muscles ripple beneath his skin,
  quiet and beautiful.
His torso is the work of a sculptor,
  hard and smooth as ivory.
He stands tall, like a cedar,
  strong and deep-rooted,
A rugged mountain of a man,
  aromatic with wood and stone.
His words are kisses, his kisses words.
  Everything about him delights me, thrills me
    through and through!

That's my lover, that's my man,
  dear Jerusalem sisters.

# 6

## THE CHORUS

So where has this love of yours gone,
  fair one?
Where on earth can he be?
  Can we help you look for him?

## THE WOMAN

Never mind. My lover is already on his way to his garden,
  to browse among the flowers, touching the colors and forms.

I am my lover's and my lover is mine.
  He caresses the sweet-smelling flowers.

THE MAN

Dear, dear friend and lover,
  you're as beautiful as Tirzah, city of delights,
Lovely as Jerusalem, city of dreams,
  the ravishing visions of my ecstasy.
Your beauty is too much for me—I'm in over my head.
  I'm not used to this! I can't take it in.
Your hair flows and shimmers
  like a flock of goats in the distance
  streaming down a hillside in the sunshine.
Your smile is generous and full—
  expressive and strong and clean.
Your veiled cheeks
  are soft and radiant.

There's no one like her on earth,
   never has been, never will be.
She's a woman beyond compare.
  My dove is perfection,
Pure and innocent as the day she was born,
  and cradled in joy by her mother.
Everyone who came by to see her
  exclaimed and admired her—
All the fathers and mothers, the neighbors and friends,
  blessed and praised her:

"Has anyone ever seen anything like this—
  dawn-fresh, moon-lovely, sun-radiant,
  ravishing as the night sky with its galaxies of stars!"

One day I went strolling through the orchard,
  looking for signs of spring,
Looking for buds about to burst into flower,
  anticipating readiness, ripeness.
Before I knew it my heart was raptured,
  carried away by lofty thoughts!

Dance, dance, dear Shulammite, Angel-Princess!
    Dance, and we'll feast our eyes on your grace!
Everyone wants to see the Shulammite dance
    her victory dances of love and peace.

# 7

Shapely and graceful your sandaled feet,
    and queenly your movement—
Your limbs are lithe and elegant,
    the work of a master artist.
Your body is a chalice,
    wine-filled.
Your skin is silken and tawny
    like a field of wheat touched by the breeze.
Your breasts are like fawns,
    twins of a gazelle.
Your neck is carved ivory, curved and slender.
    Your eyes are wells of light, deep with mystery.
    Quintessentially feminine!
Your profile turns all heads,
    commanding attention.
The feelings I get when I see the high mountain ranges
    —stirrings of desire, longings for the heights—
Remind me of you,
    and I'm spoiled for anyone else!
Your beauty, within and without, is absolute,
    dear lover, close companion.
You are tall and supple, like the palm tree,
    and your full breasts are like sweet clusters of dates.
I say, "I'm going to climb that palm tree!
    I'm going to caress its fruit!"
Oh yes! Your breasts
    will be clusters of sweet fruit to me,
Your breath clean and cool like fresh mint,
    your tongue and lips like the best wine.

## THE WOMAN

Yes, and yours are, too—my love's kisses
    flow from his lips to mine.
I am my lover's.
    I'm all he wants. I'm all the world to him!
Come, dear lover—
    let's tramp through the countryside.
Let's sleep at some wayside inn,
    then rise early and listen to bird-song.
Let's look for wildflowers in bloom,
    blackberry bushes blossoming white,
Fruit trees festooned
    with cascading flowers.
And there I'll give myself to you,
    my love to your love!

Love-apples drench us with fragrance,
    fertility surrounds, suffuses us,
Fruits fresh and preserved
    that I've kept and saved just for you, my love.

# 8

I wish you'd been my twin brother,
    sharing with me the breasts of my mother,
Playing outside in the street,
    kissing in plain view of everyone,
    and no one thinking anything of it.
I'd take you by the hand and bring you home
    where I was raised by my mother.
You'd drink my wine
    and kiss my cheeks.

Imagine! His left hand cradling my head,
    his right arm around my waist!
Oh, let me warn you, sisters in Jerusalem:
    Don't excite love, don't stir it up,
    until the time is ripe—and you're ready.

THE CHORUS

Who is this I see coming up from the country,
  arm in arm with her lover?

THE MAN

I found you under the apricot tree,
  and woke you up to love.
Your mother went into labor under that tree,
  and under that very tree she bore you.

THE WOMAN

Hang my locket around your neck,
  wear my ring on your finger.
Love is invincible facing danger and death.
  Passion laughs at the terrors of hell.
The fire of love stops at nothing—
  it sweeps everything before it.
Flood waters can't drown love,
  torrents of rain can't put it out.
Love can't be bought, love can't be sold—
  it's not to be found in the marketplace.
My brothers used to worry about me:

"Our little sister has no breasts.
  What shall we do with our little sister
  when men come asking for her?
She's a virgin and vulnerable,
  and we'll protect her.
If they think she's a wall, we'll top it with barbed wire.
  If they think she's a door, we'll barricade it."

Dear brothers, I'm a walled-in virgin still,
  but my breasts are full—
And when my lover sees me,
  he knows he'll soon be satisfied.

389

THE MAN

King Solomon may have vast vineyards
 in lush, fertile country,
Where he hires others to work the ground.
 People pay anything to get in on that bounty.
But *my* vineyard is all mine,
 and I'm keeping it to myself.
You can have your vast vineyards, Solomon,
 you and your greedy guests!

Oh, lady of the gardens,
 my friends are with me listening.
 Let me hear your voice!

THE WOMAN

Run to me, dear lover.
 Come like a gazelle.
Leap like a wild stag
 on the spice mountains.